Framing Questions, Constructing Answers

Linking Research with Education Policy for Developing Countries

Noel F. McGinn

and

Allison M. Borden

Harvard Institute for International Development

Distributed by **Harvard University Press**

Library of Congress Cataloging-In-Publication Data

McGinn, Noel F., 1934–

   Framing questions, constructing answers : linking research with
education policy for developing countries / Noel F. McGinn and
Allison M. Borden.
      p.   cm.
   Includes bibliographical references and index.
   ISBN 0-674-31715-7 : $15.00
    1. School management and organization– –Developing countries.
2. Basic education– –Developing countries.   I. Borden, Allison M., 1951–   .
II. Title.
LC2607.M34 1995   94-21886
370'.9172'4––dc20   CIP

Harvard Studies in International Development

Other Studies in the series include:

Reforming Economic Systems in Developing Countries
edited by Dwight H. Perkins and Michael Roemer, 1991

Markets in Developing Countries: Parallel, Fragmented and Black
edited by Michael Roemer and Christine Jones, 1991*

Progress with Profits: The Development of Rural Banking in Indonesia
by Richard Patten and Jay K. Rosengard, 1991*

Green Markets: The Economics of Sustainable Development
by Theodore Panayotou, 1993*

The Challenge of Reform in Indochina
edited by Börje Ljunggren, 1993

Asia and Africa: Legacies and Opportunities in Development
edited by David L. Lindauer and Michael Roemer, 1994*

Macroeconomic Policy and Adjustment in Korea, 1970–1990
by Stephan Haggard, Richard N. Cooper, Susan Collins, Choongsoo Kim, and
Sung-Tae Ro

* Jointly published by the International Center for Economic Growth.

Samples of teacher's guides on pages 112, 116, 118, 120, 122, and 124 provided with
permission by D. C. Heath and Company, Lexington, MA. Taken from **Heath
Mathematics**, Teacher's Edition, by Walter E. Rucker, Clyde A. Dilley, and David W.
Lowry. © Copyright 1985 D. C. Heath and Company.

Editorial Management: Vukani Magubane
Editorial Assistance: Sarah Newberry
Copyediting: Janet Bond Wood
Design and Production: Desktop Publishing & Design Co.
Printer: BookCrafters Inc.

Why No Table of Contents

There is no table of contents for this workbook because the material is not organized into chapters. There are, however, two main sections:

Pages 0-157, where the odd-numbered pages contain a series of questions that you will answer about education in your country; and the even-numbered pages contain information that may help you think about the questions being asked. Note that each page with questions indicates the pages from which you came; for most pages there are at least two possible sources. This is our way of emphasizing the systemic character of education.

Pages 159-244, which contain information about programs to improve education; you will be directed to this section after having answered a series of questions across the odd-numbered pages in the first section.

There are several indexes in the workbook which will help you find the information you seek:

the "even-numbered pages" index on page **245;**

the list of tables on page **248;**

the list of figures on page **249;**

key topics on page **250;** and

the index of authors and references beginning on page **254.**

There are several icons which appear throughout the workbook. These have been included to help you locate information quickly or to help you in cross-referencing the material.

Administration and Management

Buildings and Facilities

Costs and Finances

Curriculum and Materials

Policies and Planning

Students

Teachers

Women and Girls

Acknowledgements

This manual has benefitted from years of conversations and interviews with friends and colleagues in Burundi, Chile, Colombia, Egypt, Honduras, Indonesia, Jordan, Korea, Mexico, Pakistan, Sri Lanka, Thailand, and Yemen. We have talked with researchers, planners, ministers, teachers, all deeply involved in the process of improving education. The manual is an attempt to represent their understanding about how education works, and how to make it work better.

The construction of the manual required direct help in the identification of key issues. The initial concept for the manual came from suggestions by Gary Theisen. Armando Loera did early work on the development of a framework for classifying developing country research. Reed Augliere encouraged the use of an inquiry format. Based on his years of work with ministers, planners, and policy makers, Ernesto Schiefelbein made valuable suggestions about the use of information by decision makers. Lois Easton clarified the relationships between curriculum and assessment, and between instruction and classroom structure. Tom Welsh and Reed Augliere provided valuable criticisms about presentation. Tom Welsh provided valuable insights into how ministers make decisions.

The manual would not have been completed without extensive efforts to summarize and synthesize research. We are especially grateful to Sherry Squire. She is directly responsible for a number of the charts and summaries that appear in the policy section of the manual. Jennifer Haworth contributed the charts on education finance. James Williams provided access to research and program examples in the BRIDGES SHARE software program. Additional valuable help was provided by Zewditu Makonnen and Gretchen Hummon.

The manual was prepared as part of the Basic Research and Implementation in DevelopinG Education Systems (BRIDGES) Project. BRIDGES was a joint effort of the Institute for International Development and the Graduate School of Education, of Harvard University, assisted by the Institute for International Research, Michigan State University, the Research Triangle Institute, and Texas Southern University. The Project was funded between 1985 and 1992 by the Office of Education, Bureau of Science and Technology, of the United States Agency for International Development.

Introduction

This manual is written for education planners, managers and policy makers in developing countries. It was designed for people with little or no training in social science or economic research. We believe it will be most useful for people responsible for decisions that directly affect what happens in schools.[1] We hope it will contribute to the effort to obtain education for all.

The nations of the world, concerned about education for all, seek two objectives:

1. to provide some kind of education to all children; and

2. to make that education as good as it can be.

This manual relates what has been learned in recent years about access and quality in basic education. One key lesson is that access and quality are affected by many factors. In this manual, we attempt to review those factors, and to show their complex relationships. We also pose a set of issues that policy makers have to consider to improve their education systems.

Improvement in any organization depends on:

1. availability of qualified persons and physical resources that match the requirements of the situation;

2. effective actions and efficient use of resources, involving the issues of what and how and when; and

3. careful monitoring of consequences to correct the initial plan and adjust to changes in the situation.

This manual will help you to identify the kinds of qualifications that people require to improve basic education. The manual discusses the amounts and kinds of physical resources appropriate to different situations. It provides examples of programs that have been effective in other countries. The examples show how people and resources can be combined in various ways to generate change. Different goals can be met by the same combinations of resources and people . The same goals can be met through different combinations.

This manual is for people actively involved in the process of educational improvement. Progress will come faster, we believe, if you can make use of knowledge gained through experience. Use of research carried out by others can speed up the process of change. The improvement of education does not require that you become expert in research or policy analysis. On the other hand, the fruits of those activities can be of much help. By using this manual, you will become informed about what policy analysis can, and cannot, offer as tested solutions. You will be made aware of the complex set of factors that you, as policy maker, will have to take into account. Hopefully, you will also see that, although complex, the task of improvement of education is not impossible.

Note
1 A number of other sources of assistance are included in the Bibliography of this Manual. See page **161** for specific recommendations.

How to Use this Manual

There are at least four ways in which you can use the manual.

1. First, for **diagnosis.** We ask you to describe what you think is not working well in your country. The manual takes you through a series of questions intended to focus on the specific issues you consider most problematic.

Facing each page with questions is a page that reports pertinent research or statistics. These data may serve as a standard against which to compare your country.

You enter the book from page 1. Two major goals of education systems are presented:

1. enrollment of all children;

2. in programs in which they learn content valued by society.

Page 1 asks you to indicate whether you are satisfied with your country's achievement of these goals. The statement you choose as most appropriate directs you to another page. You are carried into a more detailed description of the situation, and eventually to examples of how other countries have responded to that problem.

You may already have carried out a diagnosis of your system and have identified the major problem areas. In that case, you may wish to turn to page 11, which provides a more detailed list of problems.

2. Second, the manual can be consulted as a **source of ideas for improvement.** Pages 159-244 describe a variety of policy options that different countries have adopted to improve their education systems. Each page describes what was attempted and some of the consequences of different programs.

Any new program affects and is affected by other activities in the education system. Most new programs will not work effectively if changes are not made also in other parts of the system. We provide an indication of other factors that must be taken into account if the new policy option is to work effectively.

3. Third, you may find the manual a **source of information** about which factors most influence the performance of education systems. Beginning on page 250 we present an index of all the variables and factors discussed in the book. On the page(s) indicated appears a short description of the research findings, and suggestions for further reading.

The list of research is as comprehensive as possible. If you do not find the kind of information for which you are looking, it is quite possible that educational research has not yet addressed that issue. In some cases, perhaps, you will find that research on a particular question has not yet been done in your country.

4. You could, therefore, consider that the manual presents an **agenda for research.** It suggests the kind of information useful in the policy formulation process.

Reading the Diagrams

The decisions and plans to make education systems more effective are called *policies*. In some cases the "central" management of the education system will be located at the level of the municipality or district. Sometimes management authority is held at the state or provincial, or federal or national level. In each case, policies at each level will affect what happens in classrooms.

We use diagrams to suggest the range of policies that can be taken to improve learning.

The diagrams can be interpreted as follows:

a. An arrow from one term or factor, e.g., from A to B, is read as meaning "A affects B" or "A leads to B" or "A produces B." For example, the following is read as stating that "more time spent trying to learn the curriculum results in more learning of the curriculum." The sign on the arrowhead, + or -, indicates whether increases in the first factor increase the second (+) or decrease the second (-).

b. When a particular outcome has more than one direct antecedent, all are represented. For example, the following diagram is read as saying "student absenteeism is a joint product of the distance student lives from school, frequency of illness, and family demands on time."

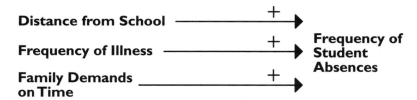

c. Some factors do not operate directly to produce outcomes, but instead facilitate or constrain the effect of another factor. For example, the impact of time spent trying to learn depends on the student's ability to learn. You can think of the vertical arrow as representing a kind of valve that regulates the flow along the horizontal arrow.

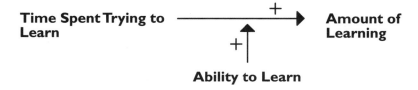

d. In some cases outcomes depend on the extent of *matching* or agreement between two factors. For example, the performance of a teacher with a given curriculum depends on the difficulty of the curriculum *and* the ability of the teacher. If the curriculum requires special skills, the teacher must have them; an easier curriculum could be taught well by a teacher with fewer skills.

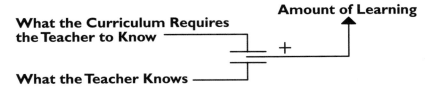

Almost all the "factors" we have included in these diagrams refer to policies that can be taken by the central management of the education system. We know, as do you, that it is what teachers do in classrooms that directly determines how much children learn. What teachers do in classrooms depends, however, on a number of factors. These include the teachers' training, access to materials, and the qualities of the students. In other words, teacher effectiveness is conditioned by the actions of others, including policy choices.

Now you can begin by turning to page:

1, to identify problems in basic education in your country; **or**

11, to find a more detailed list of problems; **or**

159, the section that identifies programs to improve education; **or**

248, which lists the tables included in the manual; **or**

250, which lists topics discussed in this manual; **or**

254, to find a list of the various authors cited in this manual; **or**

257, to find the bibliography cited in the manual.

Can We Learn Anything from Others' Experiences?

There is a remarkable variety in the organization of education, even though there are striking similarities in the goals pursued. The **purpose** of education systems is everywhere the same: the learning by students of the knowledge, skills, and values contained in the curriculum. The **means** used to achieve those objectives, however, differ according to national and local circumstances. Here are four examples.

1. In all countries, major emphasis is placed on the **learning of language**, which takes up about 35 percent of the curriculum. Mathematics is second, occupying about 18 percent of the curriculum. These emphases are constant across countries irrespective of their culture, former colonial status, or level of economic development (Benavot and Kamens, 1989).

2. The **length of the primary cycle** varies from only four years in some countries, to nine years in others, with slightly more than half the countries requiring six years to receive the primary certificate (UNESCO Statistical Year Book). Countries vary in both the number of days in the school year, and the number of hours in the school day. The worldwide average is reported to be 879 instructional hours per year, but some countries offer as few as 600 hours per year, and others report more than 1100 (Benavot and Kamens, 1989).

3. **Textbooks** are an essential element of the definition of the modern school. In some countries, however, there may be as many as 20 students per textbook. In others every student has a textbook for each subject (Paxman, Denning, and Read, 1989).

4. **Teacher certification varies widely.** There are differences in how much prior academic education is required, and in the length of the training period. In some countries, many teachers have as little as six years of schooling, while in others most are at least university graduates (Dove, 1986).

Education is everywhere similar, but different. We can learn from the experiences of other countries, even when we can not copy what they have done.

Education systems serve multiple purposes, and suffer multiple ills.

Which of the following statements best describes your major concern about basic education?

→ **Not all children enroll in basic education, either public or private.** If this statement matches your concern, go to page **3**.

→ **All children enroll, but not all complete basic education or learn as much as is expected.** If this statement matches your concern, go to page **5**.

Difficulties in Estimating the Supply of Schooling

Estimates of the supply or availability of schooling are difficult to make. This is because enrollment statistics represent the joint effect of supply and demand. We can have data on the number of schools in each country, but the term "school" can describe several situations. For example, some schools may be without buildings, others with only one or two classrooms, and others as many as thirty classrooms. Many ministries do not collect data on numbers of classrooms.

The table below presents information on numbers of teachers, and ratios of students per teacher. As you can see, student–teacher ratios are not a good index of supply. In countries in which people are widely dispersed, there may be **both** a shortage of teachers, and a low student–teacher ratio. If schools are located only in urban areas, on the other hand, the student–teacher ratio may be high. An increase in student–teacher ratio may, as in the case of Burundi, represent a change from single to double shifts. Because the Burundi government used the same teachers for both shifts, the ratio of students per teacher increased, but so did availability of schooling.

Table 1
Net Enrollment Ratios[1] and Student–Teacher Ratios 1980 and 1985 in Selected Countries[2]

Country	NER (%) 1985	Students/Teacher 1980	Students/Teacher 1985
Paraguay	95.2	27/1	25/1
R. Korea	93.9	48/1	38/1
Egypt	85.9	40/1	43/1
Turkey	75.3	27/1	31/1
S. Yemen	71.5	28/1	26/1
Nigeria	63.2	43/1	44/1
Benin	50.7	48/1	33/1
Burundi	44.4	35/1	56/1
Pakistan	42.5	32/1	33/1
Ethiopia	26.4	64/1	48/1

Notes

1 Or NER, defined as 6- to 11-year-old children enrolled as a proportion of the 6- to 11-year-old population.

2 Adapted from Lockheed and Verspoor (1991), Table A-9, pp. 289–294.

Enrollment in school is the result of two kinds of factors:

1. demand by parents for schooling for their children; and

2. the existence or supply of a school the children can attend (Anderson, 1988).

In your country, which of these two factors appears to be most important in explaining why not all children are enrolled in school?

➡️ **Because there is no school for them to attend, some children never enroll. Include here a situation in which school buildings exist, but are so overcrowded that children seeking enrollment are turned away.** If this is your situation, go to page **7**.

➡️ **Some children never enroll in school because their parents do not enroll them.** If this is your situation, go to page **9**.

⬅ For more information and discussion, see page 2

3

Figure 1
Factors that Determine Total Enrollment

Demand for Schooling ————————— + ——➤ **Number of Children Enrolled**

+ ↑
Supply of Schooling

How Can We Know How Well Schools Are Doing?

Developing country education systems do not perform as well as systems in the early-industrialized countries. This is the conclusion of studies that compare the academic achievement of students on international tests.

Table 2 below reports results from International Association for the Evaluation of Educational Achievement tests, translated into national languages.

Table 2
Comparison of Achievement in Mathematics, Science, and Reading
(percentage of correct answers)

Country	Arithmetic (grade 8)	General Science (grade 6)	Reading Comprehension (grade 6)
Japan	60	61	—
Netherlands	59	48	69
Flemish Belgium	58	53	65
Franc. Belgium	57	48	74
Hungary	57	53	70
United States	51	61	67
England and Wales	48	56	71
Thailand	43	47	—
Chile	—	36	61
India	—	36	53
Malawi	—	42	34

— indicates no data available.
Adapted from Lockheed and Verspoor (1991), p. 13.

There are several reasons why these kinds of comparisons should be regarded critically.

1. The comparisons of test scores are made only on items common to all countries. They are not necessarily a good measure of all that is learned in a subject for any country.

2. Relative standings do not indicate whether in *any* country an acceptable standard of performance is attained. What it is important to know in Malawi in general science should differ from what it is important to know in Japan, or Hungary, or the United States. How much knowledge of arithmetic is required to be a good citizen, or productive worker, or responsible family member, will vary from society to society.

3. It is also impossible to assess whether the level of difficulty of test items remains the same when they are translated from one language to another.

→ See pages **169** and **228** for critiques of standardized tests.
→ See page **227** for an example of successful use.

from page 1

Enrollment in school is *necessary* for achievement of the goal of an educated population, but is *not sufficient.*

Which of the following statements most closely approximates the situation in your country?

➜ **Many students complete the basic education cycle, but only after repeating one or more grades.** If this statement matches, go to page 129.

➜ **Many students repeat and dropout before completing the cycle.** If this statement matches, go to page 131.

➜ **Even those students who complete the cycle without failing even one grade learn too little of what is expected.** If this statement matches, go to page 11.

← For more information and discussion, see page 4

5

Figure 2
Total Learning: Enrollment and Quality

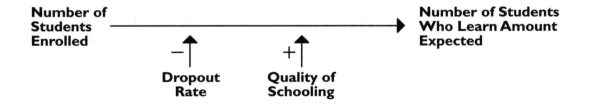

Reasons for the Gender Gap in Enrollments

The enrollment rates of boys and of girls sometimes differ because the **supply** of schooling is not the same for each group. A gap can also occur because of differences in the **demand** for schooling.

Table 3 compares the ratio of female to male students at different grade levels. In some countries (e.g., El Salvador) there is little disparity between male and female enrollments, although the gross enrollment ratio (GER)[1] is not high. In other countries (e.g., Egypt) although the GER is higher, there is a large disparity or gap between enrollments of boys and girls. For a categorization of countries according to amount of **gender gap** in enrollments see Anderson et al. (1989).

In some countries female enrollments decline in the upper grades. This may be because as girls approach the age of puberty they are withdrawn from (co-educational) schools by their parents. In some cases, this withdrawal is justified with religious explanations. In other cases, parents say they withdraw their children to work in the household or in income-generating activities. In other countries, the relative proportion of girls increases in the upper grades, as boys find wage-paying jobs in the labor force (Stromquist, 1989).

Table 3
Gross Enrollment Ratios and Ratio of Female to Male Students by Grade

	GER (1985)	Ratio Female/Male Students		
		Grade 1	Grade 3	Grade 5
Mali	21.6	.60	.60	.58
Guinea	30.3	.50	.46	.39
Ethiopia	33.7	.65	.59	.61
Sudan	49.8	.65	.67	.70
Burundi	52.5	.83	.76	.66
Benin	64.7	.52	.51	.49
El Salvador	75.1	.96	.99	1.01
Nepal	82.2	.45	.40	.37
Egypt	87.0	.81	.79	.75
Algeria	93.0	.83	.80	.76
Zaire	94.2	.77	.69	.70
Philippines	106.2	.92	.93	.98
Indonesia	117.6	.93	.93	.93

Adapted from Lockheed and Verspoor (1991), Tables A-2 and A-4, pp. 247-252, 259-264.

Note
1   The ratio of total enrollment to number of children of school age.

from pages 3, 135

Around the world, opportunities to go to school vary considerably, according to:

1. where children live;

2. their gender;

3. their physical condition and health; and

4. the stability of their residence.

Is this true in your country? If so, which of the following describe the situation of limited opportunities for enrollment?

→ **Rural children are more affected than urban children.** If this is true, go to page 13.

→ **Girls are more affected than boys.** If this is true, go to page 15.

→ **Handicapped children are affected.** If this is true, go to page 17.

→ **Nomadic children are affected.** If this is true, see descriptions of programs on page 162.

→ **Refugee children are affected.** If this is true, see descriptions of programs on page 163.

If the lack of space in school affects all groups equally, which of the following is true?

→ **There aren't enough school buildings.** If this is true, go to page 19.

→ **There aren't enough teachers.** If this is true, go to page 21.

← For more information and discussion, see page 6

7

Demand for Education

Families seek education for their children when they believe that the education will contribute to the benefit of the children or the family. These benefits can be religious, social, or economic.

There are significant differences in the amount and kind of education that families seek for boys compared to girls, and these are often justified by reference to religious teaching. These distinctions are not clear in the fundamental doctrine of world religions, but are enforced by reference to interpretations. The Koran, for example, begins with a call to **read,** and teaches complementarity between men and women. In some Islamic countries, however, education for girls is severely limited while in others men and women have equal levels of opportunity.

Differences in demand for education vary also as a result of economic expectations of parents. Children are more frequently sent to school when it is believed that their employability is greater with education. The more highly educated the parents, the higher their expectations and, therefore, the greater their demand for education of their children.

Education improves a child's social status, which can enhance the social position of the family in the community. Education may, for example, improve the ability of a family to arrange a marriage favorable to the family's interests (Stromquist, 1989).

In most countries demand for education is high, and exceeds supply. This is true even among poor and supposedly "backward" rural families. The value of education is well-understood, and poor families make proportionately greater sacrifices to educate their children than do families with greater wealth or income (Tsang, 1989).

Furthermore, demand for education increases with supply. That is, as more children go to school, the importance of schooling increases. Education, or the certification that schools give, replaces traditional methods of signalling the intellectual and social capabilities of an individual. The process is "inflationary." Once most children go to primary school, a primary school education is no longer enough to set a child apart. Demand increases for secondary education. When there are more secondary school graduates in the labor market, employers prefer to hire them over persons with only primary schooling.

In some countries not all families enroll their children in school, even when space is available. Some families look with disfavor on education of girls. In other cases, family income is too little to enroll all children. This is more likely to occur in rural areas and marginal urban areas; and when schools charge fees, or families are expected to purchase textbooks, dress their children in uniforms, or pay for transportation.

Which if any of these factors operate in your country to *limit* demand for education?

➜ **Families do not enroll some of their children because of cultural or religious factors.** If this is your situation, go to page **23**.

➜ **Families do not enroll some of their children because they can't afford to provide education for all their children.** If this is your situation, go to page **165**.

← For more information and discussion, see page 8

9

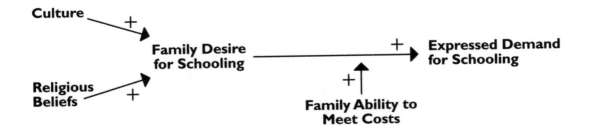

Figure 3
Factors that Influence Demand for Schooling

Factors that Contribute to Learning

The concept of **quality** is widely used in education, but often with different meanings. Among recent works on **quality of education** in developing countries are studies by Fuller (1989) and Heyneman and Loxley (1983). Consult the index for a more complete listing of research on this topic. See also page **241**.

The term **quality** is used to refer to:

1. characteristics of the factors that go into the education process;

2. aspects of the process itself; or

3. the outcomes of the process.

The diagram on page **11** is one version of how various factors affect one kind of quality, the amount of learning that students experience.

Opportunities for learning come about as the result of *policies* of the central management. Policies that affect the quality of the curriculum, instructional materials, administration and teaching, and time spent on trying to learn, can increase opportunities for learning. The impact of opportunities for learning is mediated by the "teachability" of the students, or how much students are able to learn in a given period (see page **40**).

Note that in the model, improvement of any one of the six factors will have an impact on the amount of learning. Three of the factors have multiplier or mediating effects, that is, the result of including one of these is more than a simple addition.

1. The quality of materials affects the impact of the quality of the curriculum.

2. The impact of amount of time on the task is affected by the quality of teaching.

3. The teachability of the students affects the impact of opportunities for learning.

In the diagram on page **11** we have indicated that the quality of administration affects time on task. This occurs through the actions of principals or school directors to improve discipline in the school. Improved discipline means teachers have more time to spend on instruction.

from pages 5, 57, 87, 129

You are on this page because you have stated that you are not satisfied with the outcomes of the education process in your country. The questions that follow ask only about the quality of inputs and the process that contributes to outcomes.

Which of the following do you believe is the major source of your dissatisfaction?

→ **The quality of the curriculum.** If this is critical, go to page **153.**

→ **The quality of teaching.** If this is critical, go to page **53.**

→ **The quality of administration and supervision.** If this is critical, go to page **43.**

→ **The amount of time spent on teaching and learning.** If this is critical, go to page **63.**

→ **The quality of the instructional materials.** If this is critical, go to page **111.**

We have used the concept of quality here to refer to inputs to the education system. There are, however, several other definitions of the concept of quality. Go to page **241** to read more about definitions of quality. Go to page **243** to read more about the stages of improvement in quality.

← For more information and discussion, see page 10

Figure 4
Individual Learning: Time, Quality, Expectations

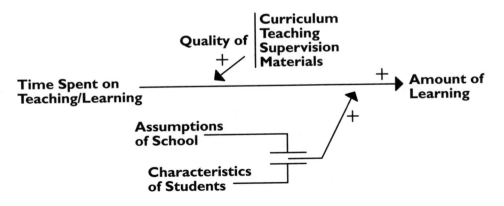

Recruiting Teachers to Work in Rural Areas

Many countries find it difficult to staff rural schools. The reasons include:

1. a perceived lack of physical amenities and cultural attractions in rural areas.

2. actual or perceived higher costs of teaching in rural areas, as these affect immediate income or opportunities for future advancement.

3. ethnic, racial, or linguistic differences between inhabitants of urban and rural areas that discourage urban candidates.

4. the failure of rural schools to graduate enough persons to supply teachers for rural schools.

5. cultural taboos, more easily enforced in rural areas, against single women living alone.

There is no comparative research on the factors that make it difficult to recruit teachers for rural schools.

Similarly, there is no systematic research on which policies are most effective in overcoming this problem.

The best we have is a careful reflection (by Dove, 1986) on the kinds of policies that might be effective. Dove analyzes the kinds of reasons persons might have for becoming teachers. Some persons are motivated primarily by economic reasons, others by cultural or intellectual reasons. The reasons for entering the profession may not be the same as the reasons for choosing to remain. For example, once a person has decided that the salary a teacher earns is sufficient, non-economic incentives may become more important.

Some countries offer financial packages to attract teachers to rural areas. These often include salary increments or premiums, and housing or a housing allowance. These may be helpful in attracting persons to rural areas. Over time, they may not be effective in keeping them there. Other incentives such as opportunities for training, or special recognition, may have greater impact.

➜ For more information on this topic see page 76.

from page 7

Enrollment in school requires the fulfillment of three conditions:

1. there has to be a building or some place identified as a school;

2. there has to be a teacher; and

3. it has to be possible for the teacher to take on another student.

Which of the following explains why some children who want to go to school do not?

➡   **There isn't enough space available in existing facilities.** If this is your situation, go to page **19**.

➡   **There aren't enough teachers.** If this is your situation, go to page **21**.

➡   **There are buildings and teachers, but there are many students repeating grades who take up space and keep out new students.** If this is your situation, go to page **129**.

⬅ For more information and discussion, see page 12

13

Figure 5
Supply of Schooling and Repetition

Investing in Education of Girls

Poor countries that provide education equally to boys and girls, do better on health, population growth, and economic growth.

Countries that have spent more on providing primary education to girls tend to have

- "higher economic productivity,
- lower infant and maternal mortality, but also lower fertility rates, and
- longer life expectancy for both men and women..."

than do countries that have spent less (King, 1990, p. 6).

Also important is the disparity or *gap* between spending for girls and spending for boys. The closer the amount of spending for the two groups, the greater is the contribution that education makes to development and economic growth. In those countries where there is a large gap between education of boys and the education of girls, economic growth and social development lag behind.

Why should we expect the education of women to be so important?

1. In many poor countries women make an important contribution to agricultural production. Education of farmers in general increases their productivity; provision of primary schooling to women may make the difference between subsistence and surplus conditions.

2. Women also make an important contribution to the nutritional and health status of the home. Particularly where men are drawn into the wage labor force and are absent from the household, mothers have primary responsibility for child-rearing, food purchasing, and food preparation.

3. In some economies women increasingly are participating in the labor force, either as single mothers or as wives. Educated women earn higher incomes than those without education. They can apply that income to the improvement of conditions in the home, such as improved nutrition.

4. Development requires the coordinated effort of all citizens. A large gap between the education levels of women and men makes it difficult to achieve that coordination.

→ See page 215 for ways to increase education for girls.

14

from page 7

The means by which education systems discriminate against girls in favor of boys can vary from country to country.

How is it in your country?

➜ **Your country requires separate buildings for boys and for girls, but there are not as many facilities for girls as for boys.** If this is true, go to page **27**.

➜ **Your country has co-educational facilities, but not enough schools for all boys and girls. Boys are admitted first.** If this is true, go to page **19**.

➜ **Discrimination against girls occurs because your country requires female teachers for girls, and there are not enough female teachers.** If this is true, go to page **21**.

15

In developing countries expenditures on women's education have a greater impact on economic growth than do expenditures on education for boys (Crouch, Spratt and Cubeddu, 1992). From the point of view of national development it would make sense to remove all barriers to education of women.

See also Floro and Wolf (1990).

← For more information and discussion, see page 14

Who is Handicapped?

The term **handicap** varies in definition and in acceptability. Generally the term includes children who are blind (sometimes called **visually impaired** or **visually disabled**), children who are deaf (**hearing impaired**, **hearing disabled**) and children with other physical impairments that limit their participation in activities considered important to the learning process. Sometimes the term includes children who are termed **mentally impaired**, that is, those who are thought to lack the intellectual ability or mental stability to be able to benefit from schooling.

Persons with "handicaps" often develop special skills to compensate for their "deficiency." For example, the blind develop a keen ability to distinguish and remember sounds. Deaf persons often develop a capacity to understand speech from the movement of a speaker's lips. Persons without these impairments less often develop these abilities. They also place a lesser value on these abilities than on those they themselves have developed.

The "handicap" of a person is, therefore, in relation to the abilities of the majority. Other, less-often recognized "handicaps" might include lack of familiarity with the dominant culture, lack of fluency in the dominant language, or, in some circumstances, not being of the dominant gender.

Schooling often is designed only for the dominant. In this case schools ignore the diversity of the population that makes up a dynamic and progressive country. In effect, schooling *creates* handicaps for some students.

A few countries have provided **separate** educational opportunities for these children. In most cases the education provided is of lesser quality than that provided in most public schools.

Other countries have decided that it is unjust to deny these children access to the education provided to others different from them. As a result, handicapped children are now being incorporated into the daily routine of regular public schools.

The process is called **mainstreaming.** Research shows that handicapped children learn more when they are **mainstreamed** than they do in special facilities. There is no negative effect on the cognitive learning of children without "handicaps"; on the contrary, their social development is enhanced by contact with persons different than themselves. Also clear is that the learning capacity of these "handicapped" children exceeds what is generally presumed.

from page 7

In your country, which of the following is why there are not enough opportunities for handicapped children to attend school?

→ **Separate facilities are required for handicapped children, and there aren't enough buildings to accommodate them.** If this matches your situation, go to page 19.

→ **Specially trained teachers are required and there aren't enough.** If this matches your situation, go to page 21.

For an example of a program for handicapped children, go to page 177.

← For more information and discussion, see page 16

How Much Should be Spent on School Construction?

If students learn as much in inexpensive school buildings as in expensive buildings, we should build less expensive schools. Saved resources can be used to expand access, or to improve quality.

Data from the World Bank (Lockheed and Verspoor, 1991) indicate that Sub-Saharan African schools built with local materials cost only one-third as much as schools built to "international" standards.

Table 4

Cost per Student Place for Local versus International Construction Materials (US$)

Country	"Brick and Mortar"	Local Materials
Senegal	$593	$175
Central African R.	$478	$176
Burkina Faso	$549	$203
Mauritius	$355	$183
Chad	$460	$156
Mali	$417	$ 226

Source: Lockheed and Verspoor (1991), p. 179.

At most there is only very weak evidence that quality of buildings makes a difference to learning. Although some sort of building is necessary for a school to operate effectively, many studies show little or no relationship between: the type of construction; the amount of ventilation and illumination; physical condition of the roof, walls, or furniture; and student learning (Fuller, 1987).

For example, in Pakistan researchers found no difference between schools with high scores on an external achievement test in mathematics and science, and those with low scores, with respect to the condition of the building and whether children had desks or chairs (Warwick, Reimers, and McGinn, 1990).

Perhaps *other* factors are much more important in producing student learning. For example, suppose the difference between effective and ineffective teachers is very large, much larger than the effect of buildings. Suppose also that teachers are assigned randomly to buildings. In this case we would see only the effect of teachers.

A few studies do report that quality of the building makes a difference (Mwamwenda and Mwamwenda, 1987). It may be that in these studies teachers are assigned according to the quality of the building, and what we really are seeing is the impact of effective teachers.

➜ For another point of view see page 78.

from pages 7, 13, 15, 17, 45, 91, 133

Thehere are at least three ways to overcome limited availability of school buildings.

The first is, of course, to construct more.

Do any of the following account for the lack of buildings?

→ **There isn't enough money for construction.** If this is so, go to page **29**.

→ **Land isn't available for school sites.** If this is so, go to page **31**.

→ **Poor planning. Buildings were put in the wrong places, not enough buildings were put up in time.** If this is so, go to page **45**.

A second response to a projected shortage of school buildings is to attempt to extend the useful "life" of those currently built. This can be achieved through improved maintenance. See page **230** for two examples.

It is also possible to use buildings more efficiently and intensively. See page **166** for examples.

A third possible response is to make use of other structures not originally designed to be schools.

Would it be possible to use other buildings as sites for schools?

→ If **YES**, see page **213** for policy options.

← For more information and discussion, see page 18

19

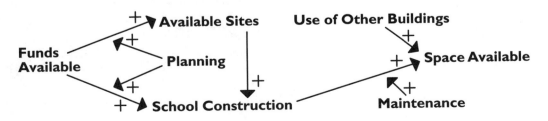

Figure 6
Increasing Available Space

Salaries for Teachers Explain Most of Cost of Education

Education is a "labor intensive" industry. Salaries and benefits for teachers are the largest line item in the budget of all ministries of education. Salaries generally amount to more than 90 percent of the total.

The starting level of teacher salaries varies from country to country. The amount depends on the relationship between demand for and supply of teachers, the structure of wages in the country, and the political strength of teacher associations or unions.

In most countries teachers receive salary increments in relation to years of service and to further training and education. This means that two countries with identical starting levels of salaries may spend sharply different amounts on salaries because teachers in one country have more years of service than teachers in the other.

In recent years teacher salaries in many countries have declined as a proportion of GNP/capita. In some countries teacher salaries in 1985 in units of constant currency were only 50 percent of what they were in 1970 (International Institute for Educational Planning, 1989).

This decline has been attributed (e.g., by Reimers, 1990) to decisions that governments have made about how to respond to pressures from the International Monetary Fund to reduce overall government expenditures. Some countries chose to reduce spending on education. In most cases this was accomplished by not matching allocations to education with the inflation rate or expansion of enrollments. Teacher salaries were held constant. Not only did the **real income** or **purchasing power** of teachers decline, but governments also did not hire enough teachers. Class sizes increased.

It is politically easier for governments to hold teacher salaries constant when there are more than enough candidates for positions. This oversupply occurs when the number of persons trained as teachers exceeds the number of available positions, independent of whether all children are enrolled in school or the ratio of students to teachers.

The net effect of reduced salaries appears to be a reduction in the **quality** of education. Repetition and drop out rates have increased, and public complaints about how little students learn are more common.

→ See page **84** for some data on teacher salaries relative to GNP.

Some countries have had great success in producing teachers. The supply of teachers has been used in several ways. First, countries have enrolled all children in school. Some have then reduced class sizes. Others have raised requirements for certification.

Even countries with relatively low levels of GNP per capita have been able to produce enough teachers.

The factors involved are:

1. the overall supply of persons with the level of education considered necessary to be a teacher;

2. the level of teacher salary compared to other persons with similar education;

3. the cost of training; and

4. how long people stay in teaching once trained.

Which of these statements applies to your country?

→ **There's not enough money to hire additional teachers.** If this is your situation, go to page **33**.

→ **There is a rapid turnover rate in the teaching force.** If this is your situation, go to page **77**.

→ **There aren't enough people who want to be trained to be teachers.** If this is your situation, go to page **85**.

→ **Too few people achieve the minimum level of education necessary to become a teacher.** If this is your situation, go to page **87**.

See page 214 for ways to increase training for rural teachers.

← **For more information and discussion, see page 20**

21

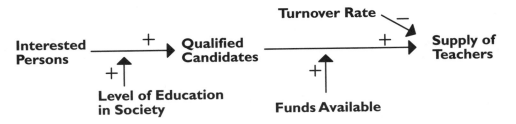

Figure 7
Supply of Teachers: Recruitment, Funding, and Turnover

Demand for Schooling

Planners distinguish between *total demand* for education, and *expressed demand*. The *total demand* for basic education is the number of children within the ages of compulsory schooling. This number of children is the same as that enrolled when a country has achieved Universal Basic Education.

Expressed demand is the number of children who **seek** enrollment, that is, who would enroll if there were space in a school. Expressed demand can be greater than the total enrolled. In some situations the *supply* of schools and/or teachers is not enough, that is, demand **exceeds** supply. For example, the number of students who want to get into higher education often is more than the number of places available.

Among the factors that limit enrollments in school is the **distance** of the school from the homes of children of school age. Research reports that the farther children must travel from home, the less likely they are to enroll in school (Anderson, 1988). In addition, the farther children live from school, the more likely they are to stop attending, that is, to drop out.

Among the reasons why parents delay or prevent entrance of their children in school is fear about their **safety** en route to and from the school. This concern is greater for girls than for boys. Research in Pakistan and Egypt shows that enrollments of girls increase sharply when a school is one kilometer or less from the home.

Demand is also limited by the **costs** of schooling to the household. Direct costs include fees, uniforms, and textbooks. Indirect costs may include transportation and clothing. Opportunity costs are the income that the household gives up by sending the child to school.

Demand is further reduced when the **perceived benefits** are low. Families are more likely to enroll children they see as having high potential than those without. Children who fail in school may be withdrawn because parents believe the child is unlikely to ever succeed.

For more information on demand factors see Anderson (1988).

from page 9

Which of the following statements is true for your country?

→ **Some families do not enroll their children because they fear for children's security.** If this is your situation, go to page **168** for possible solutions.

→ **Some families do not enroll female children because education for girls isn't valued.** See page **215** for policy options to resolve this problem.

← For more information and discussion, see page 22

How Many Teachers are Required?

The number of teachers a system requires to teach the students enrolled can be changed by changes in the curriculum.

The effectiveness of a teacher depends, among other factors, on:

1. the ability of the teacher to teach the curriculum;

2. the ability of the teacher to manage the students;

3. the cultural disposition of students to behave according to requirements of the curriculum;

4. the availability to teachers of instructional materials that hold students' attention;

5. the availability of materials for self-instruction;

6. the heterogeneity of students' abilities and interests; and

7. the physical environment in which instruction takes place, both the climate and the building.

Research states that better trained teachers can handle more students with no decline in learning outcomes.

Large classes with instructional materials do as well or better than small classes without materials. See page **90**.

Of particular importance is to be able to assign teachers to the subjects and levels for which they are prepared. Supply is inadequate when there are not enough teachers for a given subject, such as mathematics or science (Dove, 1986).

Some instructional technologies, such as interactive radio instruction, have been shown to permit teachers to handle larger classes effectively. See page **199**.

from pages 153, 166

Which of the following best accounts for the difficulties you have with implementation of the curriculum?

→   **Teachers are ignorant of the approved curriculum.** If this is true, go to pages **112, 116, 118, 120, 122,** and **124** which provide examples of an effective teacher's guide to the curriculum.

→   **Teachers know what the approved curriculum is, but do not implement it.** If this is true, go to page 157.

→   **The approved curriculum conflicts with what is tested.** If this is true, go to page **207**.

→   **The requirements of the curriculum aren't matched by the quality of teaching.** If this is true, go to page **37**.

→   **The requirements of the curriculum aren't matched by the quality and/or quantity of instructional materials.** If this is true, go to page **39**.

→   **The requirements of the curriculum aren't matched by characteristics of the students.** If this is true, go to page **41**.

→   **The requirements of the curriculum aren't met because teachers lack the time to put it into practice.** If this is true, go to page **63**.

For suggestions on how to evaluate curriculum, go to page 237.

← **For more information and discussion, see page 24**

Differential Participation in Education of Girls and Boys

As Table 5 below shows, in all parts of the world women are more likely than men to have received no schooling. Similarly in all parts of the world the school completion rate of men is higher than that of women.

The ratio of educational attainment by women to that by men is above .90 in the industrialized market economies, in Eastern Europe, and in Latin America and the Caribbean. Women receive almost as much education as do men. In other regions of the world, however, the ratio is lower. It is lowest in the Middle East and North Africa where women complete only half as many years of schooling as do men.

Table 5
Percentage of Women and Men Who Receive *No* Education

Region	Number of countries	Women %	Men %
Sub-Saharan Africa	14	57.7	46.0
Middle East/N. Africa	7	72.2	48.0
South Asia	5	65.0	51.4
East Asia and Pacific	12	20.7	9.7
Latin America/Caribbean	17	24.3	20.2

Adapted from Stromquist (1989) Table 1, p. 152.

Can the differences in educational attainment be explained by a short **supply** of education for women? **There appear to have been no systematic studies on the *provision* of education to women compared to men.** A review of 90 empirical studies on women's participation in education (Stromquist, 1989) reports few studies from the Third World. None of the studies appear to have included information about differential **opportunities** for attending school for girls compared to boys. Instead, the studies focus on how **demand** for schooling varies according to the gender of the child.

Systems that maintain separate schools for boys and for girls may report enrollments by gender. They may even indicate numbers of teachers classified by gender. They do not, however, indicate the numbers of classrooms with teachers that are available to girls compared to boys. It is possible, therefore, that lower school attendance by girls is partly a result of a lower **supply** of education.

from page 15

Is this correct for your situation?

➡ There is not enough money for construction or for rental of buildings. If **YES**, go to page **29**.

➡ There are enough funds, but planning has been poor. If **YES**, go to page **45**.

← For more information and discussion, see page 26

How Much Money is Enough for Education for All?

Third world countries vary widely in the amount of their national "income" that is spent on education. In 1989 the Government of Tunisia spent 5.5 percent of the gross national product on education. That is, education accounted for 5.5 percent of the total of goods and services that were exchanged in Tunisia in a given year. In the same year, other countries spent less than two percent of their gross national product on education.

Data of this kind are sometimes used to make an argument that countries vary in the "effort" they make to provide a public education system.

These data may be misleading. Central government expenditures may be only a fraction of total public expenditures. In some countries a significant proportion of the education is provided by non-governmental organizations. The *cost* of providing education varies considerably.

Table 6 shows central government expenditures on education, for the years around 1989, and the proportion of the age group enrolled in primary school. There is no relationship between either the percent of government expenditures for education, or government expenditures as a proportion of GNP, and the net enrollment rate in primary.

Table 6
Central Government Expenditures on Education around 1989

EXPENDITURES ON EDUCATION

	As % of Total Gov't Expend.	As % of GNP	% Age Group in Primary
Ethiopia	10.6	3.7	26
Malawi	12.3	3.6	55
Mali	9.0	2.6	18
Burkina Faso	14.0	1.6	27
Indonesia	10.0	2.1	100
Bolivia	20.3	3.4	83
Cameroon	12.0	2.5	80
El Salvador	17.6	1.8	72
Tunisia	14.6	5.5	85
Turkey	15.7	3.7	84
Costa Rica	17.0	4.7	85
Mexico	12.3	2.6	99
Rep. Korea	18.5	3.1	100

Source: World Bank *World Development Report 1991*, Table 11, pp. 224–225.

from pages 19, 27

Which of the following best explains why there is not enough money for basic education?

→ **More money needs to be allocated to education in general.** If you think the problem is how to generate more revenue in general, go to page 172 for possible solutions.

→ **What money is available needs to be spent more efficiently.** For suggestions on how to get more for your money, go to pages 171 and 175.

← For more information and discussion, see page 28

29

Choosing School Locations

There are excellent aids to assist in the planning of school locations (e.g., Gould, 1978; Hallak, 1977). There is a scarcity, however, of aids to help in obtaining sites on which to locate buildings.

Most work on school location planning or school mapping has focused on how to locate schools to respond most effectively to the distribution of potential students.

Cost is undoubtedly a major factor in the selection of sites for schools. *Land* costs are a major contributor, but *preparation* costs may also be high, as when the land provided has an unsuitable subsoil or is subject to flooding.

A second factor is access of the client population to schools. This problem is most serious for primary grades; and most serious in rural areas in which students are widely scattered. Time and mode of travel to school have been shown to affect regularity of attendance (of both teachers and students), They have an indirect effect on amount of learning (see pages **100** and **104**).

Recommended distances and time durations vary by the urban or rural nature of the site, age and gender of the students, and level of violence. A current rule of thumb is that no child should have to walk more than one and a half kilometers to reach a primary school.

When land is not available for schools, educational planners have shown great ingenuity in re-designing programs and buildings. In crowded urban areas, schools can be built vertically, that is, with multiple floors. Playgrounds can be located on roofs, or in central areas accessible by transport. Similarly, workshops and laboratories can be concentrated in school clusters (Cummings, Gunardwardena and Williams, 1992) in rural areas. Page **213** suggests alternative sites for schools. Page **223** describes the effective use of a cluster system. See also Wheeler, Raudenbush and Pasigna (1989).

For additional reading see Almeida (1988), Gould (1978), and Hamel (1977).

from page 19

A chronic problem in large cities, especially those growing rapidly, is procuring sites for school construction. Urbanization can increase the price of land to the point that the education system can not afford to buy school sites. The government may not have either the political will, or the political power, to requisition land at a price it can afford.

Similar problems are found in rural areas. In some countries the government relies on large landowners for donations of land for school sites. Some landowners do not cooperate; they fear that educated children may not be willing to work under the same conditions as their fathers and mothers.

What is the situation in your country?

➡ **In urban areas land is too expensive for the Ministry of Education to purchase.**

➡ **In rural areas the landowners will not donate or sell it for school construction.**

➡ **Procuring and preparing land takes a great deal of time.**

If any of these situations is true for your country, go to page **213** for suggestions about alternative locations for schools.

← For more information and discussion, see page 30

How Much Money is Needed for Teachers?

In every education system *salaries of teachers* is the largest single cost item. The total is often above 90 percent of total recurrent expenditures. This is consistent with our understanding of education as a "labor intensive" activity.

As overall spending on education increases, the proportion of the budget that is for teacher salaries declines. More is spent on administration, and on instructional materials and training.

All evidence indicates that investment in education is a fundamental requirement for economic growth as well as political and social development. Spending on education contributes to development by

1. slowing down the rate of population growth;

2. helping to improve overall health;

3. increasing participation in the labor force; and

4. increasing productivity.

Should increased spending on education go to higher salaries for teachers, or for increased spending on administration, or instructional materials?

Increased spending for teachers could be used to hire more teachers. If teacher/students ratios are held constant, this permits an increase in enrollments.

Increased funds could be used to raise teacher salaries, to improve quality of teaching. See page **84** for a comment on research on this issue.

Increased funds could be used for training to improve quality of education. See pages **52**, **66**, and **82** for a discussion of training and quality of teaching.

Increased funds could also be spent on instructional materials. In Brazil, research shows that spending on basic materials such as chalk, paper, pencils and textbooks is much more cost-effective (more impact on learning per unit cost) than are training courses for teachers (Lockheed and Verspoor, 1991); see also page **60**.

The balance between spending on teacher salaries, administration, and materials, will vary according to the kind of instructional technology adopted. Some ways of delivering education are less *labor intensive* than others. For examples see page **199**.

from page 21

Which is the reason why there is not enough money to hire additional teachers?

→ **More money needs to be allocated to education.** If this is so, go to page 172 for possible solutions.

→ **Money available for education is allocated to other areas in addition to teacher salaries.** If this is so, go to page 175 for possible solutions.

If it is not possible to increase the supply of persons who, with adequate training, can become good teachers, it may be necessary to introduce other methods that make up for what teachers lack. See page 220 for examples of distance education methods that can be used when it is not possible to generate an adequate supply of good teachers using conventional methods of training.

← For more information and discussion, see page 32

33

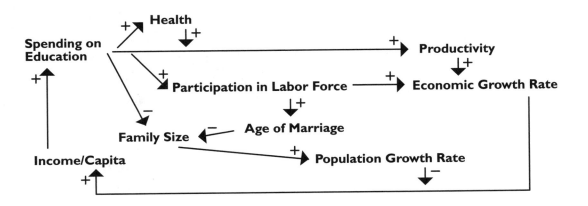

Figure 8
How Education Contributes to Economic Growth

Instructional Design versus Curriculum Design

There are two basic perspectives on how curriculum should be designed. The first emphasizes "correct" coverage of the subject matter. This perspective argues that each *discipline* or subject matter contains its own *logic*. Content should be presented according to this logic. Those persons most expert in the discipline are those best qualified to develop the curriculum. For convenience, we refer to this as a **curriculum design** approach.

A second perspective emphasizes amount of learning of the subject. This view insists that presentation of content should be organized according to how students learn. The psychology of the learner is more important than the logic of the expert in the discipline. Curriculum should be developed according to research on learning. This is called the **instructional design** approach (Gagne & Briggs, 1979; Richey, 1986).

There is a growing body of research that shows that **learning technologies based on instructional design methods:**

1. enable teachers to handle larger class sizes with no reduction in learning outcomes;

2. enable students to learn the same amount of content in less time (or to learn more in the same time); and

3. permit less qualified teachers to be as effective as qualified teachers using **traditional technologies.** (Thiagarajan and Pasigna, 1988).

Instructional design methods emphasize the following principles:

1. Students (and teachers) should be clear about what is to be learned, that is, about instructional objectives.

2. It should be possible to assess whether these objectives have been achieved, that is, whether the student has learned.

3. Assessment should be fairly frequent, to allow for adjustment of the *pace* of presentation.

4. Lessons (instructional units) should be relatively short.

5. The *sequence* of units should be organized according to the logic of the learners.

➜ See pages **38**, **216** and **217** for further information.

from pages 47, 77, 153, 157, 181

Which of the following factors best accounts for the low quality of the curriculum?

→ **Content is not relevant to the students.** If this so, go to page **51**.

→ **It does not clearly specify what students are expected to learn.** If this is so, go to page **237** for suggestions of how to evaluate the curriculum.

→ **It does not clearly specify how the teachers are supposed to teach the content.** If this is so, go to pages **112**, **116**, **118**, **120**, **122**, and **124** for an example of a teacher's guide to a curriculum.

→ **There is inadequate pacing of the presentation of materials.** For an example of pacing of subject matter in a textbook, go to page **122**.

→ **There is inadequate and/or incomplete sequencing of units within subjects.** For an example of sequencing, go to page **124**.

← For more information and discussion, see page 34

Figure 9
Factors that Determine Student Learning

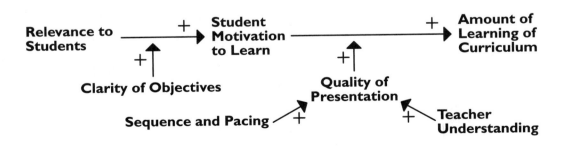

Summary of Research on Background Characteristics of Teachers Identified as Effective

We can define an *effective* teacher as one who generates high levels of student learning. If we knew the characteristics of persons who become effective teachers, we could develop criteria for selection and training that would improve learning outcomes. However, how effective a teacher is depends in part on circumstances beyond the control of the teacher. For example, how much students learn depends also on characteristics of the students (see page **40**).

As a consequence, studies that link characteristics of teachers with student learning outcomes do not produce consistent results. Here are some of the findings that often, but not always, appear:

Characteristics of Effective Teachers	*Implications for Selection and Training*
Higher verbal ability, sometimes measured by IQ, sometimes by social class	Screen for verbal ability.
High expectations for learning	Screen on beliefs about learning capacity of students. Train teachers to set high standards for themselves and their students.
Knows many teaching methods	Train teachers to use wide variety of pedagogical practices. Provide examples of different methods in practice.
High knowledge of subject	Extend academic training of candidates. Use in-service training to broaden knowledge.
Clear definition of purpose	Select candidates familiar with real conditions of classroom, purpose of schooling.
Sense of humor	Select candidates on basis of interpersonal skills.

For more information see Gumbert (1990) and Rugh (1991).

from page 25

Effective teaching requires that the teacher meet requirements
established in the curriculum. The minimum requirements are:

1) knowledge of the language in which the curriculum is to be taught;

2) knowledge of the subject matter of the curriculum; and

3) ability to carry out the methods specified in the curriculum.

Which of the following statements best describes the situation in your country?

➜ **Teachers can't teach in the language in which the curriculum is written.** If this matches your situation, go to page **47**.

➜ **Teachers don't know the subject matter required in the curriculum.** If this matches your situation, go to page **49**.

➜ **Teachers lack the skills needed to teach the curriculum.** If this matches your situation, go to page **53**.

← For more information and discussion, see page 36

37

Figure 10
Determinants of Quality of Teaching

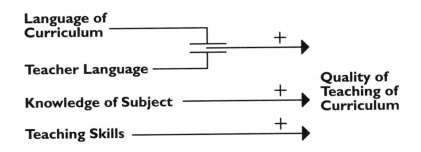

Instructional Materials and Curriculum Requirements

Students learn what they are taught (Fraser, Walberg, Welch and Hattie, 1987). The curriculum is the education system's plan for the learning of specified content. As a plan, the curriculum includes goals (learning objectives) and programs (which specify the activities to reach the objectives). The success of the system depends on implementation of the curriculum.

Like many plans, however, curricula often fail because of faulty implementation. Proper implementation depends on knowledge of and commitment to goals, and the ability to carry out programs. Teachers often lack knowledge of official learning objectives, and of the specific content they are supposed to teach.

The Textbook as Source of Curriculum Knowledge

Day to day knowledge of the official curriculum can be provided by textbooks matched to the curriculum. For many teachers, without manuals and without in-service training, the textbook is the only source of knowledge of the curriculum.

In many countries, students do not have access to textbooks (Paxman, Denning and Read, 1989). In some countries this is because few textbooks have been printed, in others it is because poor parents can not afford to purchase books for their children. Rural students are most affected by shortage or cost of books.

In many countries what books are available do not match the requirements of the curriculum. In some cases, books are not available in the language of instruction used in the classroom. In other cases, the content of the textbooks is not consistent with official curriculum objectives.

An analysis of texts in 15 countries reports that curriculum content is often presented in a form that makes it difficult for students to learn. Textbooks spend too little time on initial learning tasks, too quickly skip to more sophisticated material that few students can master (Cope, Denning, and Ribeiro, 1989).

The Teacher's Guide as Source of Curriculum Knowledge

An alternative or complementary source of information about the curriculum is a guide written for teachers. The guide can accompany the textbook, and contain suggestions for how the text is to be used. Or it can be a stand-alone manual for implementation of the official curriculum. However, teacher guides are even more scarce than textbooks.

➜ See page 110 for information about the importance of textbooks.

from page 25

For materials to contribute to teaching and learning of the curriculum they must meet requirements specified in the curriculum. These requirements include:

1) that materials be written in the language in which the curriculum will be taught;

2) and that materials match the content of the curriculum in pacing, sequence, and emphasis.

Which of the following matches the situation in your country?

→ **Materials are not written in the language of the curriculum.** If this is your situation, go to page **123**.

→ **The content of the materials does not match the content of the curriculum.** For an example of one attempt to resolve this problem, go to page **181**.

Your country may experience two other kinds of problems with materials.

Which of the following matches your situation?

→ **There are not enough materials.** If this is the case, go to page **109**.

→ **There are no teachers' guides for instructional materials.** For an example of what one country did, go to page **181**. See pages **112**, **116**, **118**, **120**, **122**, and **124** for sample pages from a teacher's guide.

← For more information and discussion, see page 38

39

The Teachability of Students

The success of the formal school, as a means for providing large numbers of children with basic education, lies in its specification of content and procedures. The formal school specifies

- who can teach,

- what they will teach,

- how it will be taught,

- what materials will be used,

- how student learning will be assessed.

To make these specifications, *planners make assumptions about the characteristics of children* who will attend the school. The school works best when there is a close match between the assumptions of the school, and the characteristics of its students. Students who do *not* match the assumptions, often experience failure.

Low levels of learning by some children may, therefore, be explained by their lack of readiness for school. This lack of "readiness" may be attributable to several factors:

1. a family background that did not provide the **self-discipline** expected by the school. After all, schools expect children to obey teachers, and to be able to sit still for relatively long periods of time.

2. a family background that did not provide the **learning skills** expected by the school. Some schools, for example, expect children to arrive at school knowing their alphabet, colors, and numbers. They expect children to have learned to listen and remember.

3. differences in language and culture that make it difficult for the child to understand the teacher.

Schools can improve their **ability to teach** students by changing their own assumptions. They also can provide special training to children to ready them for school. **Pre-school** programs are designed to accomplish this.

Effective pre-school programs provide children with opportunities to learn the social skills and habits required by the first grade of school. Children learn self-discipline, respect for others, and obedience to the teacher. They also may be taught learning skills expected by the first grade curriculum.

Research shows clearly that pre-school programs can reduce failure in the early grades of primary school (Halpern, 1986; Raudenbush et al., 1991), especially among poor children.

➜ For further discussion of pre-school programs see page **210.**

from page 25

Which of the following statements describe why students can't meet the requirements of the curriculum?

→ **They lack the language of the curriculum.** If this is your situation, page **198** suggests a series of questions to help decide which language of instruction to use.

→ **Teaching in the previous level was inadequate and the students are not prepared.** If this is your situation, go to page **125**.

→ **Classes are too heterogeneous.** If this is your situation, go to page **127**.

→ **Attendance problems.** If this is so, go to page **105**.

← For more information and discussion, see page 40

Sources of Problems in Administration of Education

The *administration* or management of education became a critical issue beginning in the seventeenth century. Schooling was seen as an effective means to produce citizens loyal to the new European nations (Ramirez and Boli, 1989).

Mass education was designed to employ techniques of control similar to those developed in factories. This included standardization of inputs such as furniture, teachers, and texts. It also meant the designation of persons responsible for seeing to the proper use of those inputs.

Those who managed schools were in turn managed by district inspectors who in turn responded to a national ministry. The form of most ministries of education was laid down in the early 1800s and has not changed significantly.

The following are among the sources of problems faced by managers at all levels:

1. *Lack of clarity in objectives.* The goal statements of most education systems are highly abstract. Few systems have developed *indicators* or measures of **outputs**. Plans often focus only on inputs. As a consequence, managers at various levels may have conflicting views of which activities are most important.

2. *Imprecise and overlapping job definitions.* Failure to specify responsibilities leads to duplication of effort. Perhaps worse, it may lead to a tendency to push decisions up to the highest ranking official in the system. Managers at the top of the hierarchy end up carrying out tasks of lower level managers.

3. *Insufficient resources to carry out responsibilities.* Ministries of education often have no control over their own budgets. Funds are allocated by a ministry of finance or some other agency. The first budget items to be cut are those that support activities of managers, such as transportation and communication. This makes it difficult for managers to visit units for which they are responsible.

4. *Lack of planning; time consumed with 'fire-fighting' or routine tasks.* Many plans are merely extrapolations of current activities. No effort is made to anticipate the petty and serious crises that every system faces during a year. Managers have to attend to solving "urgent problems" rather than studying how to improve long-term performance.

We have some descriptions of the kinds of problems faced in administration of education (Toronto, 1990; UNESCO, 1984) but no studies on how to solve these problems. See pages 142 and 144.

from pages 11, 79, 101, 117

Today we know that management can make an important contribution to the *quality* of education. Teachers have the most impact on how much and what students learn; but, school administrators, and their managers, also can improve quality.

Which of the following is the major source of your dissatisfaction with the quality of administration in your country:

→ **Administration as it directly affects the quality of teaching**. Go to page **71**.

→ **The quality of administration at the central or national level**. Go to page **139**.

→ **The quality of administration at the regional or district level**. Go to page **141**.

→ **The quality of administration at the local or school level**. Go to page **143**.

← **For more information and discussion, see page 42**

43

The State of Educational Planning at the End of the 1980s

Many observers worldwide agreed that by the end of the 1980s educational planning was in a state of confusion. Most planning had been *normative*, based on an assumption that it is possible to anticipate the future and therefore that it is meaningful to specify in advance what should be done. Norms dictated from the center by "experts" were to be applied uniformly throughout the system. Critics commented that there was a naive perception regarding the ease of educational planning and a presumption that it would automatically have a positive effect on economic growth (Hallak, 1989). As a consequence, planning was carried out to satisfy international funding agencies such as the World Bank, USAID, and UNDP. They required governments to make educational plans in order to receive loans. Governments created plans without substance and direction (Morales Gomez, 1989). Because planning was dictated from outside the countries, there was little micro-planning. World planners underutilized indigenous researchers, creating a disparity between educational planners and the actual conditions in the developing societies (Morales Gomez, 1989).

In most cases, central planners had little knowledge of actual conditions in schools; the information with which they worked, often out of date, generally was limited to quantities of inputs. There was little knowledge of variations in qualities of inputs, about the process of instruction that took place in classrooms, or the impact of inputs and process on learning outcomes.

Several new forms of planning have emerged that may or may not resolve the issues named above. These include:

a. micro-planning, often called school mapping (Hallak, 1977). This technique uses detailed information at the level of the school.

b. contingency planning (Rondinelli et al., 1990). An effort is made to anticipate the range of situations that can occur and to be ready to respond to them. Strong emphasis is placed on implementation.

c. strategic planning (Bryson, 1988). The methods of long-range planning are utilized to generate consensus among those who will implement the plan, about objectives and ways to attain them.

Central to the improvement of planning is the generation of timely, comprehensive and accurate information about the performance of the system. Planners have to be able to link variations in inputs to the system, with variations in outputs and outcomes. The development of an education management information system permits the education organization to learn from its mistakes.

For more information on educational planning see Hallak (1989), Lewin (1988) and page **239**. For a description of education management information systems, see page **202**. For more information on sustainability of externally-funded projects, see page **194**.

from pages 19, 27, 79

Which of the following accounts for lack of space?

➡ **This need was not anticipated.**

➡ **The need was anticipated, but the buildings were not built.**

➡ **Buildings were constructed but not maintained.**

If any of these explanations is appropriate go to page **180** for a description of planning in Pakistan. Go to page **213** for alternatives to school construction. Go to page **230** for comments about maintenance.

➡ **Buildings were constructed, but not in the right places. Buildings were too far from where students live.** Go to page **212** for a discussion of how school size affects availability.

If none of these descriptions describe your situation, go back to page **19**.

45

← For more information and discussion, see page 44

Teacher Language and Student Learning

There are several reasons why education systems in multilingual countries should provide instruction in more than one language.

1. There is abundant research that shows that students learn to read more quickly when taught in their first language ("mother tongue" or L1).

2. Students that have learned to read in their L1 learn to read in a second language (L2) more quickly than do those who are first taught to read in the L2.

3. Students taught to read in their L1 more quickly acquire academic learning skills. (See page 114 for details.)

Unfortunately, many countries do not have enough qualified teachers who speak languages other than the official language of instruction. In this situation L2-speaking teachers often allow students to use their L1 to help explain the lessons. Research shows that in most cases this is not as effective as an explicit bilingual program. Students do not learn well in either L1 or L2.

The most successful teachers in bilingual programs are native speakers of the students' L1, *from the same community*. Often there are not enough qualified teachers from the community. Good results have been obtained by training indigenous speakers as teachers.

Bilingual teachers (whose "mother tongue" is the language of instruction but who speak the students' L1 as a second language) are also effective. We know little, however, about how proficient teachers have to be in the students' language. **There is very little research on student learning that measures teachers' language proficiency as an independent variable.**

Teachers' attitudes toward the indigenous language are important to the success of the program (Corvalan, 1985). Also important are the attitudes of parents and the community. Negative attitudes toward use of the indigenous language for instruction are found when:

1. the indigenous language lacks prestige in the society at large; and

2. not learning the L2 has negative consequences for employment.

For more information see Heise-Baigorria (1991).

from pages 37, 59

Which of the following factors explains why teachers can't teach in the language of instruction?

→ **The inadequate process of selection of teacher candidates.** If this fits your situation, go to page **184** for a discussion of issues in selection of teachers.

→ **We need to train more people from rural areas.** If this fits your situation, go to page **214**.

Another kind of solution to the problem of not enough teachers might be to improve the curriculum.

→ If this is possible in your country, go to page **35**.

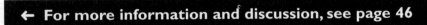

← For more information and discussion, see page 46

Should Teacher Training Emphasize Subject Matter or Pedagogy?

An effective teacher needs to know both the subject taught, and how to teach it. As the chart on page **86** shows, countries vary in how much time is spent on training in skills, and teaching of subject knowledge. **We have almost no research about the proper balance between training in teaching skills, and teaching of subject knowledge.**

There are several reasons why this is so.

1. *Most research is not comparative.*

Some studies show that teacher knowledge is important for student learning (Fuller, 1987). These studies did not, however, include measures of pedagogical skills. Other studies include measures of training in skills, but do not analyze which combination is most effective (Tatto, Nielsen, and Cummings, 1991).

Research is selective in its attention. Studies on teacher competencies emphasize training in subject matter. On the other hand, research on teaching strategies gives priority to pedagogical training (Organization for Economic Cooperation and Development, 1989).

2. *It is difficult to study the training process.*

Little research has been done on what actually takes place in teacher training programs (Dove, 1986). Many teacher training programs do not have a formal curriculum.

Teaching of subject knowledge and training in skills may be combined in the same class. This makes it difficult to assign levels of effort to each. We do not have well-developed methods to measure how teachers have been transformed by their training.

3. *It is difficult to distinguish effects of teacher knowledge from effects of teacher skills.*

The impact of variations in teacher knowledge and teacher skills on student learning varies as a result of:

a. teacher motivation;

b. students' ability levels;

c. working conditions in the classroom; and,

d. the specific content (by subject and level).

from pages 37, 59

In your country, which of the following statements is correct?

→ **Elementary classroom teachers are the ones who don't know the subject matter.** If this is true in your situation, go to page **67**.

→ **There are not sufficient subject area specialists.** If this is so, go to page **73**. If there are enough specialists, go to page **65**.

← **For more information and discussion, see page 48**

Obstacles to the Development of Relevant Curriculum

There are few published evaluations of new curriculum, and few studies on the obstacles to making curriculum more relevant. The following case study illustrates some of those obstacles.

In 1986, Botswana developed a new curriculum to accompany the establishment of a nine-year basic education cycle. The curriculum was intended to be more practical, and related to "the needs of the country." Some new subjects (such as agriculture) were included, others (e.g., mathematics) were modified. The intent was to make it easier for school-leavers to find employment or become self-employed. The new curriculum included guidelines and materials for English, Setswana, math, science, agriculture, and social studies. It included as four optional subjects: art, home economics, religion, and social studies.

Implementation of the curriculum in grades 7, 8, and 9 was evaluated during 1987 to 1988. The researchers visited schools, observing classes and interactions between teachers and students. The study concludes that there was little "practical curriculum" actually taking place. Instead,

a. the curriculum actually used was heavily teacher centered;

b. emphasis was placed on transfer of information from teacher to student;

c. repetition and drill were the most frequently used instructional methods; and

d. little attention was given to the knowledge and values that students brought with them.

Four explanations are offered as to why the new curriculum failed in implementation to be "practical" or relevant.

1. The language of instruction often was a second language for students. (See pages **46** and **114** for a discussion of importance of language of instruction.)

2. Teachers were not competent in the students' languages, and were unwilling to deviate from the text, to adapt it to the local circumstances. This led to reductions in content taught.

3. Teachers preferred to reinforce existing skills of students rather than introduce the new material in the curriculum.

4. Parents pressured teachers to prepare students for an external certification examination not matched to the "practical" curriculum (Prophet and Rowell, 1988).

→ For more on problems of **implementation** see page **218**.

→ For information on **sustainability** of externally-funded projects, go to page **194**.

from page 35

Some experts argue that **relevance** of the curriculum should be our primary concern. The term **relevance** is used in several ways. For example, lower enrollment rates for rural children are explained by arguing that the curriculum is not relevant to the interests of rural communities. Relevance is understood as the connection between the content or outcomes of education, and objectives of some group.

Parents are not, of course, the only group to define what education should do. In most countries curriculum is defined primarily by experts in the various academic disciplines. Employers may complain that graduates do not have proper work habits or skills. Minority groups often find that curriculum does not represent their values or cultural heritage.

The problem of relevance is compounded because in some societies educated persons may end up living and working far from their communities of origin. Which group should be taken into account when deciding on relevance?

In your country, which of the following describes why curriculum is not relevant?

→ **It is specific to one group.** Go to page 181 for a possible solution to this problem.

→ **It is written in an unfamiliar language.** Go to page 181 for possible solutions to this problem.

← For more information and discussion, see page 50

Does Teacher Training Improve Quality of Education?

Research on the effects of teacher training is not conclusive. In some countries teacher training clearly makes a difference for student learning, in others it does not (Fuller, 1987; Lockheed and Komenan, 1989).

Several reasons are offered (Chapman and Snyder, 1989) as to why the impact of teacher training is not more evident.

1. Out-of-school factors (malnutrition, little time for study) limit how much learning can occur (see page **104**).

2. The quality of training is too low for it to make much difference. This explanation has several parts:

   a. training is too short;

   b. training fails to provide required knowledge and/or skills;

   c. trainees do not have an opportunity to practice what is learned in their classrooms; and

   d. there is too much difference between what is taught, and actual conditions in classrooms.

3. Variations in conditions of work in schools (materials, physical facilities, student characteristics), not taken into account in the study, may mask the true effectiveness of training.

This last explanation emphasizes how local context can affect the impact of training provided in central facilities. The *general academic* education a teacher receives more often accounts for student learning than does the *professional training* received. Professional training is more likely to be specific to certain situations and, therefore, inappropriate in others.

This is not an argument against teacher training. On the contrary, training has to be adapted to actual conditions in classrooms. This can best be done when planners visit classrooms, or teachers participate in planning.

(For additional research see: Anderson and Postlethwaite, 1989; Avalos, 1986; Chapman and Carrier, 1990; Husen, Saha, and Noonan, 1979.)

from pages 11, 37, 99, 111, 117, 166

There are various factors that influence the **quality** of teaching.

1. Quality of teaching depends on the qualities of the persons who become teachers, such as their intelligence, character, personality.

In your system, is the quality of teaching affected because the quality of the candidates entering the teaching profession is poor?

➜ If YES, go to page **65**.

2. Training is the major means by which countries attempt to improve upon the qualities of persons who want to become teachers. Training programs themselves can vary in quality or impact.

Are you satisfied with the contribution made by:

➜ **pre-service training programs?** If NO, go to page **67**.

➜ **in-service training programs?** If NO, go to page **69**.

If none of these questions match your situation, go to page 55.

← **For more information and discussion, see page 52**

53

Figure 11
Quality of Teachers and Teaching

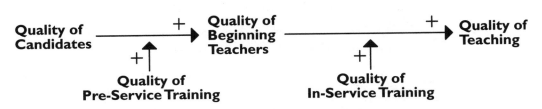

Dimensions of the Behavior of School Administrators

The behavior of school administrators depends in part on personal characteristics. But school administrators also respond to incentives from central administration, and can be trained to be more effective. The following findings are summarized by an evaluation of the impact of management reforms in Sri Lanka. The major reform involved moving responsibility for many school functions down to the level of a cluster of ten schools.

Management behavior was assessed by interviews with school administrators. Questions covered three sets of behaviors:

1. management initiative. This refers to the extent to which administrators (in Sri Lanka, principals) make decisions for themselves.

2. management practice. Did administrators:

    a. carry out goal definition and planning;

    b. encourage local curriculum development;

    c. supervise teacher behavior in classrooms;

    d. concern themselves with the welfare of students; and

    e. involve the school in community activities?

3. management style. Did administrators:

    a. involve teachers in decision making;

    b. delegate responsibilities; and

    c. communicate upward and downward?

The study found that administrators tend to focus either on attention to academic activities in the school, or on activities that promote student welfare and strong community relations.

Administrators who include teachers in decision making also include public officials and the community. Those who are not inclusive, prefer to give responsibility for implementation to others.

Administrators who stressed academic leadership put less emphasis on relations with students and parents.

Trained administrators who participated in the reform were: much more active in school management; had better relations with their teachers; and developed closer relationships with communities. Student performance (promotion rate) improved in schools where administrators became more active. Better relations with the community resulted in larger donations of money and volunteer labor (Cummings, Gunawardena, and Williams, 1992).

➜ See also page 142.

from pages 53, 75

At one time school administrators were **master teachers** whose main responsibility was to help less-qualified persons become better at teaching. A good master teacher provided a model that less qualified teachers could imitate to become good teachers. The school administrator also resolved problems of student discipline. This freed teachers to spend more time on instruction.

Are you satisfied with the contribution made by administrative practices to the quality of teaching?

→   If NO, go to page **71**.

Administrative practices also affect the motivation of teachers, and the conditions in which they work.

Which of the following describes your quality of teaching?

→   **Affected by teachers who are not motivated.** If this is true, go to page **77**.

→   **Affected by working conditions in schools.** If this is true, go to page **79**.

If none of these statements are appropriate for your system, go to page 57.

← **For more information and discussion, see page 54**

55

Figure 12
Motivation and Quality of Teaching

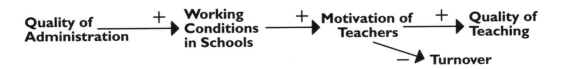

Table 7

Availability of Qualified Teachers in Latin America and the Caribbean[1]

	Percentage of teachers *without* certificates
Colombia	29.4
rural areas	39.2
Cuba	16.1
El Salvador	2.3
rural areas	0.0
Guyana	35.2
Honduras	32.3
rural areas	45.6
Jamaica	9.1
Nicaragua	50.5
rural areas	73.6
Peru	43.2
Venezuela	14.9

[1] Adapted from Table 22 in UNESCO/OREALC (1990).

from page 55

T he quality of teaching is affected by several other factors, some of which can be controlled by central administrators, others not.

Which of the following *other* factors affect how much students learn?

➜   **The teachers' qualities do not match requirements of the curriculum.** Go to page **59**.

➜   **Characteristics of materials do not match requirements of curriculum.** Go to page **61**.

➜   **Quality is lowered by the heterogeneity of students.** Go to page **127**.

If none of these statements apply, perhaps quality of teaching is not a major problem for you. In that case, go back to page **11**.

Table 8
Certification Requirements for Primary Teachers

Algeria	Must have completed either five or six years of post-primary education. One-year course at Institute of Technology of Education (ITE), followed by one year of practice leads to **certificate**.
Bahrain	**M.Ed.** in Science Education and **Postgraduate Diploma in Education** offered by University College of Arts, Science and Education.
Bangladesh	Eight-month course at a Primary Training Institute leads to a **Certificate**.
Botswana	Two-year course at a teacher training college leads to a **Primary Teacher's Certificate**.
Brazil	During the professional training period in secondary school pupils can take teacher training. Training over three years qualifies one for the **Diploma de Professor do Ensino de 1er Grau**.
Burma	After completion of middle school, a one-year training program at a teacher-training institute or college leads to certification as a **Primary Assistant Teacher (PAT)**.
Burundi	Teachers are trained on a seven-year secondary-level courses. Completion of full course leads to secondary school certificate and the **Ordinary Teachers Diploma**.
Egypt	**Elementary Teaching Certificate** awarded students who complete five-year course in which they specialize in the last two years.
India	**Teacher Training Certificate** awarded after completion of a one- to two-year course at a Teacher Training Institute.
Ivory Coast	Training is at upper secondary level and leads to the qualification of **Instituteur**.
Kenya	Two-year teacher training course after four years of secondary education leads to **P1, P2 or P3 Certificate** depending on exam results.
Malawi	T3 teacher training colleges admit students with the **Junior Certificate of Education** and run a two-year program which leads to a **T3 Teachers Certificate**.
Panama	The **Certificado de Maestro Normal** is awarded at the end of the last three-year cycle of secondary education in a teacher institution.
Peru	A three-year upper secondary course leads to the title of **Maestro Normal**.
Zimbabwe	Four-year course after five GCE O-level passes leads to **Certificate in Education of the University of Zimbabwe**.

Source: British Council (1987); Postlethwaite (1988).

58

from page 57

Countries differ in the requirements set for **who can become a teacher**. In many countries the shortage of qualified teachers makes it necessary to hire persons who do not meet the requirements. Among the more important requirements for teachers are:

1. ability in the language of instruction;

2. skills in teaching; and

3. knowledge of the basic subject matter.

Teachers' knowledge of the subject matter generally is linked to having completed a specified level of education.

The assessment of whether the candidate has the kinds of pedagogical skills required to implement the curriculum generally is supposed to occur during a trial period. Many countries lack sufficient supervisory staff for this to be effective.

Which of the following is a correct statement of problems that you have in your country?

➡ **Many teachers don't speak the language of instruction.** If this is your situation, go to page **47**.

➡ **Teachers don't have skills required by the curriculum.** If this is your situation, go to page **67**.

➡ **Many teachers don't have the level of knowledge expected in the curriculum.** If this is your situation, go to page **49**.

← For more information and discussion, see page 58

59

The Effect of Increased Spending on the Quantity and Quality of Instructional Materials

Research shows that spending on instructional materials improves student learning and reduces student failures. As a consequence, **investments in instructional materials can be cost-effective.**

These examples are taken from Lockheed and Verspoor (1991).

1. The Brazilian government was concerned with low student performance in the schools of the northeast, the poorest region of the country. Budgets were increased for physical facilities, furniture, teacher training, textbooks, student writing materials and other school supplies.

Evaluations over a six-year period showed significant improvements in student performance. Increased learning reduced failure and repetition rates, and dropouts. As a consequence, the average length of time that students take to move from grade 2 to grade 4 was reduced by .13 years. Total costs for educating a student through grade 4 were reduced by US$4.03, less than the cost per student of the program.

The largest returns were from expenditures on textbooks and writing materials: four times the original cost was saved by reductions in repetition and dropouts.

2. Grades 4 and 5 in rural schools in Fiji were provided with a selection of well-illustrated story books considered to be of high interest to children of that age. Each class in the experiment received 250 books.

In half the classes, teachers were trained in methods for using the books in instruction. Teachers were taught how to involve students in discussion of the book's contents, and how to read aloud to them. In the other half of the classes, students read silently on their own for 30 minutes a day. A third group of children received no books, only a course on English taught using a conventional approach. Tests of reading were applied before and eight months and one year later.

In the first eight months, classes that received the books improved reading levels by 8.5 months more than classes without the books (15 months to 6.5 months gain). At the end of two years, gains were even more impressive, and had also improved more than the control group in writing, grammar and other subjects. Pass rates on the national English examination were over 70 percent for classes that received books, and only 37 percent for those who did not receive books.

➜ See also pages **108** and **110**.

from page 57

The production of materials requires an up-front capital cost that may be resisted by ministries of finance. As a consequence, instructional materials are seldom a significant part of the education system's annual budget. In many countries materials are in short supply.

Materials should, of course, be in the language of instruction actually used in the classroom. Effective use of the materials for teaching the curriculum is more likely when teachers are provided with instructions on how they are to be used.

Which of the following best describes your materials situation?

→ **There aren't enough materials.** If this is your situation, go to page 109.

→ **Materials are written in a language which doesn't match the teachers' language.** If this is your situation, go to pages 181 and 198 for possible responses.

→ **There are no instructions for the use of the materials.** If this is so, go to page 121.

← For more information and discussion, see page 60

61

How Much Time is Spent on the Task?

Suppose each unit of time spent on teaching the curriculum is of equal value for student learning. If so, the more time spent teaching the curriculum, the more students will learn. Time spent teaching the curriculum (by teachers) or learning from the curriculum (by students) is called *time-on-task*.

There is probably an upper limit to time-on-task, after which learning starts to taper off. A ten-hour school day, for example, might be too much.

Table 9 below indicates the range of differences in the length of the school year. These totals are obtained by multiplying the number of days in the official school year by the number of hours in the official school day. In fact there is variation from school to school in the same district in number of days of actual classes and hours in the school day.

→ For a discussion of the importance of time-on-task see page **92**.

Table 9
Length of School Year in Hours per Year, Grade 6

Argentina	950	Ghana	800
Benin	1080	Guyana	1200
Brazil	800	Jamaica	950
Burkina Faso	1290	Jordan	1074
Central African Republic	885	Korea	1088
Chile	1140	Malawi	930
China	1320	Malta	1120
Costa Rica	800	Philippines	1200
Cote D'Ivoire	1140	Suriname	725
Ecuador	833	Venezuela	875

Source: International Institute for Educational Planning (1991), p.1.

from pages 11, 25

Most education managers worry that not enough time is being spent on teaching the curriculum, that is, **on task**. To overcome this problem, managers look for ways to increase time spent.

Is this reasonable? Does length of day and school year make a difference in student learning?

The answer is yes, but a simple extension of the school year will not necessarily produce increased learning. Research suggests that **hours in the school day are more important than length of school year.** More important than either is student attendance and coverage of the curriculum.

That is because:

1. spending to increase student attendance will produce greater gains in learning than spending to lengthen the time the teacher spends in the classroom.

2. helping teachers to teach the official curriculum more completely will produce more learning than will lengthening the time teachers spend in the classroom.

Which of the following best describes why teachers are unable to spend enough time on curriculum?

➜ **Teachers are distracted from their work by classroom disorder.** If this is true, go to page **81**.

➜ **Teachers are distracted from their work by other factors.** If this is true, go to page **93**.

← **For more information and discussion, see page 62**

63

The Profession of Teaching

The teaching profession began at a time when the process of teaching was seen as the transfer of book knowledge from one person to another. The main qualification for becoming a teacher was to be "educated" in the sense of having read a lot of books. Initially most teachers were men, and from religious orders (which educated all their members) or from relatively prosperous families that could afford to allow some of their members to become "intellectuals."

Industrialization in the West created other sources of employment for educated men, but not for educated women; teaching became one of the few professions that an educated woman could take up. With the Meiji Restoration in Japan in the late 1800s, professional warriors (samurai) were converted into teachers. In countries achieving independence in the 1900s there often was a shortage of teachers as new governments absorbed those few persons working in education under the colonial regime.

Although "teachers" had existed for a long time, it was only in the 1700s, with the expansion of primary schools in France, that special attention was given to how to train persons to carry out this role most effectively. Significantly, these developments occurred much at the same time that manufacturers were experimenting with new forms of organization of work. Later to be defined as "bureaucracy," these new organizations specified in detail the tasks to be carried out to insure a product of high quality with a minimal use of resources. Workers were trained to follow rules of production that had been learned by observing skilled artisans.

In education, the challenge was to teach persons without a "gift" for teaching how to produce learning in a large class of children. The religious order of Christian Brothers in France learned in the 1700s that if they arranged children by ages, and prepared books that included learning assignments appropriate to those ages, they could then train their young novices to become effective teachers.

In the early 1800s, this principle was re-discovered in England by Lancaster and Bell, who found they could use older children to teach younger ones. The older children were taught a series of norms or rules that permitted them to be effective teachers. The French meanwhile had "normal schools" that prepared teachers. Other countries soon began to adopt the French solution to the shortage of educated teachers. The first formal teacher training institution in the Americas was begun in 1832.

from pages 49, 53

The availability of teachers depends not just on how many persons have been prepared for the profession of teaching, but also on how many prepared persons decide to enter the profession.

Sometimes the best persons do not go into teaching. This is likely to occur when teaching salaries are low, working conditions are poor, and opportunities exist in other fields.

In your country, which of the following best accounts for the low quality of teachers?

→ **Not many people want to become teachers.** If this is the case, go to page **85**.

→ **Inadequate selection processes.** Go to page **184** for policy options to improve selection processes.

← For more information and discussion, see page 64

Pre-Service Training of Teachers

Mass education requires many teachers. Most countries met this requirement by creating schools to train persons to teach. In many cases these *pre-service* institutions (normal schools, teacher training colleges) were residential; some guaranteed employment.

The pre-service schools were intended to accomplish several tasks:

1. allow planners to anticipate future supply of teachers;

2. insure that new teachers knew the subject matter content; and

3. provide teachers with the teaching skills expected by the curriculum.

Over time countries have differed in:

a. the level (secondary, tertiary) at which teacher training is offered;

b. the amount of training provided;

c. the relative emphasis of training on subject matter knowledge, or on teaching skills; and

d. the inclusion of supervised practice as part of the training program.

The level of education provided for teachers increases with the average level of education of the population. What were secondary normal schools become university-level teaching colleges. In some instances these have become full-blown universities. A further step requires all teachers to have a basic university degree and one or two years of graduate level training in education (Ghani, in Rust and Dalin, 1990).

These trends are compatible with research that shows that level of academic education is the best predictor of teacher effectiveness when effectiveness is measured as students' achievement.

Keep in mind that raising teachers' education levels also raises teachers' salary expectations. Some countries have not raised teachers' salaries to match general trends in society. Cummings (in Rust and Dalin, 1990) argues that the result is that new teachers now come from a lower cultural stratum and are seen as providing a lower quality education.

See Rust and Dalin (1990) for a discussion of teacher training in developing countries.

➜ For an alternative to raising levels of academic training, go to page **187** for ways to upgrade teachers in-service.

➜ See page **199** for an instructional technology that does not require highly educated teachers.

The curriculum is a defining characteristic of the formal school. The use of curriculum requires a person with special knowledge and skills. The profession of *teacher* implies therefore special training.

In most countries this training is given before persons are allowed to practice the profession, that is, to teach. This *pre-service* training generally tries to strike a balance between the *techniques* of teaching, or *pedagogy*, and knowledge of the subject matter.

The best pre-service training programs include the following elements:

1. basic education in subject matter content;

2. exposure to the instructional objectives and methods specified in the curriculum;

3. exposure to classroom management techniques; and

4. opportunities for student teaching, that is, supervised practice teaching.

67

Which of the following statements describes pre-service training programs in your country?

➜ **Fail to provide opportunities for student teaching, that is, supervised practice teaching.** If true, go to page 192 for possible ways to accomplish this.

➜ **Fail to provide enough basic education in subject matter content.** For policy options to improve teacher knowledge of subject matter, go to page 185.

➜ **Fail to provide sufficient exposure to the instructional objectives and methods specified in the curriculum.** Go to page 187 for some policy options.

➜ **Fail to provide sufficient exposure to classroom management techniques.** If this is true, go to page 106 for suggestions of how to overcome this.

Descriptions of teacher training programs are provided on page 189.

← For more information and discussion, see page 66

The Functions of Supervision in Schools

Supervision is the monitoring of the work of teachers and principals in schools. In some education systems, supervision of teachers is carried out by the principal or master teacher. In other systems, this responsibility is assigned to an external *supervisor* or *inspector* (see page **102**).

The work of supervisors falls into two distinct categories:

1. observation of the work of teachers (and principals) to insure that they conform to expected patterns or standards. This can be called the *administrative* responsibility of supervisors.

2. working with teachers to improve their teaching practices. This is the *in-service training* element of supervision.

In some systems there is, in fact, little supervision of either kind, except in urban schools. This occurs because there are few supervisors. They reside in urban areas, and there is limited budget for transport. Rural school teachers may see the supervisor only once a year.

Administrative supervision is the most common variety, for these reasons:

1. given heavy work loads supervisors cannot spend time in classrooms;

2. supervisors are used by the central administration to carry information to and from schools;

3. few systems provide supervisors with specific training in how to observe teachers. Supervisors don't learn how to help teachers improve their teaching practices; and

4. there are strong pressures, from friends and from unions, for supervisors to avoid any evaluation of teachers in classrooms.

Research indicates that supervision can have more effect on teacher performance in classrooms than other kinds of in-service training. This may be because good supervisors can generate the five components that make in-service training effective:

1. conceptualization of good teaching;

2. "modeling" or demonstration of teaching techniques;

3. opportunities to practice in a non-evaluative situation;

4. immediate feedback on classroom practice; and

5. suggestions on how to apply teaching practices in new settings (Joyce and Showers, 1980).

Effective supervision can be provided by external supervisors or by the school principal (Eisemon, Schwille, and Prouty, 1989; Raudenbush et al., 1991).

from pages 53, 107

The amount of pre-service training teachers receive does not always have a strong impact on student learning. Go to page 52 for a summary of the research.

There are several reasons why training may not have a big impact on learning. First, the effects of good training may diminish over time.

1. Teachers, like students, forget what they learn, and develop improper teaching methods.

2. Curriculum and materials change over time. Teachers who are not brought up to date persist in methods and content no longer appropriate.

3. Teacher motivation may be reduced by poor working conditions or poor administrative practices.

Second, the initial training may not have been appropriate. There may have been a poor fit between content of training and actual conditions in classrooms.

There are two main methods to overcome problems of the kind listed above:

1. **supervision** and training of teachers in classrooms; and

2. regular **in-service** training.

Which of the following is most appropriate as a description of what happens in your country?

→ **Most teachers receive some in-service training during the school year.** If this is true, go to page **89**.

→ **Supervisors observe teachers while they are teaching, and provide feedback.** If this is *not* true, go to page **103**.

← For more information and discussion, see page 68

69

The Importance of the School Administrator

There are two major reasons for assignment of an administrator or manager to a school:

1. to provide on-site in-service training for teachers. This is the **headmaster** or **headmistress** model of school administration.

2. to manage the human and physical resources of the school. The responsibilities of **directors, principals,** and sometimes **administrators** include attendance, finance, and discipline.

School administrators contribute to positive learning outcomes by:

1. developing a positive school climate;

2. focusing attention of teachers on goal-directed activities; and

3. setting clear and high standards for student achievement (David, 1989; DeBevoise, 1984).

Although almost all countries have administrators, little research has been done in developing countries on what makes an administrator effective.

A study in Thailand suggests what happens when administrators are not properly trained.

"If the principal went into the classroom and the teacher asked some key words about the new curriculum, he couldn't answer. He felt that if he stayed at the school he would suffer a loss of face...so he moved out of the school....So when the researcher went to visit the schools...[he] couldn't find any principals. So teaching was very poor. There was no supervision and no monitoring." (Wheeler, Raudenbush, and Pasigna, 1989, p. 13).

Students in schools with trained administrators have higher achievement scores than those in schools without trained administrators (Fuller, 1987).

For a summary of recent innovations in school administration in the United States, see Keith and Girling (1990).

For a review of developing country studies see Georgiades and Jones (1989).

from pages 43, 55

The quality of teaching depends to an important degree on the actions of both local and central administrators. Good administrators contribute to conditions in which teaching quality is maximal. One way is through improvements in physical conditions of work.

Which of the following is what administrators need to work on to improve quality of teaching?

→ **Maintenance of physical facilities and equipment.** If this is a problem, go to page **230** for policy options.

→ **Supply and distribution of instructional materials.** Go to page **119**.

If neither of these two options is appropriate, go to page 73.

← For more information and discussion, see page 70

How Administrators Contribute to Student Learning

Effective schools are those in which students learn the curriculum even when conditions are not optimal, for example when:

1. students come from families with limited education;

2. teachers have low levels of academic knowledge;

3. pre-service training of teachers has not been adequate;

4. the central ministry provides few resources for equipment and school maintenance; and

5. there is a shortage of instructional materials.

Some schools are able to graduate students with high levels of learning, despite these conditions.

Effective schools have three major characteristics that distinguish them from less-effective schools:

1. clearly defined goals and high expectations for student learning that are accepted and promoted by teachers, students, and the community;

2. clearly defined and applied standards for student behavior that are accepted by students and teachers; and

3. mobilization of community resources to compensate for insufficient resources from the central school agency (Purkey and Smith, 1983).

These characteristics are reflected in a high sense of community in the school, and high levels of time-on-task (see page **62**).

The presence of these characteristics depends on the leadership of the school principal or director (headmaster or headmistress).

Research on school directors or principals in developing countries is limited. A few studies have shown that directors are most successful when they use *participatory* methods to generate consensus among teachers and students about goals, and methods to achieve them (Georgiades and Jones, 1989; Cummings, Gunarwardena, and Williams, 1992; Levin, 1992).

➔ For an example of a successful program for training directors in-service see page **226**.

from pages 49, 71

A second way in which administrators can improve quality of teaching involves actions to train teachers, and to match teachers to schools and subjects.

Which of the following would you like administrators to do to improve quality of teaching?

→ **Supervision and training of teachers in classrooms.** Go to page 103.

→ **Actions to improve teachers' morale and motivation.** Go to page 77.

→ **Monitoring teacher attendance.** Go to page 101.

If none of these options is appropriate, go to page 75.

73

← For more information and discussion, see page 72

The Importance of School-Community Relationships: A Case from Sri Lanka

Educators often emphasize the importance of good relationships between school and community. We found no studies on this topic, other than that reported below.

The Sri Lanka study was based on information from 273 schools randomly selected in six districts chosen for geographic, ethnic and economic diversity. School principals responded to a questionnaire. Detailed interviews were carried out in 21 schools.

Most (69 percent) of the principals reported some contribution from the community to the school. Contributions take the form of cash, volunteer labor, or donation of materials (e.g., paint, lumber). Contributions are more common in urban (and wealthier) than in rural (and poorer) communities. Poor and rural communities typically provide their contributions in the form of labor and materials.

As rural (and poor) schools charge smaller student fees, contributions are an important source of income. Contributions improve the physical condition of the building and furniture, which contributes to student and teacher morale.

The School Development Society is the channel for contributions to the school. The level of contributions is associated with level of attendance at Society meetings. Teachers who live close to the school are more highly involved, as are teachers with higher morale.

The principal is the major factor in the success of the School Development Society. The more importance the principal gives to the Society, the more successful is the Society in raising money for the school. **Principals who received district level management training generated the highest level of contributions.** Principals who have positive attitudes toward the community and teachers, and who delegate responsibility, are most successful in fund-raising.

Source: Anderson et al. (1989).

from page 73

A third way in which administrators contribute to improving the quality of teaching is through student discipline and relationships with the community.

Which of the following do you wish administrators would do more often, to improve quality of teaching?

→ **Maintain student discipline**. Go to page **81**.

→ **Set goals and standards for the school**. Go to pages **98** and **224**.

→ **Establish relationships in the community**. Go to page **74**.

If none of these options fit your situation, go back to page **55** and reconsider the basis for your dissatisfaction with administrative practices.

← **For more information and discussion, see page 74**

Teacher Motivation and Performance

Motivation of teachers becomes a critical policy issue when:

1. turnover rates become so high it is impossible to fill available positions;

2. teachers organize and protest against their conditions of employment; or

3. the government seeks to increase efficiency or improve quality, but wants to avoid increasing costs.

Incentives are defined as benefits intended to motivate increased or improved performance by workers. These may include:

1. monetary offers such as salary, allowances, fringe benefits; and

2. non-monetary offers such as training opportunities, materials, transfers, or public recognition (Kemmerer, 1990).

Almost all studies of the incentives that affect teacher behavior have been done in the United States. Most of that research has been done on *job satisfaction,* that is, on factors that reduce teacher turnover. Recognition and approval (including salary increases) contribute to increased satisfaction (Chapman, 1983; Jenkinson and Chapman, 1990).

But increases in teacher satisfaction do not necessarily lead to improvements in the quality of teaching. Low satisfaction encourages turnover and protest, but high satisfaction may lead to resistance to change. A study of junior secondary teachers in Botswana found no relationship between how teachers conduct their classes, and their level of satisfaction with teaching (Chapman, Snyder, Burchfield, 1991).

➔ See page **12** for a further discussion of non-material incentives to attract teachers to rural areas.

from pages 21, 55, 73, 83, 101

Motivation of teachers is an important contributor to the quality of education. Some of the factors that contribute to low teacher morale, and poor motivation for performance, have little to do with what takes place in the classroom itself.

In your country, what are the major factors outside the classroom that account for low motivation?

→ **People who enter the teaching profession lack an adequate understanding of what teaching involves.** If this is true, go to page **83**.

→ **Some teachers think the curriculum is not well-designed.** If this is true, go to page **35**.

→ **Difficult working conditions in schools.** Go to page **79**.

→ **Salaries (and/or benefits) are considered to be too low.** Go to page **193** for suggestions of ways to motivate teachers without raising salaries.
Go to page **172** for suggestions of ways to increase funds available for teacher salaries.

← **For more information and discussion, see page 76**

77

The Impact of Physical Facilities on Students and Teachers

Although it is obvious that it is possible to have too many students in a classroom, it is not clear how many "too many" is. **Most studies in developing countries have shown no significant differences in levels of achievement of students according to number of students per teacher** (Haddad, 1978). A review of research done in the United States found that high student density in a classroom has a negative effect on achievement in *complex* tasks (Weinstein, 1979).

An ethnographic study of schools in four countries in Latin America describes how poor material conditions affect the quality of work of teachers. One teacher observed:

> "...the premises are not adequate. In winter the room is very dark. It is too long, the children at the back cannot hear nor see well. And so I have to keep running backwards and forwards. The children are on top of each other. *One cannot teach.*" (Avalos, 1986, p. 129; italics in original).

One can imagine this particular teacher running backwards and forwards. A very good teacher could produce high levels of learning, confounding an attempt to associate quality of facilities and level of achievement (see page **18**). Over time, however, these poor working conditions might well drive even the best teachers out of the profession. Some research (in Malta) has shown that teacher satisfaction is higher when physical facilities are good (Farrugia, 1986). **In general, however, there is little research on this topic.**

Teachers who live in the community in which the school is located participate more actively in school-community relations, are less frequently absent from the school, and have students with higher average levels of achievement (Anderson et al., 1989; McGinn et al., 1992). Government provision of housing is an important incentive to attract people into teaching (Chivore, 1988; Kemmerer and Thiagarajan, 1989).

from pages 55, 77

Working conditions in schools are influenced by two kinds of actions: local administrative decisions, and policy decisions made by the central ministry.

Which of the following best accounts for poor working conditions in schools in your country?

→ **Primarily a result of overcrowding, i.e., too many students per class.** If this is true, go to page **91**.

→ **Primarily a result of insufficient supplies of materials.** If this is true, go to page **113**.

→ **Primarily a result of the physical condition of the school buildings.** If this is true, go to page **45**.

→ **Primarily a result of actions, or inaction, of the school administrator.** If this is true go to page **43** for a list of problems.

← For more information and discussion, see page 78

79

How Physical Conditions and Classroom Management Skills Affect Time-on-Task

The following is offered as description of a typical classroom in a school in Latin America. It might apply to any part of the developing world.

"Where there are no benches, chairs are brought in by students from their homes, or desks are provided. Sometimes there are so many desks or benches that students have to walk across them to reach the blackboard…. Lighting is…provided by only one large window…. The blackboard shines as it has been painted …to give it a smooth surface for the chalk to move on. Materials are scarce, especially chalk and pencils.

A roll call is taken by the teacher while students are asked to take out notebooks or textbooks from the locked cabinets. This activity takes up about 15% of the allocated time. About one-third [of the remaining] time is spent on discipline…. Teachers discipline students either openly within the group or by taking students aside to reprimand them." (Montero-Sieburth, 1989, pp. 6-7)

Moving about a crowded classroom takes time that could be given to instruction and learning. Montero-Sieburth (1989) reviews research on how classroom management skills contribute to more effective use of time (see also page 92).

Little research has been done, however, on how teachers in developing countries distribute their time. Little is known about how much time is taken from instructional activities in order to punish or discipline students. Studies in Pakistan and Honduras (Warwick and Reimers, 1992; McGinn et al., 1992) show that frequency of discipline is related to student achievement. Achievement scores rise as frequency of punishment by teacher declines.

from pages 63, 75

Which of the following explains the level of classroom disorder in your schools?

→ **There are too many students in the class.** Go to page **91**.

→ **Teachers do not know how to maintain discipline.** If this is true, and if the problem is in *pre-service* training, go to page **67**. If the problem is with *in-service* training, go to page **89**.

→ **Administrators do not set and maintain standards.** If this is true, go to page **224**.

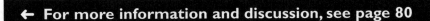

← For more information and discussion, see page 80

The Relationship Between Pre-Service and In-Service Training

The expansion of education to enroll all children requires a supply of qualified teachers. Some countries train persons before they begin teaching. This is called *pre-service* training. Its objective is to insure that beginning teachers have required knowledge and skills.

In-service training is used as a means to *up-grade* the quality of all teachers. It is offered to those who received training as teachers before beginning work and those who did not. In some countries, most new teachers are without specialized training prior to beginning work. In-service training is used to provide these persons with required knowledge and skills.

Teachers require three kinds of education or training:

1. in knowledge of the subjects that are to be taught;

2. in knowledge of and ability to use the methods most appropriate for teaching the subject; and

3. in the management skills required to make most efficient use of material resources and time.

Little research has been on the relative costs, and relative effectiveness, of different kinds of pre- and in-service programs. A recent study provides this information.

Residential pre-service training works best

1. when emphasis is on training a few, but excellent teachers; and

2. candidates are given a year of supervised practice teaching.

Up-grading programs, in which experienced teachers return to a residential institution to take additional training, work best:

1. to maintain motivation of current teachers; and

2. to raise levels of knowledge of and ability to use appropriate teaching methods.

Distance education training works best

1. when instructional materials are used together with visits by tutors, and

2. when large numbers of unqualified persons need to be trained as teachers, at relatively low cost. (Tatto, Nielsen, and Cummings, 1991).

For other studies see Andrews and Thomas (1986); and Greenland (1983).

➜ For a description of various kinds of in-service programs see page **187**.

from page 77

Which of the following describes the situation with respect to teacher training in your country?

➜ **Pre-service programs provide opportunities for prospective teachers to better understand the profession.** If this is *not* true, go to page **67**.

➜ **In-service programs provide opportunities for teachers to better understand the profession.** If this is *not* true, go to page **89**.

If both of these statements are true for your country, go back to page 77.

← For more information and discussion, see page 82

Will Raising Teacher Salaries Improve Quality?

There is considerable variation across countries in terms of how much teachers are paid. To take into account variations in cost of living, Table 10 below compares teacher salaries with per capita income. In some (very poor) countries, teachers are paid much more than the per capita income. In other countries, teachers are paid close to the per capita income.

Table 10
Average Teacher Salary as a Proportion of Gross National Product per Capita

Country	Year	Salary in 1985 Dollars	As a Multiple of GNP/Capita
Mexico	86	1733.3	0.9
Dominican R.	86	898.5	1.3
Haiti	86	491.7	1.4
Venezuela	84	5125.1	1.5
Ghana	86	787.9	2.0
Bangladesh	86	309.1	2.1
Liberia	79	1833.6	2.7
Trinidad & Tobago	85	18369.0	2.9
Tanzania	79	1072.0	3.0
Madagascar	85	750.5	3.5
Tunisia	84	4225.6	3.9
Nepal	80	575.4	4.3
Morocco	79	2900.3	5.7
Togo	84	1369.2	6.3
Burundi	84	1704.0	7.2
Rwanda	81	3135.8	10.4

Adapted from Lockheed and Verspoor (1991), p. 103.

Several factors are at work here. First, the education requirements to become a certified teacher vary widely (see page **58**). In some countries teachers may be among the best educated persons in the community. In some countries strong teacher associations have won salary concessions from the government.

Across countries, there is no relationship between teacher salary (as compared to GNP per capita) and quality of education. Within countries, teacher salary is not related to student learning. In the U.S., *merit pay plans* (paying teachers more when test scores go up) have not produced significant increases in learning outcomes (Murnane and Cohen, 1986).

On the other hand, lowered teacher salaries have been linked to a decline in quality of education in Latin America. See page **20**.

from pages 21, 65

Why don't enough people want to become teachers?

➔ **Salaries and benefits are low as compared to other careers or occupations.** It may not be possible to raise teacher salaries. Go to page **193** for suggestions of ways to get teachers to work without raising salaries. Go to page **172** for suggestions of ways to increase funds available for teachers salaries.

Sometimes, there just aren't enough persons who, even with adequate training, can become good teachers. In these cases, it may be necessary to introduce other methods to make up for the shortage of good teachers. Go to page **220** for examples of distance education methods that can be used when it is not possible to generate an adequate supply of good teachers.

← For more information and discussion, see page 84

Comparison of Pedagogical Training Instruction in Teacher Training Colleges in Three Countries

Significantly more time is spent on academic training than actual pedagogical training in teacher colleges in Haiti, Yemen, and Nepal. New teachers, because of the attention paid to general academic learning during training, lack pedagogical skills. Teachers with a wide variety of teaching skills are more effective than those with a more limited repertoire (Fuller, 1987).

The few studies that have addressed the effectiveness of teacher subject matter knowledge and student achievement in developing countries indicate a positive effect of teacher subject matter knowledge on student achievement (Lockheed and Verspoor, 1991).

We know little about the most effective proportions of subject matter and pedagogical knowledge in teacher training programs. On the other hand, it is widely accepted that teachers need to know effective ways to transmit their subject matter knowledge. Teachers need to know not only what to teach, but how to do it.

Table 11
Teacher Training in Haiti, Yemen and Nepal

Subject	Haiti average hours/week three-year course		Yemen average hours/week five-year course		Nepal total credit hours two-year course	
Academic Training	17.7	53%	25.4	70%	General: 500	
					Special: 1050	86%
Pedagogical Training	7.7	23%	5.4	15%	150	8%
Introduction to education	0.0		0.0		50	
Philosophy of education	0.0		0.0		0	
Professional ethics	0.0		0.0		0	
General pedagogy	1.0		0.0		0	
History of education	0.3		1.2		0	
Theories of education	0.3		0.0		0	
Psychology	2.3		1.2		100	
General didactics	1.0		0.0		0	
School administration	1.0		0.0		0	
Special pedagogy	0.7		0.0		0	
Methods of teaching	0.0		1.8		0	
Instructional materials	0.0		1.2		0	
Student Teaching	0.0		2.0	5%	100	6%
Social Education	3.3	10%	0.0		0	
Practical Training*	4.7	14%	3.8	10%	0	
Total	33.3	100%	36.6	100%	1800	100%

Source: Lockheed and Verspoor (1991), p.99.
See also page **48**.

To some extent, the certification levels set for teachers are arbitrary. As indicated in Table 8 on page **58**, there is wide variation across countries in levels of education and training required for teachers.

These variations occur for several reasons. When there is an *over-supply* of educated persons in the labor market, then it is reasonable to raise certification requirements. Research shows that the level of academic education of the teacher is related to student achievement.

Is there, however, a *minimal* level of academic education below which we should not hire persons to be teachers? What is that level?

The level depends on the *content* of the curriculum, and on the *methods* required to teach that content.

It may be possible to introduce methods that can be handled effectively by persons with lower levels of academic training.

In your country,

➜ **Is it politically feasible to *lower* the minimum academic requirements to become a teacher?** If it is, it may be possible to use as teachers persons with lower academic qualifications. Go to page **199** for examples.

➜ If it is not possible to use persons with lower academic qualifications, you will have to consider other kinds of changes in the system. You can return to page **11 to review other factors that affect the system.**

← For more information and discussion, see page 86

87

The Impact of In-Service Training in Sri Lanka

One form of in-service education for teachers in Sri Lanka is provided by using Distance Education. The course emphasizes subject knowledge (31 percent) and primary school teaching (49 percent). Content of the program is provided through self-study printed materials. A tutor visits each teacher three times during the academic year, observes their teaching and provides feedback. Trainees also meet in Regional Centers, in two 2-day sessions and one 5-day session to discuss experiences.

As a group, all trained teachers do better than untrained teachers. Teacher training makes a difference in what the teachers do in the classroom, and what teachers do is related to student achievement.

Teachers who go through the in-service program gain *less* in mathematics than do graduates from pre-service programs. The in-service graduates gain more in knowledge of mother tongue during the program, but these gains are lost after they leave the program. Pre-service trainees gain more in mathematics and mother tongue teaching skills.

The students of teachers who receive pre-service training have higher mathematics and achievement scores, controlling on school type and pupil and teacher backgrounds, than do the teachers who received in-service training.

Pre-service training in a residential institution, with supervised practice instruction, is the most *effective* training, but it is also the most expensive. In Sri Lanka, the per year cost for a trainee is US$1,401 for residential pre-service training, and $251 for Distance Education.

As a consequence, Distance Education is a more *cost-effective* method of training. Although residential training produced larger gains in student achievement, **the cost per unit of student achievement for residential training was *4.5 times* that of student achievement for Distance Education training.**

The impact of Distance Education training tends to fade over time. The research indicates that continuation of contact with a supervisor (or tutor) and with fellow teachers, can help to maintain gains from distance training.

Based on Tatto, Nielsen, and Cummings (1991).

➜ For more about the Sri Lanka study see page **82**.

➜ For more about *distance education* for training teachers, see page **220**.

from pages 69, 81, 83

Which of the following describes the in-service training programs in your country?

Are they related to the content of the curriculum?
Are they related to teaching methods?
Do they provide opportunities for professional enrichment and renewal?
Do they provide training in classroom management?

→ For examples of successful in-service training, go to pages 187 and 189.

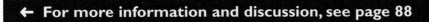

← For more information and discussion, see page 88

Is Overcrowding a Serious Problem?

Overcrowding is a relative term. In a small room, 25 students might seem to be too many. A school with six classrooms and 300 students may be overcrowded if classrooms are used by only one shift of teachers.

As noted elsewhere (see page **78**), large class sizes have no effects on achievement in some countries, but do in others (Haddad, 1978). Several factors determine what student–teacher ratios constitute overcrowding.

1. *Teacher's ability.* Experienced, well-trained teachers can handle larger classes without reducing quality.

2. *Subject matter.* Subjects differ in the extent to which the teacher must be directly involved in the learning process. Topics that permit students to learn on their own can be handled successfully in larger classes.

3. *Instructional materials.* The availability of textbooks and other self-study materials permits larger classes without losing quality.

4. *Characteristics of students.* Class sizes can be larger when students are motivated to learn and are healthy.

The use of the same building for more than one "shift" of teachers (or students) may reduce crowding. Teachers complain that double (and triple) shifts reduce time for instruction. For example, in Burundi the introduction of double shifts was accompanied by a reduction of time on agriculture and home economics (Eisemon, Schwille and Prouty, 1990).

But there are enough hours in the day to permit a full program in two shifts. Some countries offer the same number of hours of instruction per week in single and double shift schools. The number of instructional hours in the school week is not different from than in countries with only single shift schools, that is, between 20 and 25 hours per week.

Research on achievement of students in single- and double-shift schools is, like that on class size, ambiguous.

1. *Able teachers* manage to teach as much material in shorter periods of time.

2. Some *subjects and topics* are more flexible with respect to time than are others.

3. The use of *instructional materials,* especially textbooks, allows students to learn outside of class (see page **199**).

For more information on double shifts and achievement, see Bray (1989). For research on class size, see Haddad (1978), and Glass et al. (1982). See also page **166**.

from pages 79, 81

Which of the following best explains why there is overcrowding in your system?

➔ **There aren't enough school buildings.** Go to page 19.

➔ **There aren't enough teachers.** Go to page 21.

← **For more information and discussion, see page 90**

How Important is Time-on-Task?

Would lengthening the school year, or the school day, lead to an improvement in student learning? *Not necessarily,* according to research in the United States, where because of local control of schools there is considerable variation in length of year and day.

One study found no relationship between length of school year and student achievement in basic subjects (Lee, 1981). Another found no relationship between time allocated to reading instruction and reading ability (Guthrie, 1976). A review of research on instructional time summarizes by stating that most results are not significant (Rosenshine and Berliner, 1978).

These results go against our common sense. Teachers know that time is an important factor in the learning process. Giving more time to a subject increases the likelihood that students will achieve learning objectives.

But we also know that the passage of "time" by itself is not enough. What happens during that time is most important. Lengthening the school year, with no change in teaching practices is likely to have little effect on teaching practices. Unless teachers spend additional time *on the subject,* using effective methods, why should we expect more learning?

Recent studies have been more precise in definition of time. Now reference is made to **academically engaged time**, or **opportunity to learn.** These concepts focus on exposure to the curriculum, in a way that encourages student learning. These measures are different from *allocated time,* that is, how many minutes and hours are assigned to instruction by the rule books. Studies show wide disparities between actual practices and allocated time (Fisher, 1980). Teachers alter the curriculum, student discipline distracts from instruction, the teaching-learning process is interrupted by events outside the classroom.

Instead of time-on-task, we can focus on **opportunity to learn**. The length of time teachers in Pakistan state they allow each week for instruction in math and science is unrelated to achievement test scores in grades 3 and 5. On the other hand, the number of pages covered in the textbook is directly related to achievement scores. (Warwick, Reimers and McGinn, 1989). Time spent studying mathematics was the only classroom-level factor associated with achievement in Thailand (Montero-Sieburth, 1989).

from pages 63, 117

There are four general explanations of why too little time is spent on teaching and learning.

Which of the following best describes your situation?

→ **Factors outside the classroom are the major cause of too little time on teaching and learning.** If this is your situation, go to page **95**.

→ **Various factors in the classroom reduce the time available for teaching and learning.** If this is your situation, go to page **97**.

→ **Teachers don't make good use of the time that is available.** If this is your situation, go to page **107**.

→ **The time available for teaching and learning the content is adequate, but there are other problems.** If this is your situation, go to page **99**.

← For more information and discussion, see page 32

93

Restrictions on Time-on-Task

In Mexico, a typical teacher uses about 50 percent of the scheduled school week on actual instruction. The rest of the time is lost to absences, leaving early, administrative interruptions, and classroom disturbances (Munoz Izquierdo, 1979). In Colombia, off-task time has been estimated at about 40 percent (Arancibia, 1987). One third of instructional hours in Malawi are lost because the teacher's voice is drowned out by rain on metal roofs (Lockheed and Verspoor, 1991). In Indonesia actual instructional time in early grades is less than half that specified by the central ministry (Lockheed and Verspoor, 1991).

Although there is no mechanical relationship between time-on-task and student learning (see page **92**), it is clear that opportunities for learning are reduced when the teacher is not present, when the teacher is present but is not teaching, or when teaching is ineffective.

Many education systems collect and report information on student attendance. Few systems collect information on teacher attendance, and perhaps none report that information. **There is little research on frequency or determinants of teacher absences, or on effects of teacher absenteeism on student achievement.**

The reasons that teachers fail to attend school include:

1. personal reasons, including sickness, attendance to personal affairs;

2. lack of transportation, which applies to teachers who do not live in or near the community in which the school is located, and which increases in frequency during inclement weather.

3. attendance to school-related matters. This may mean going to get paid, cashing the check, going to the central Ministry to straighten out a mistake in payment, asking for a transfer, attending a training session.

The impact of teacher absenteeism can be great in schools with few teachers. For example, one-teacher schools are closed when the teacher does not come. In a school with several teachers, one teacher may include the students of an absent colleague. Some education systems may have enough resources to hire short-term substitute teachers. This is not feasible for outlying rural schools if decisions are made centrally.

Rural teachers in Honduras make up for their absences by changing the pace of instruction, or skipping material. There is no relationship between frequency of teacher absence and student achievement (McGinn et al., 1992).

from page 93

Which of the following factors external to the classroom explain why too little time is spent on teaching?

→ **Not enough teachers are available.** If this is true, go to page **21**.

→ **Teachers are frequently absent.** If this is true, go to page **101**.

→ **Supervision of teachers is inadequate.** If this is true, go to page **103**.

← For more information and discussion, see page 94

Improving Time Spent on Teaching and Learning

Effective teachers are defined as those whose students score higher than would be expected given the students' background. Effective teachers use a series of practices that increase both the time spent on learning by students, and the *efficiency* of that time use.

Effective teaching requires the organization of available instructional time to maximize student involvement in learning tasks. This is accomplished by:

1. achieving an *orderly environment,* in which rules are understood and followed by students, and in which there are few distractions from outside the class.

2. use of an *orderly sequence* in the teaching of lessons. This sequence includes review of previous lessons, statement of learning objectives for this lesson, linking the subject to students' interests or experience, presentation of new information, practice by students in using the new information, and feedback by teacher on that use, and homework to continue the learning process outside school.

3. *variety* in the specific methods in which material is presented. This helps maintain high levels of attention by students.

4. *pacing* presentation of material to individual students. This is accomplished by dividing the class into groups according to their knowledge of the particular topic, permitting individual work, using more advanced students to teach some of the groups.

Research indicates that there is no single style of teaching that is most effective. The best teachers combine different methods and vary them according to circumstances.

But student learning is generally higher when:

1. students are *actively* engaged in the learning process;

2. what is taught is practiced by students until they assimilate it; and

3. student learning is recognized through frequent assessment by student or teacher, and this information is used to guide selection of the next learning tasks.

For more information see Lockheed and Verspoor (1991); Rugh, Malik, and Farook (1991).

from page 93

Which of the following best explains why too little time is spent on teaching and learning?

→ **High rates of student absenteeism.** If this is true, go to page **105**.

→ **A lack of instructional materials for student use.** If this is true, go to page **109**.

→ **A lack of materials for teacher use.** If this is true, go to page **111**.

→ **Teachers don't have enough information about how much students have learned.** If this is true, go to page **207**.

→ **The lack of discipline in the classroom and school keeps teachers and students from teaching and learning.** Go to page **182** for suggestions of ways to improve discipline.

← **For more information and discussion, see page 96**

97

What Makes for an Effective School?

We know many of the factors that contribute to one school having higher levels of achievement than another. Bright students with educated parents, highly trained teachers, good facilities—we associate these conditions with high achievement. From that perspective, the only way to achieve Better Education for All is to spend more money, to make the schools of the poor like the schools of the rich.

But some high achieving schools are in poor areas of the city, or in isolated rural areas. Some high achieving schools are in poor buildings. Some have high levels of achievement even though many of the teachers are not certified. How can this be explained?

The term *effective schools* has been used by some researchers to refer to schools whose levels of achievement are above those expected.

The essential elements of an *effective school* are summarized as follows:

1. Presence of a philosophy of education that informs the actions of the school's members. This philosophy is often seen as an ideology or a set of spiritual beliefs, rather than a technical theory. The philosophy focuses on the ends of education, rather than on means.

2. Organization of the school according to the philosophy. Curriculum, administration, training, discipline, even recreation are organized consistent with the principles of the philosophy.

3. The process of organization of the school according to the philosophy involves administrators, teachers, students, parents and sometimes the larger community. This involvement *empowers* participants, in terms of increasing their influence on what happens. It also makes participants *responsible* for the school's welfare. For example, parents and the community are expected to contribute to support of the school.

4. This involvement affects the curriculum, both in terms of content and pedagogy. Content is made more "relevant" to the concerns of the community. Teachers use active teaching methods which require the student to assume some responsibility for learning.

For an example of effective schools, see page **199** (Escuela Nueva). For a list of common features of effective schools, see page **224**. For more information on research on effective schools and fostering positive student achievement, see Teddlie and Stringfield (1990).

from page 93

Which of the following best describes the other problems your system has?

→ **Poor quality teaching.** Go to page **53**.

→ **Poor quality and/or inadequate quantity of instructional materials.** If this is true, go to page **111**.

→ **A lack of fit between the assumptions of the school and curriculum, and characteristics of students, prevents effective teaching.** If this is true, go to page **115**.

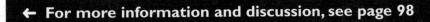

← **For more information and discussion, see page 98**

Causes and Effects of Teacher Absences

There is almost no research on causes and effects of teacher absences. (See page 94.)

Teacher absence is a behavior, and behaviors can be explained by reference to three kinds of factors:

1. *Knowledge of what is expected.* Some organizations permit their workers a certain number of absences per year, for illness, personal affairs, professional improvement. If persons know that some absences are allowed or overlooked, they will sometimes be absent.

2. *Motivation.* Some research links absences to "burnout," even when the official explanation is illness. Burnout occurs when teachers spend long and hard hours doing routine tasks for which they receive little recognition. The causes of burnout are located primarily in the school environment (especially administration) rather than in the personality of the teacher (Friedman, 1991). Motivation is a response to incentives in the environment.

3. *Ability to respond.* Sometimes motivated teachers are unable to attend school, as for example when the road is washed out, or the bus drivers have gone on strike.

Teacher absences affect the system in at least two ways.

1. *Economic cost.* There may be an immediate cost, as when substitute teachers are hired. Indirect costs are felt when students repeat grades, or when graduates are less productive.

2. *Support for Education.* Teacher absences have a direct effect on public support for education. Absent teachers mean that students are home, requiring supervision. Frequent absences convince parents their children are receiving a low quality education.

from pages 73, 95

Which of the following best explains why teachers are absent?

→ **They live far from the school where they work.** There is little information available about how to respond to this problem.

→ **They are not monitored.** If this is true, go to page **103**.

→ **They need to go to the central office to arrange salaries, promotions, transfers, etc.** If this is true, go to page **43**.

→ **They lack motivation.** If this is true, go to page **77**.

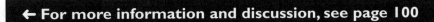

← **For more information and discussion, see page 100**

Effective Supervision to Improve Learning Outcomes

Supervision (or inspection) involves the monitoring of the behavior of school directors, teachers, and students. Supervision is intended to meet one or more of the following objectives.

1. *Insure compliance* with system policies, rules, and regulations. This includes correct use of the official curriculum, proper handling of community funds, attendance.

2. *Collect data* about system performance. This includes routine statistical information, director and teacher comments on curriculum and instructional materials, vacant positions, repair of buildings, etc.

3. *Provide guidance and training* to school directors and teachers in order to improve their performance.

Supervision limited to the first objective assumes that compliance with the *plan* will insure achievement of system objectives.

Supervision as data collection was originally intended to permit central management to make critical decisions, but could also contribute to a decentralized management system.

The third objective for supervision is consistent with decentralization of management, and makes the supervisor part of the *in-service* training team.

Anecdotal information suggests that in many countries supervisory visits to schools are irregular and infrequent. Most supervision is consistent with the first or second objective. Supervisors make few visits to classrooms, and seldom offer advice to teachers to help improve their performance.

When supervision occurs, it can have a positive effect on learning outcomes. More frequent visits to schools by supervisors in Pakistan were associated with reduced teacher absences, improvements in quality of teaching, improved student attendance and improved information flow from school to central management (Warwick, Reimers, and McGinn, 1992). In Bangladesh, twice-monthly visits of supervisors to schools has improved teacher attendance (Verspoor, 1989). The level of supervision is an important factor in the implementation of school improvement programs (Verspoor, 1989). **There is very little research on the behavior, or effectiveness, of different patterns of school supervision.** See page 54 for research on principals.

The *school cluster system* is an effort to move supervision closer to the school. See page **223** for an example. See also Wheeler, Raudenbush, and Pasigna (1989)

from pages 69, 73, 95, 101, 107, 157

Which of the following best describes why supervision at the local level is inadequate?

→ **Supervisors have few incentives to enforce the standards.** If this is true, go to page **188** for suggestions of ways to improve supervision.

→ **There are too few supervisors and/or they have too much work.** If this is true, go to page **193** for suggestions of ways to make up for shortage of supervisors.

→ **Supervisors do not observe teachers in their classrooms.** If this is true, go to page **192** for examples of supervisory programs.

← For more information and discussion, see page 102

Causes and Effects of Student Absences

A major determinant of total student *time-on-task* (see pages **92** and **94**) is attendance. In most schools, most learning of the curriculum takes place within the classroom. (See page **96** for a discussion of learning outside the classroom.) Students who are absent from school do not receive instruction from the teacher, in many schools do not have access to textbooks, and miss opportunities to learn from their peers.

There are no comparative statistics on rates of student attendance and few studies on the causes and effects of student absences. Some countries collect daily attendance data. This is common in countries in which annual allocations to schools are based on detailed information about student attendance. Jamaica, for example, includes in its annual statistics average rates of attendance by day of the week. Between September (beginning of the school year) and December, enrollment declined from 318,384 to 232,436. That is, as many as 27 percent of the students may have dropped out. (Ministry officials are not certain because some of the students may have enrolled in more than one school in September.) Daily attendance of those enrolled averaged 79 percent in September, and 57 percent in December. Girls had higher attendance rates than boys. Average daily attendance ranged from 73 percent in the capital, to 43 percent in an outlying district (Planning Institute of Jamaica, 1992).

But Jamaica, like most other countries, has carried out few studies on why children fail to attend and what can be done to increase attendance. Student absences are often higher when teachers are frequently absent. When teachers have low expectations for their students' achievement, student attendance is lower (Munoz Izquierdo and de Arrive, 1987; Montero-Sieburth, 1989).

Absences are most common among poor children in rural areas. Poor children are more likely to be ill and to come from families which from time to time require their help at home. Rural children face topographic and climactic obstacles to regular school attendance.

Female absences are highest in countries or regions in which enrollment of girls is considerably lower than enrollment of boys. When girls achieve parity in enrollment with boys, they tend to be absent less frequently. (Baker, 1988). This would appear to be linked with the economic utility of the child at home or employment opportunities outside of the home.

Student absences are a predictor of repetition (McGinn et al., 1992). Student absences can, therefore, be a major source of *ine*fficiency in an education system.

from pages 41, 97

Which of the following best explains why students are absent?

➡️ **They have to travel long distances to attend classes.** Go to page 179 for suggestions of solutions to this problem.

➡️ **Because of their poor academic performance during the school year.** Go to page 195 for suggested policy options.

➡️ **Other activities compete with school time, for example, children must harvest crops.** Distance education methods might help. Go to page 222. It may also be possible to adjust the school calendar.

← For more information and discussion, see page 104

105

What is Classroom Management?

The concept of *classroom management* considers the teacher as a producer of learning. The amount and quality of learning that is generated depends (in part) on the ability of the teacher to use effectively the resources available, and to affect the behavior of students.

The resources include physical facilities, equipment, instructional materials, and time. Increased spending on facilities, equipment, or materials may have little impact on learning outcomes if teachers are not trained in how to use them effectively. Returns to improvements in teachers' management skills are probably higher than improvements in the stock of physical resources. **There is, however, almost no research on the interaction between classroom management skills and the effectiveness of improved physical resources.**

Time is a special kind of resource. There is a growing body of research that shows that increased time spent on teaching of curriculum results in increased learning outcomes (see page **92**). Teachers' ability to manage time use in the classroom is, therefore, an important contributor to the amount of learning.

The management of time includes action to increase

1. total time available to instruction; and

2. efficiency in the use of time.

An effective classroom manager has high student attendance rates, and spends little classroom time on non-instructional activities. This is accomplished by actions to motivate attendance, and to control student behavior in class. Physical resources (classroom conditions, instructional materials) make it easier for a teacher to *engage* students in learning activities, but their effective use involves management skills.

Little is known about the impact of conventional teacher training on classroom management skills. Alternative instructional strategies (see page **199**) based on instructional design concepts (see page **34**) emphasize careful attention to pacing and sequence, that is to use of time. The Reduced Instructional Time Project (see page **219**) was able to reduce the time required by students to learn, and to reduce the time spent by teachers in instruction.

For additional information see Montero-Sieburth (1989).

from page 93

Which of the following best accounts for why teachers don't make good use of instructional time?

→ **They are not adequately monitored.** If this is true, go to page **103**.

→ **They do not receive adequate in-service training.** If this is true, go to page **69**.

→ **They do not receive adequate pre-service training.** If this is true, go to page **67**.

→ **They have trouble maintaining order in the classroom.** Go to page **182** for comments on problems of discipline.

← For more information and discussion, see page 106

The Importance of Instructional Materials

Instructional materials are an essential element in the formal school. The term **materials** includes not just textbooks, but also workbooks, reference books, tapes, posters, maps, globes, slides, movies, charts, models, and a variety of other devices to facilitate the instructional process.

Instructional materials make three important contributions to the school:

1. Properly prepared instructional materials provide access to the curriculum. That is, instructional materials provide the content that is specified in the curriculum.

    This may be important for teachers whose training did not include adequate preparation in the content of the curriculum. Instructional materials can carry the content of new or revised curriculum units.

2. Instructional materials can contribute to the teaching process. Good instructional materials carry suggestions as to how the material can be used.

3. Instructional materials can extend engaged time-on-task by allowing students to learn on their own without direct contact with the teacher. This may be important in crowded, heterogeneous or multigrade classrooms. Instructional materials can make it possible for a teacher to work with one group of students while another learns on its own.

Instructional materials can be used by students to learn at home, alone or with the supervision of their parents.

➡ See page **199** for a discussion of **self-instructional** materials.

from pages 39, 61, 97, 119

In your country, which of the following best explains the shortage of instructional materials?

→ **The education system doesn't have enough money to develop them, or to provide them.** Go to page **172** for some ways to overcome this problem.

→ **Families cannot afford to purchase them.** Go to page **196** for possible solutions.

← **For more information and discussion, see page 108**

The Importance of Textbooks

Textbooks are the most common type of instructional materials used in schools, especially at the primary level. The importance of textbooks can be attributed to several factors:

1. Textbooks can compensate for low quality of teaching.

   a. Textbooks can carry the curriculum, which may be ignored by the teacher.

   b. Textbooks can present material in a sequenced, graded fashion that makes learning easier.

   c. Textbooks allow the student to learn even when the teacher is not teaching.

Research shows that **students with textbooks learn more than those without**, holding teaching quality and student abilities constant. In two separate studies students who were given textbooks scored significantly higher on end-of-year achievement tests than their companions without books (Jamison et al., 1981; Heyneman, Jamison, and Montenegro, 1984). In Brazil, students who had textbooks over a five-year period did significantly better than students who did not have books (Armitage and others, 1986).

2. Textbooks are relatively inexpensive. Government provision of textbooks to all students in all grades can cost less than two percent of total expenditure on education.

3. Use of textbooks in classrooms makes it easier for teachers to manage heterogeneous groups of students. One group of students reads, while the teacher works with another group. **With textbooks teachers can handle larger classes without declines in learning.**

4. The student's textbook may be the only contact parents have with printed material. The textbook can contribute to the intellectual growth not only of the child, but also of adults.

The positive effect of textbooks is achieved only when certain conditions are met. **Some textbook projects have failed to deliver expected results**, because of qualities of the textbooks themselves, or because of the ways in which they were used in the classroom.

Not much research has been done on the impact of instructional materials, other than textbooks. There is little research on how variations in the qualities of textbooks, or in their form of use, affect their impact. For example, a classroom may have adequate numbers of textbooks, but the books may have not been written for use at that particular grade level. Sometimes, in an effort to preserve textbooks for as long as possible, the teacher locks them in a closet or uses them infrequently.

Educational development is a growth process which occurs in stages (Beeby, 1966 and 1986). Mismatches between the level or stage of a teacher's training, for example, and the textbooks to be used contribute to the failure of textbook programs. Go to page **243** for more information on the stages of educational development and the improvement of quality in education.

from pages 11, 97, 99

What is it about the instructional materials in your system that concerns you?

➡ **Is the problem with the materials themselves?** If so, go to page 113.

➡ **Are the materials adequate, but teachers are not trained to use them?** Go to page 53 to review issues related to training.

For information on the production of textbooks see Gardner (1982), Paxman, Denning, and Read (1989), Pearce (1982 and 1988), Searle (1985).

← For more information and discussion, see page 110

This is a page from the teacher's guide for a grade 6 math textbook (Rucker, Dilley, and Lowry, 1985). The information provided helps the teacher prepare lessons, teach them, and then evaluate student learning. On this page from the guide, information is given about pacing and learning objectives. The overview of the chapter and background information help the teacher teach this chapter successfully.

→ Please turn to page **116** for another page from the same teacher's guide.

112

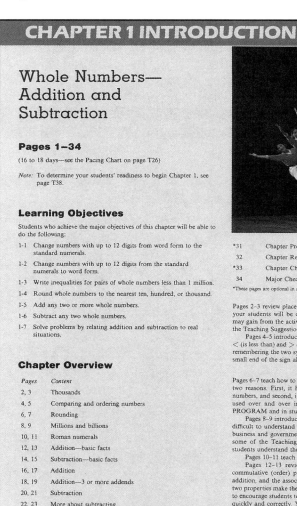

CHAPTER 1 INTRODUCTION

Whole Numbers— Addition and Subtraction

1

Pages 1–34

(16 to 18 days—see the Pacing Chart on page T26)

Note: To determine your students' readiness to begin Chapter 1, see page T38.

Learning Objectives

Students who achieve the major objectives of this chapter will be able to do the following:

1-1 Change numbers with up to 12 digits from word form to the standard numerals.

1-2 Change numbers with up to 12 digits from the standard numerals to word form.

1-3 Write inequalities for pairs of whole numbers less than 1 million.

1-4 Round whole numbers to the nearest ten, hundred, or thousand.

1-5 Add any two or more whole numbers.

1-6 Subtract any two whole numbers.

1-7 Solve problems by relating addition and subtraction to real situations.

Chapter Overview

Pages	Content
2, 3	Thousands
4, 5	Comparing and ordering numbers
6, 7	Rounding
8, 9	Millions and billions
10, 11	Roman numerals
12, 13	Addition—basic facts
14, 15	Subtraction—basic facts
16, 17	Addition
18, 19	Addition—3 or more addends
20, 21	Subtraction
22, 23	More about subtracting
24, 25	Estimating sums and differences
26, 27	Problem solving
28, 29	Problem solving—reading a chart
30	Chapter Checkup

1a

*31	Chapter Project
32	Chapter Review
*33	Chapter Challenge
34	Major Checkup

These pages are optional in a minimum course.

Pages 2–3 review place value for numbers with up to 6 digits. Most of your students will be quite familiar with place value. However, some may gain from the activities with manipulative objects that are given in the Teaching Suggestions.

Pages 4–5 introduce comparing two numbers and using the symbols < (is less than) and > (is greater than). Students will have some trouble remembering the two symbols, so we suggest this little memory aid: the small end of the sign always points to the smaller number.

$$6 < 8 \qquad 8 > 6$$

Pages 6–7 teach how to round numbers. This is a very important skill for two reasons. First, it helps students develop an intuitive feel for the numbers, and second, it is used extensively in estimating, a skill that is used over and over in the rest of the HEATH MATHEMATICS PROGRAM and in students' lives as well.

Pages 8–9 introduce millions and billions. These large numbers are difficult to understand in any concrete way but are so widely used in business and government that students should begin to use them. Use some of the Teaching Suggestions and Lesson Follow-ups to help students understand these numbers.

Pages 10–11 teach some of the characteristics of Roman numerals.

Pages 12–13 review the basic addition facts, along with the commutative (order) property of addition, the adding 0 property of addition, and the associative (grouping) property of addition. The first two properties make the facts easier to memorize. Page 13 is a speed drill to encourage students to learn the facts so well that they can be recalled quickly and correctly. You may find it valuable to use this and similar sets of exercises regularly.

Page 14 has a similar speed drill for the basic subtraction facts, and page 15 provides practice with the basic addition and subtraction facts.

Pages 16–17 review the addition algorithm with various regroupings that are usually necessary. The text provides an explanation of why the algorithm works by using pictures of a physical model. Although most

from pages 79, 111, 117

Instructional materials increase student learning of the curriculum when the following conditions are met:

1. The materials are consistent with and cover curriculum content. In some countries, authors do not take curriculum objectives and content into account when developing materials.

2. The scope and sequence of the materials' content matches students' abilities. Textbooks, for example, vary considerably in level of difficulty (Lockheed and Verspoor, 1991). When materials are too difficult, or too easy, students do not learn.

3. The language of the materials matches that used by students. A textbook produced in Honduras used words familiar to urban children, but not used in the rural areas where most of the population lives (McGinn et al., 1992).

4. The content of the materials is interesting to students.

5. The pedagogical style of the materials matches that of the teacher, or teachers are trained in the pedagogical style that the materials assume will be used.

6. The materials provide students with an opportunity to use what they have learned. This can be in the form of quizzes or exercises, or in activities to be carried out at home or in the classroom.

7. Students actually use the materials. This comes about through teacher use of the materials in instruction, or as seat-work for students, or when students take materials home.

Which of the following best describes the problem you face with instructional materials?

→ **There aren't enough materials.** If this is the case, go to page 119.

→ **The materials are of poor quality.** If this is the case, go to page 121.

← **For more information and discussion, see page 112**

113

Does Bilingual Instruction Work?

In which language should children entering school for the first time be taught?

1. The language they speak at home, here called *L1*?

2. A second language, either an official national language or an "international" or "metropolitan" language, *L2*?

Assume that the objective for the language policy is adult proficiency in L2. What is the best way to achieve that objective? Three kinds of bilingual education programs have been tried. The results are as follows:

1. *Transitional Bilingual Programs.* This approach uses the student's "native" language or L1, to teach the curriculum until proficiency is attained in L2. These programs often begin 1st grade with all instruction in L1, but reduce the proportion of instruction in L1 in each successive grade.

   Results. This approach has had mixed results. About half the evaluations are positive as measured by achievement in basic subjects, the rest neutral or negative. One major factor is language ability of the teacher. It often is difficult to find teachers who are competent in minority L1 languages.

2. *Maintenance bilingual programs.* This approach seeks to strengthen the student's ability in his/her L1, in addition to achieving proficiency in L2. L1 is used as the language of instruction at least through completion of primary school. L2 is taught as a second language.

   Results. In the few applications of this approach, students learned as much or more of academic subjects as do L2 students, and in addition learned L2. There is strong resistance, however, by L1 parents to this kind of program.

3. *Immersion programs.* Students begin instruction in L2, with L1 added as a second language subject after the 1st grade. They differ from an official-language-only policy, in that parents choose to have their children participate, and L1 has high prestige in the community.

   Results. This approach has been most successful in Canada, where students whose L1 was English had French as language of instruction in primary school, learning both French and English and academic subjects as well as students taught in their L1.

Which language of instruction should be used depends on three factors: 1) students' age, social class, and language ability; 2) attitudes of teachers, parents, and community; and 3) the role of each language in the society.

→ For an application of these factors see page **198**.

from page 99

The technology of the formal school is based on assumptions about the children who become students. The school makes assumptions about:

1. the knowledge and abilities the child has on entering school;

2. the ability of the child to conform to the discipline of the school;

3. the child's ability to attend to what teachers present, and to work for a sustained period of time in the confines of the classroom.

The school works best when children in a classroom are alike in abilities and interest. Heterogeneity makes the teacher's job more difficult. If there are discrepancies in what the school expects, and what children are like, the efficiency of the school is reduced.

Which of the following best describes the situation in your country?

➜ **Many students do not speak or understand the language that is used for instruction.** Go to page **198** for a description of a process of assigning children to different languages of instruction.

➜ **Children enter school without the cognitive skills that teachers expect.** Go to page **210** for a discussion of pre-primary education as a means of providing children with expected skills.

➜ **Some students are not physically able to attend to the teacher.** Go to page **209** for an example of a program to improve student nutrition.

➜ **Some students fail at the next level because they are not ready or prepared.** Go to page **125**.

➜ **Heterogeneity of classes is a problem.** Go to page **127**.

You may decide, after going through these questions, that it is important to look at other factors. If so, go to page 117.

← For more information and discussion, see page 114

115

This is another page from the teacher's guide for a grade 6 math textbook (Rucker, Dilley, and Lowrey, 1985). The smaller box is an actual copy of a page in the student's text. The larger box which surrounds it is in the teacher's guide. The page provides the teacher with a great deal of information. The teacher is offered vocabulary, an example of a readiness sheet, suggestions for using the textbook and optional materials, and the answers to the questions and exercises found on the student's page.

→ Please turn to page **118** for additional pages from the teacher's guide.

116

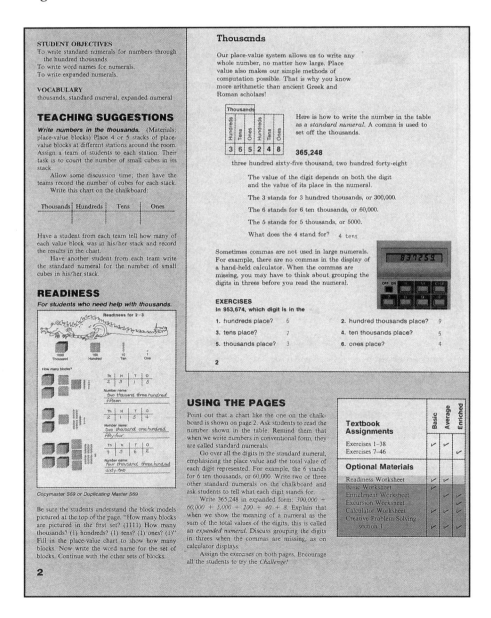

from page 115

In your country, is one of the problems...

→   **the quality of the curriculum?** If so, go to page **153**.

→   **the quality of teaching?** If so, go to page **53**.

→   **the lack of instructional materials?** If so, go to page **113**.

→   **insufficient time on task?** If so, go to page **93**.

→   **the quality of administration?** If so, go to page **43**.

← **For more information and discussion, see page 116**

The smaller box is from the student's book. The students complete the chapter checkup and give it to the teacher. The teacher uses the diagnosis and remediation paragraphs to help students learn from and correct their mistakes.

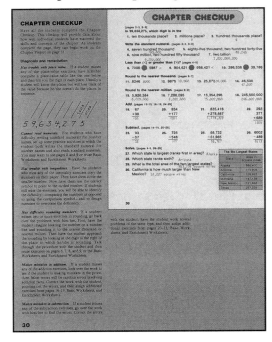

Once again, the smaller box is a page from the student's book. The students complete this page in order to practice taking standardized tests. This also helps the teacher know that the program content is related to standardized tests. Please turn to page **120** for additional pages from this teacher's guide (Rucker, Dilley, and Lowrey, 1985).

A number of studies have shown that students with "more" instructional materials learn more than those with "fewer." For example, in Chile (Schiefelbein and Farrell, 1982) the more textbooks students have, the more they learn. This effect is greater for students from poor families.

But there is relatively little research on the question of how much is sufficient in terms of instructional materials. One of the few studies was carried out in the Philippines. Investigators found that there were no achievement differences between schools in which there was one book for every two students, and schools in which each student had a book. In both sets of schools students learned much more than students in schools in where there was only one book for every ten students (Heyneman, Jamison, and Montenegro, 1984).

The questions below call attention to the fact that quantity is not the only factor to keep in mind.

Which of the following is correct with respect to your country?

→   **There are sufficient materials for all students.** If this is *not* the case, go to page **109**.

→   **There is sufficient variety in the level of difficulty of materials to match the range of student abilities in a class.** If this is *not* the case, go to page **199** for suggested solutions.

→   **The materials are such that teachers can assign some students to work on them on their own, while the teacher works directly with other students.** If this is *not* the case, go to page **199** for examples of programs that use self-instructional materials.

← For more information and discussion, see page 118

Students will complete one of these two pages after they have done the Chapter Checkup. Those who had difficulty with the Chapter Checkup will be assigned the Chapter Review. The rest of the class will complete the Chapter Challenge.

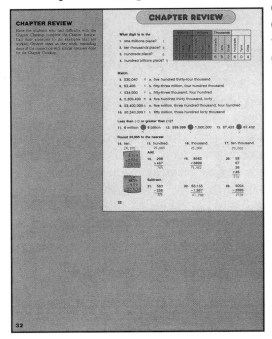

Teacher's Guides are complemented by worksheets, overhead transparencies, filmstrips, and other instructional materials.

See page **122** for another sample page from Rucker, Dilley, and Lowrey (1985).

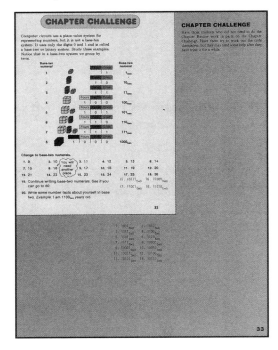

from pages 61, 113

The number and variety of instructional materials required depends on:

1. the content of the curriculum;

2. the instructional technology used;

3. abilities of the teachers; and

4. characteristics of the students.

In your country, which of the following describes why the quality of materials is not satisfactory?

→ **They are not written in the appropriate language.** Go to page **123**.

→ **Their content is not linked with the expectations of the curriculum.**

→ **They do not clearly specify what students are expected to learn.**

→ **They do not clearly specify how teachers are supposed to teach the content or how students are supposed to learn on their own.**

→ **The sequencing of units within the subjects is inadequate or incomplete.**

→ **The presentation of material is paced too fast or too slow for the students.**

Go to page **237** for a discussion of the criteria to take into account in the design of materials.

Go to page **238** for a checklist to be used in evaluation of textbooks and other instructional materials.

← For more information and discussion, see page 120

121

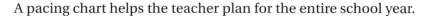

A pacing chart helps the teacher plan for the entire school year.

It suggests how much time should be spent on each chapter. It also allows the teacher to be flexible when planning for faster or slower learners.

→ Please turn to page **124** for one more page from this teacher's guide (Rucker, Dilley, and Lowrey, 1985).

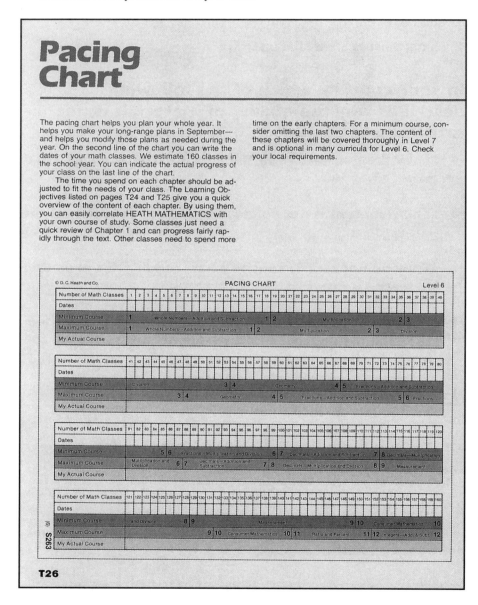

Pacing Chart

The pacing chart helps you plan your whole year. It helps you make your long-range plans in September—and helps you modify those plans as needed during the year. On the second line of the chart you can write the dates of your math classes. We estimate 160 classes in the school year. You can indicate the actual progress of your class on the last line of the chart.

The time you spend on each chapter should be adjusted to fit the needs of your class. The Learning Objectives listed on pages T24 and T25 give you a quick overview of the content of each chapter. By using them, you can easily correlate HEATH MATHEMATICS with your own course of study. Some classes just need a quick review of Chapter 1 and can progress fairly rapidly through the text. Other classes need to spend more time on the early chapters. For a minimum course, consider omitting the last two chapters. The content of these chapters will be covered thoroughly in Level 7 and is optional in many curricula for Level 6. Check your local requirements.

© D.C. Heath and Co.   PACING CHART   Level 6

T26

from pages 39, 121

Which of the following best describes why the language of materials is not right?

→ **The language of the materials doesn't match the language which the teacher uses.** For possible policy options, go to page 198.

→ **The language of the materials doesn't match the language which the students use.** For possible policy options, go to page 198.

← For more information and discussion, see page 122

123

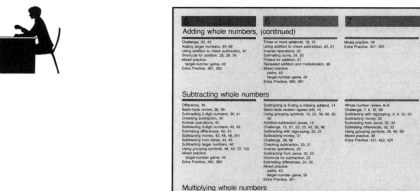

This page from the teacher's guide (Rucker, Dilley, and Lowrey, 1985 illustrates part of the scope and sequence chart. It compares the grade 6 program (second column) with the grade 5 program (first column) and the grade 7 program (third column). This helps the teacher understand what the students studied during the previous school year as well as what will be expected of them during the next school year.

This page from the same guide lists the learning objectives for each chapter in the textbook. This grade 6 math book has a total of 12 chapters. For a minimum program the students would have to complete chapters 1–10. Other pages from this guide are found on pages **112, 116, 118, 120** and **122**.

from pages 41, 115, 195

Which of the following best explains why students coming from a lower grade are not prepared to do the work?

➡ **Standards are too low, which allows unprepared students to go to the next grade.** Go to page **224** for the importance of setting and maintaining high standards.

➡ **Assessment methods are inadequate.** See page **207** for programs that improved assessment methods.

⬅ For more information and discussion, see page 124

Should We Eliminate Multigrade Classrooms?

The single grade classroom, in which all children receive the same curriculum and are about the same age, is a relatively recent invention. Prior to the nineteenth century, most schools grouped children on the basis of their knowledge of the subject matter. A beginning primary class might, therefore include adults as well as children of all ages. What they had in common was their illiteracy. All were taught using a common method of instruction, despite varying levels of intellectual and emotional maturity.

This worked well enough with educated and dedicated persons as teachers. But the rapid expansion of education in Europe in the 1700s (see page **64**) required use of less-well educated persons as teachers. The problems of handling learners of different ages grew to be too much.

The solution was the *graded* school, in which learners were divided up by age groups, more homogeneous in both ability and maturity. The homogeneous grouping of learners made it possible to train relatively uneducated persons to be effective teachers.

Single grade classrooms were possible, however, only in areas with enough students. Isolated areas with few children could not afford a teacher for every grade. In these situations, the policy chosen was to combine students at different levels of development in the same room. This came to be referred to as the *multigrade* classroom.

Some multigrade classrooms can still be found in the United States (Miller, 1987). There are as many as 11,000 one-teacher schools in France. UNESCO (1989) reports common (but not predominant) use of multigrade classrooms in many developing countries.

Should countries attempt to eliminate multigrade classrooms? Research indicates that students **can** learn as much in multigrade classrooms as in single grade classrooms (Schiefelbein, 1991a). Learning in a heterogeneous classroom has important social and education benefits as well (Pratt, 1986). But these gains are possible only when additional inputs are provided in the multigrade classroom. Those inputs include:

1. training for teachers on how to handle diverse groups of students;

2. instructional materials that permit students to work without direct supervision; and

3. physical facilities that permit division of the class into separate work groups.

For examples of programs that combine one or more of these elements see pages **187, 199, 208** and **217**, and Bray (1987), Miller (1987), Thomas and Shaw (1992), and UNESCO (1989).

from pages 41, 57, 115

To which of the following is the problem of heterogeneity related?

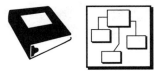

→ **Multigrade classrooms**. Go to page **208** for possible ways to improve quality in multigrade classrooms.

→ **High rate of failure and repetition.** If this is true, go to page **129**.

→ **Single grade classrooms with wide ranges of student interests and abilities.** Heterogeneous classrooms can best be handled using the same concepts and procedures as the multigrade classroom. Go to page **208**.

← For more information and discussion, see page 126

Repetition and its Costs

In 1986 approximately 20 million children in Latin America enrolled in, or *repeated*, the same grade of primary school in which they had been enrolled in 1985. The average cost per student per year is $161. That means that the total cost of providing repeaters a second year of schooling is about US $3 billion (Schiefelbein 1991b).

Rates of repetition are highest in grade 1, where they are estimated to be above 40 percent of students enrolled, declining to about 20 percent by grade 5 (Schiefelbein and Heikinnen, 1991).

Each year some children in Latin America who have not yet completed the primary cycle *drop out* of school, that is, do not enroll. This figure is about eight percent of enrollment in grades 1 and 2, declining to slightly more than one percent by grade 5. Most children who repeat do so in grade 1, and almost all of those who drop out have repeated grades 1 or 2. **Very few children drop out without first having repeated a grade.**

Factors Associated with Repetition

Repetition is most often the result of a decision that the student's academic abilities at the end of the year are not sufficient to insure that the student will benefit from exposure to teaching in the next highest grade. That is, children are failed by teachers.

In most cases, the decision that a child should repeat is made by the teacher, in some cases by parents who may even request that the child repeat a grade even though the teacher has promoted the child. In both cases, the assumption is that repetition of the grade will result in the child learning the knowledge, skills, and attitudes required to learn effectively in the next highest grade.

There is *no* research evidence to support the assumption that repetition in early grades *increases* the learning capacity of the student. In the early grades, students who fail are labeled as less qualified than others, and often receive less instruction as a result. The likelihood of future failure often increases with repetition (Grissom and Shepard, 1989).

Repetition does not overcome failure to learn. It reduces motivation to learn.

from pages 5, 13, 127

There are two basic reasons why students repeat grades in school:

1   teachers or parents decide the student has not learned enough to go on to the next grade; or

2   there is no higher grade to attend and parents wish the child to remain in school.

In your country, which of the following statements best accounts for why students repeat grades?

➜   **The teacher fails the students because s/he believes they have not learned enough.** Go to page 11.

➜   **Children repeat not because they fail, but because there are no higher grades for them to attend, and parents/teachers feel they can learn more by repeating the grade.** Go to page 133.

➜   **Parents keep children back because they feel they have not learned enough, no matter what the teacher says.** Go to page 132.

← For more information and discussion, see page 128

Why Students Drop Out of School

We say that a student *drops out*, or *deserts* school when she or he leaves before completing the cycle (e.g., primary, middle, secondary). Some countries distinguish between *within-year* dropouts, and *between-year* dropouts. In primary schools, most *within-year* dropouts actually **repeat** the grade in the following year (Schiefelbein and Heikinnen, 1991). They do not meet our definition of a drop out as a student who leaves the system permanently.

Because dropouts are not easily "accessible" to the researcher, it is hard to ask them why they dropped out. For this reason there is little solid research on causes.

Two Possible Reasons for Dropping Out

Some students do not continue their schooling simply because there is no higher grade to attend. This is most likely to be true in rural areas in which schools do not have all grades, or where the nearest secondary school is too far away.

But the primary reason why students drop out of school is that they (more likely their family) see less value in continuing in school than in pursuing other activities. This value can be in terms of immediate or expected future economic gain, or it can be in terms of intellectual or spiritual improvement. Page **136** describes the kinds of factors families take into account.

The perception that there is less value in continuing school is based on information from the school itself. For most dropouts, especially those who do so in the lower grades of primary school, their earlier failure in school is the signal that there is little reason for continuing.

Research shows that children who fail and repeat are more likely to drop out than those who never fail (McGinn et al., 1992). There are several reasons why this is so:

1. Student failure lowers mothers' expectations for their children's future success, reducing pressures on the child to study (Lembert, 1985).

2. Teachers, especially in large and heterogeneous classrooms, are not able to spend the time necessary to provide corrective instruction.

3. Students older than the "correct" age for their grade are sometimes asked, sometimes required to leave.

→ Is **automatic promotion** the answer? See page **132**.

from page 5

In your country, which of the following are reasons why children drop out of school before completing the cycle?

→ **There is no school with a higher grade for them to attend.** Go to page 133.

→ **They reach working age before completing the cycle and they or their parents believe that they can contribute more to the household by going to work rather than continuing schooling.** Go to page 135.

→ **Parents believe the possible gains from education are too little compared to the cost.** Go to page 137.

→ **They get pregnant or are married, or parents withdraw them to prepare for marriage.** Go to page 135.

← For more information and discussion, see page 130

Is Automatic Promotion the Answer to High Repetition and Dropout Rates?

Repeating grades after academic failure is not good for students;

- it lowers their self-esteem, and

- it seldom overcomes the teaching or learning situation that led to failure the first time.

Students who repeat two or three times are much more likely to drop out than are students who never repeat.

One apparent way to solve this problem is to promote all children, regardless of their levels of learning. This policy, called *automatic promotion* (sometimes social promotion), increases the number of years low achieving students spend in school before dropping out. It is assumed that this increases their total learning. Automatic promotion also clears out the backlog of repeaters in grades 1 and 2, creating space for new students.

Chile promotes all children, irrespective of grades, up to the 4th grade. Egypt and El Salvador promote automatically in grades 1, 3, and 5, and children who fail in grades 2 and 4 can repeat only once and are then promoted. In Korea less than one percent of children fail to complete primary school in six years.

But Does it Work?

If a policy of automatic promotion is implemented with no attempt to eliminate the factors associated with school failure, problems of learning in the early grades may only be passed on, reducing the efficiency of teaching in the upper grades. Automatic promotion by itself increases the range of different abilities among children, increasing the difficulty faced by the teacher.

Countries that once favored automatic promotion are now turning away from it. Panama and Puerto Rico, faced with increasing numbers of illiterate primary school graduates, reversed a policy of automatic promotion (Munoz and Arrive, 1987). Ellwein and Glass (1989) describe the efforts of one U.S. school district to "raise standards" by elimination of automatic promotion in kindergartens and grades 2, 5, and 7.

Internal efficiency can be symbolically improved by automatic promotion, but a real improvement requires attention to the causes of low learning in school.

➜ See page 117 for questions to help you analyze the causes of low learning in school.

from pages 129, 131

ncomplete schools, that is, schools that do not offer instruction in all the grades in the cycle, occur principally in areas of low population density. The ministry of education may decide that there are too few students for the upper grades to warrant assignment of a teacher or use of a classroom.

In a few countries, there simply are not enough classrooms, or teachers to teach in them, to go around, even in urban areas.

In your country, which is the main reason why some children do not find a higher grade to attend?

→ **The small number of students does not merit assignment of a teacher or use of an existing classroom.** If this is true, go to page **231** for several ways to overcome this problem.

→ **There is a shortage of buildings.** If this is true, go to page **19**.

→ **There is a shortage of teachers.** If this is true, go to page **21**.

133

← For more information and discussion, see page 132

School and Employment

Poor families face a difficult choice. Should children be sent to school, or put to work?

Arguments for sending a child to school are based on an expectation that this will increase the child's life chances. This expectation has two parts:

1. The child will do well in school, and achieve a significant level of education.

2. Education will lead to achievement of goals such as greater social status, a better marriage, higher levels of income, deepened spirituality.

Families may decide not to educate a child if:

1. their immediate situation is such they must have the benefits of the child's labor;

2. they cannot afford the costs of schooling; and

3. they believe that the rewards of education are smaller than those of immediate employment.

The following quote is from a parent in India:

"...schools do not prepare for careers...our primary schools are worthless. The children do not learn....These are precious years for learning their trade, and these preparatory years would be gone if they went to school....The poor children who go to school will not complete their education and they will not get a degree. Most probably they will drop out of school and not go to college. So if they go to school, they are suited for nothing." (Weiner, 1991, pp. 59-61)

Families in which parents have some education are less likely to put their children to work (Psacharopoulos and Arriagada, 1989).

In an attempt to increase the relevance of primary education, some countries have primary school students do manual work. The objectives have been to provide useful skills and make school seem more relevant. Most of these programs have failed. Primary school teachers are not competent to provide skills training or to teach basic agriculture. Primary school children are seldom skilled or efficient workers; their products do not earn them respect from society, nor contribute significantly to school costs. Children from these schools do not develop an affinity for manual labor (Psacharopoulos, 1986).

→ See also pages **130** and **136**.

For more information see Bequele and Boyden (1988), Chakravarty (1989), and Mendelievich (1979).

from page 131

The reason(s) why many students reach working or marriage age before completing the basic education cycle is that:

→ **They started late in grade 1.** Delayed enrollment occurs when schools are too far away for young children to attend. Go to page 168 for a few solutions.

→ **Delayed enrollment also occurs when there is no space available in the local school.** If this is a problem in your system, go to page **7**.

→ **They repeated one or more grades.** Go to page 128 for a discussion of factors associated with repetition.

→ **The working age is too young.** This is a political problem that requires national legislation. Most students do not leave school before age ten or 11.

→ **The marriage age is young.** This age often depends on cultural and religious traditions. Experience shows, however, that as levels of education increase, age of marriage increases. See Crouch, Spratt, and Cubeddu (1992).

← For more information and discussion, see page 134

135

Why Parents and Students Lose Interest in Schooling

Families take several factors into account when deciding whether to continue the education of a child:

1. the educability of the child, that is, how far the child can be expected to go in school.

2. the direct costs of schooling, which can include fees levied by the teacher; cost of textbooks, notebooks, pencils and other learning materials; clothing; transportation; and food.

3. the immediate opportunity cost or benefit lost if the child continues in school. What could the child earn, or learn, or enjoy, if he or she were not in school?

4. the likely benefits at some time in the future. What would the child earn, learn or enjoy in the future?

The critical information for this estimation of costs and benefits comes from the school principally, secondarily from the larger society.

1. Success or failure in school (marks, teacher comments, promotion) help parents estimate how far the child can be expected to go in school.

2. Repeated failure raises the direct cost of each completed grade of schooling.

3. Failure also increases the opportunity costs to the child. The world outside the classroom looks more and more attractive with each failure and rebuke. At entry age (e.g., six years) the economic benefit of children might be quite small, but each failure and grade repetition pushes the child closer to a "productive" age threshold.

4. Once a student is of "working" age, the expected return to one more year of schooling in grades 1 or 2 seems small. The expected return to completing grade 6, on the other hand, is tangibly larger.

This analysis is consistent with research (Cuadra et al., 1990; Schiefelbein, 1991b) that shows that very few students drop out of school before age ten or 11. Furthermore, few students drop out of school who have never failed.

Parents and students lose interest in schooling when their experience, in school, tells them there is little to be gained from continuing.

from page 131

Which of the following best explains why parents believe that possible gains from education are not worth the cost?

➜ **Central education officials have failed to report adequately on the objectives and accomplishments of the system, and of the importance of education for society.** Go to page **235** for suggestions of ways to improve reporting on progress of the education system.

➜ **Teachers have told parents their children are not likely to go far in school.** Go to pages **205** and **206** for suggestions of how to improve the information teachers can provide parents.

➜ **Parents believe the possible gains from education are too little in comparison with the immediate, direct costs of sending children to school (fees, books, transportation, clothing, meals, etc.) are too high.** Go to page **165** for ways to reduce the costs of schooling.

➜ **Parents believe the possible gains from education are too little in comparison with the economic benefit they lose by sending the child to school, for example, from labor in the house or income gained outside the house.** See page **165** for suggestions of ways to reduce the conflict between participation in labor and attendance at school.

← For more information and discussion, see page 136

137

Problems of Education Administration

Three broad tasks have been proposed to improve the capacity of countries to manage their education system. These are:

1. improve organizational structures;

2. increase managerial capacity; and

3. develop effective information systems (Lockheed and Verspoor, 1991).

Unfortunately we have few guidelines for these proposed changes. **Almost no research has been done on the organizational, personnel, or informational capacities of national ministries of education.** What studies are available describe the inadequacies of current forms of organization.

    a. Overall goals are poorly defined and not understood by many members of the organization. Many organizations operate without annual goals.

    b. Tasks and functions of units are unclear, and often overlapping.

    c. The structure of the organization encourages data to flow from bottom to top; there is little horizontal communication between units.

    d. Planning is most often defined as a staff function, with little influence on actual operations.

    e. The organization has no "memory." From year to year there is little or no evaluation, no attempt to associate previous actions with present outcomes — to learn from experience.

Most ministries of education are staffed by persons who have been promoted up from teaching and school administration, on the basis of seniority. No special training is provided, either in general administration or in specific functions of the units in which they work.

Most ministries do not have sufficient funds to maintain close contact with districts and schools. They operate in ignorance of what actually takes place in schools. Most data are about inputs to the system, rather than outputs. Data often arrive too late to permit use in annual planning and budget-making. Decisions about allocation of schools and teachers often lag behind current needs.

For a detailed description of the central ministry of an education system, see Toronto (1990). For a comparison of ministries of education in Colombia and Venezuela see Hanson (1986).

from page 43

Which of the following best describes your concerns with the quality of administration at the central or national level?

→ **The quality and/or quantity of personnel.** If this is true, go to page 145.

→ **Organizational or structural factors.** If this is true, go to page 147.

→ **The resources available for education.** If this is true, see page 149.

← For more information and discussion, see page 138

139

District or Regional Education Administration

Many countries have one or more layers of administration between the central ministry and local schools. Even in relatively small countries, schools may be grouped together (e.g., in clusters, districts, regions — the specific terminology varies widely). The purpose of this grouping is to facilitate communication and control by the center.

In Egypt, for example, the central ministry supervises the operation of 42 *mudirriyya*, or regions. Within each region are from ten to 20 *idaaras*. Within each idaara there are sectors, within sectors sections, and within sections schools. This series of hierarchically organized units provides a *chain of command* that permits the central ministry to communicate its orders and requests downward to teachers, and to receive information upward (Toronto, 1990).

General research in organizations suggests that an ideal ratio of manager to managed is about 1:7. As the number of managed units increases, the manager's ability to keep track of what is going on in each unit is reduced. The larger the ratio, the more likely it is that "managed" units will not receive information or supervision from the center.

Prior to the most recent administrative reforms in Sri Lanka the central ministry supervised 26 regional offices. Each regional office supervised three to five circuit offices, but there were 50 to 100 schools for each circuit office. Messages came down to the circuit offices, but did not reach all the schools (Cummings, Gunawardena, and Williams, 1992). This contributed to unwanted variability in the quality of schools.

Too many layers of management may also reduce the effectiveness of an organization. In Egypt, for example, information from teachers has to pass across many desks before it reaches the central ministry. Prior to recent reforms, statistical data often arrived too late to be of use. As a consequence, each unit within the central ministry created its own information system. Local officers felt they were unheard in the center and often failed to communicate important facts about their schools. The Minister complained that he had no way of knowing what was really going on in schools.

Egypt is pursuing a double-pronged approach to this problem. First, it is speeding up the capacity of the central ministry statistics department to collect, record, and publish data on schools. The objective here is to discourage each central office from collecting its own data. This approach is good but not sufficient. Egypt is also transferring some aspects of management of schools down to the regional offices. This will relieve pressure on the central ministry, which hopes to spend more time on national policy issues. See pages **146** and **148** for a discussion of some of the issues involved in this form of decentralization.

from page 43

Which of the following describes your concerns with respect to the quality of administration at the district or regional level?

→   **The quality and/or quantity of personnel.** If this is true, go to page 145.

→   **Organizational or structural factors.** If this is true, go to page 147.

→   **The resources available for education.** If this is true, go to page 149.

← For more information and discussion, see page 140

How Can the Quality of School Administrators be Improved?

Available research offers few clues as to the most effective ways to improve the quality of school administrators. Not much research has been done. Much of the research that has been done has been descriptive, either of the behaviors of administrators or of opinions about their performance. The few studies that compare administrator characteristics with achievement scores of their students report conflicting results. For example, years of experience is associated with higher achievement in some countries, but not in others (see Georgiades and Jones, 1989).

Countries differ widely in terms of policies and practices with respect to selection of school administrators. In some countries they are selected from the most experienced and senior teachers. In some countries school administration is seen as an unattractive job (because salary increments do not compensate for additional responsibilities). The persons who actually accept appointments are not always the most senior, or best, teachers. Few countries have special academic requirements for administrators. Few appear to require prior certification.

As a consequence of no common definition of job responsibility, and no convincing research, **there is no agreement on what are the most important skills and knowledge and values of an administrator.** There is no agreement on how best to select for these skills, knowledge, or values. Nor is there agreement on the best time and method to train persons who do not yet have these skills. In other words, you will have to develop your own answers.

The required qualities of an effective administrator will vary according to the:

1. objectives set for the school;

2. quality of teachers;

3. characteristics of the community and parents; and

4. characteristics of the school organization itself.

Schools that emphasize academic achievement will need one kind of administrator, those that emphasize moral development another. Schools with experienced teachers may perform very well with a young and unskilled administrator, while schools with young teachers will require a seasoned manager. Similarly, the quality required of the administrator will vary according to the support and level of development of the community. Schools that encourage high teacher participation in decision making will require one kind of administrator, those in which the administrator makes all decisions will require another.

➜ See also page 54.

from page 43

Which of the following best expresses your concerns with the quality of administration at the local or school level?

→ **Quality and/or quantity of personnel.** If this is a concern, go to page **226** for an example of an in-service training program for school administrators. For policies to create a training program for administrators, go to page **234**.

→ **Organizational or structural factors.** If this is a concern, go to page **147**.

→ **The resources available for education.** If this is a concern, go to page **149**.

← For more information and discussion, see page 142

Personnel for the Central Ministry

There is a striking absence of studies on the kinds of persons who work in the central education organizations. We know little about: how people are hired into a ministry of education; whether qualified persons are available; what kinds of persons work most effectively; and what kind of training is provided for new staff. As a consequence, there is little we can say about which policies to improve personnel or the organization are most effective.

The effectiveness of a given person in an organization depends on the organization in which she or he works. A ministry that emphasizes adherence to rules and regulations requires one kind of person, a ministry that encourages initiative requires another. Research on organizations argues that the latter kind of organization is more effective, especially in a changing environment. But to introduce innovative persons into a rules-oriented organization may actually reduce levels of productivity and efficiency.

The process of *organizational analysis* (or *audit*—see Sack, 1992) begins with a characterization of the basic management philosophy and structure of the ministry. The organizational charts that each country produces are not a sufficient guide to this philosophy. **What is essential to know are the criteria that are used to assess the performance of persons and units in the organization.** Organizations that evaluate compliance with rules, and measure levels of activities or inputs, are distinct from those that assess the extent to which goals are met, or which evaluate the quality and quantity of product or outcomes.

The organizational analysis typically divides the ministry into levels of organization. A conventional division is according to functions: strategy, pedagogy, and administration. An alternative approach divides the ministry into a *policy* level, an *executive* level, and an *operational* level. In each case, the analysis looks for problems in the operation of the organization, such as missed deadlines, insufficient resources, idle staff, lack of information.

See Toronto (1990) for an organizational analysis of the ministry of education in Egypt.

The International Institute for Educational Planning, in Paris, has developed a methodology for carrying out an organizational audit.

See page **225** for a case study of use of indicators to monitor the performance of an education system.

from pages 139, 141

An educational administration works well when all positions are filled with qualified and trained staff who are motivated.

Where do you locate the problem with administrative personnel?

→ **The selection process for filling administration positions does not permit stability or continuity of programs.**

→ **There are not enough administrative staff to respond to regional or local concerns.**

→ **Administrative staff are poorly trained.**

→ **Administrators are not well motivated.**

→ **Administrative staff do not reflect national diversity in terms of language or ethnic groups.**

For possible solutions to these problems, see pages **226** and **234**.

← For more information and discussion, see page 144

Modes of Centralization and Funding

Education systems vary widely in terms of the extent to which policy making, planning, and management are centralized. Education was once primarily a private affair, but with the creation of nation-states governments took on responsibilities for the provision, and control, of education. This process took place over several hundred years, beginning first in Prussia in the early 1700s.

The specific economic and political circumstances of the country determined the particular mode of provision and control that developed. Cummings and Riddell (1992) summarize the complex process as follows.

1. The earliest systems developed in the now-industrialized countries. Those models were then exported to (and often imposed upon) developing countries.

2. The earliest developed systems took longest to be constructed.

3. The more recent, autonomously developed systems are the most centralized.

4. Few systems have made radical changes in the extent or form of central control.

5. Decentralized systems have more levels of administration, and more administrative staff.

6. Most countries (about 84 percent) in 1975, even those that were centralized, had some private schools. (The exceptions were all in "socialist" countries.)

7. As participation rates increase, central government involvement increases in the higher levels of education, and private participation declines in relative terms.

8. Centralized control tends toward mass provision of education, but does not insure equality of access.

9. There is no conclusive evidence that centralized systems are less efficient, or effective, than decentralized systems.

10. Private schools may be, but are not always, more efficient or effective than public schools.

→ See page **148** for information on varieties of funding and mode of control.

→ See page **232** for an assessment of four experiences in decentralization in Latin America.

from pages 139, 141, 143

Which of the following applies in your country?

➡ **Excessive centralization makes it difficult to improve the quality of the education system.** If this is true, go to page **151**.

➡ **Current organizational processes are inadequate or inefficient.** If this is true, go to page **226** for how one country trained local administrators to handle more responsibility.

← For more information and discussion, see page **146**

147

Different Modes of Finance of Education

There is considerable variation in both sources and application of funding for education. The table below presents information about 127 countries classified in terms of:

1. how much government funding for education is centralized. The horizontal dimension of the table moves from most to least centralized.

2. the extent of public funding of private education. The vertical dimension of the table moves from least to more public funding of private education.

Minimal private means less than five percent private enrollment in primary, and no more than ten percent in secondary. Government funding of higher education generally parallels that of secondary education.

Table 12
Alternative Models of Source and Recipient
of Funding in 127 National Education Systems in 1975

Source of Funding	Central Govt Only		Central & Local Govt		TOTAL
	No Private or Regulated Private only	Regulated/ Subsidized Private	No Private or Regulated Private only	Regulated/ Subsidized Private	
Emphasis in Funding					
No Private	14	—	7	—	21
Minimal Private	14	4	1	5	24
Private Secondary	15	8	8	4	35
Private Primary	4	4	4	9	—
Primary and Secondary	10	8	3	6	27
Minimal Public	2	8	—	1	11
TOTAL	59	32	20	16	127

Source: Cummings and Riddell (1992).

→ See also pages **172** and **175**.

from pages 139, 141, 143

Which of the following applies in your country?

➔ **More resources are needed for education.** If this is a problem, go to page 172 for several sources of funding.

➔ **Resources currently available for education are not properly allocated within education.** The information on page 175 may be of assistance.

← For more information and discussion, see page 148

Figure 13
Alternatives for Financing Primary Education

149

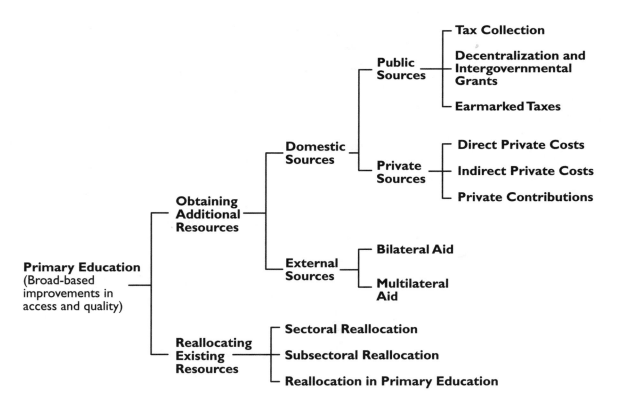

Based on Tsang (1989).

When Is Centralization Excessive?

Most countries have relatively centralized education systems. A ranking of 100 national governments on degree of regulation, on a scale in which 1 = total local control and 7 = total national control, produced an overall average of 5.46 for primary education (Ramirez and Rubinson, 1979).

These patterns of centralized governance are the product of a long process marked by considerable conflict. Whether centralization is excessive depends on the perspective of the group affected. Centralization of education benefits some groups, decentralization benefits others.

From a strictly *technical* perspective, it can be argued that some aspects of governance should be centralized, but others should be decentralized. **The most effective governance system is one that gives the persons with most information about the particular situation requiring a decision the authority to decide how best to achieve objectives set at a higher level.**

Teachers are the persons who have the most information about students' progress in learning; they should have the authority to decide which methods to use, and the pace and sequence of lessons.

Principals are the persons with most information about conditions in the whole school; they should have authority to decide about matters which affect the whole school.

Teachers know more about teaching and curriculum, but parents know more about local values and economic requirements of the community.

District supervisors or education officers know best the overall problems of the district and the resources available to distribute, but school principals have more information about the kind of teacher required in their particular school.

The central ministry may have more information about the overall requirements for school construction, but district officers will know better where new buildings should be located.

From this perspective, centralization is excessive when decisions are located too far from the source of information. Decentralization, on the other hand, is excessive when decision-makers at one level do not have information about the effects of their actions on the level immediately below.

For more information see McGinn (1990, 1992); Winkler (1988).

150

from page 147

Which aspects of your education system are most affected by excessive centralization?

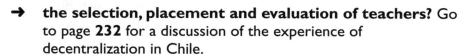
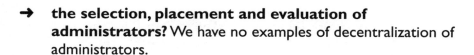

→ **the selection, placement and evaluation of teachers?** Go to page **232** for a discussion of the experience of decentralization in Chile.

→ **the selection, placement and evaluation of administrators?** We have no examples of decentralization of administrators.

→ **the selection of curriculum content?** Go to page **181** for an example of local involvement in curriculum.

→ **the selection of teaching methods?** Go to page **181**.

→ **the evaluation of students?** Many countries expect teachers to evaluate students until the end of the cycle. Go to page **228** for comments on the risks of using centralized achievement tests.

→ **the construction of buildings?** Many countries now expect local communities to assume responsibility for school buildings. Go to page **232**.

→ **the funding of schools?** Go to pages **172** and **175** for alternative forms of finance.

→ **the allocation of resources?** Go to page **232**.

→ **in-service training?** See page **226** for an example of a centrally-organized program that permitted local involvement in in-service training.

← For more information and discussion, see page 150

151

Integrated Curriculum and Assessment

With curriculum and assessment issues often at the center of public debate about improving school quality, one problem is that innovations or changes in curriculum are not usually integrated with similar and simultaneous modifications in assessment.

Research on effective schools (Fielding, 1989) reveals that high performing schools have a common commitment to a set of challenging, well-defined learning goals for students. Such schools also have a process for monitoring student progress toward accomplishing learning goals.

Some of the questions that can be asked to determine the degree of integration between curriculum and assessment are:

1. Is there a well-rounded, academic-oriented core curriculum which will, with some modifications, benefit all students?

2. Are tests, exams, and other forms of assessment based on the goals of the curriculum?

3. Is the assessment process designed to be managed at the local level?

4. Were the assessment methods developed by the same group that developed the curriculum?

5. Do the assessment methods determine if

   a. students have the prerequisites to move to the next level?

   b. students are making satisfactory progress?

   c. students are attaining learning goals?

6. Are any or all of the following included in the assessment methods used in the education system (in addition to standardized achievement tests or national exams)?

   a. Portfolios (see page **205** for more information about portfolios)

   b. Exhibitions

   c. Profiles

   d. Open-ended problem solving exercises

   e. Essays and oral exams

Adapted from Fielding (1989).

from pages 11, 117

The specification of content to be taught and learned often involves indicating:

1. the prior knowledge students should have;

2. methods to be used, including the language of instruction;

3. appropriate materials;

4. methods and content of evaluation of learning; and

5. the abilities required of the teacher.

Which of the following is correct with respect to your country?

→ **The curriculum itself is of poor quality.** If this is true, go to page **35**.

→ **There are difficulties with implementation of the curriculum.** If this is true, go to page **25**.

→ **Assessment of student outcomes is of poor quality.** If this is true, go to page **155**.

→ **The curriculum itself is not evaluated.** If this is true, go to page **237** for suggestions on how to evaluate curriculum.

← For more information and discussion, see page 152

153

Educational Assessment and Standardized Testing

"Curriculum" can be defined as what is taught. "Assessment" refers to what has been learned. School reform efforts usually focus on changing curriculum or transforming assessment, but rarely on integrating the two.

Although there are many ways to assess academic achievement, standardized test results are often used by policy makers and the public to attack or defend school quality. There is increasing pressure on schools to prove that investments in education are producing higher levels of achievement for all students. This has resulted in increased reliance on the use of tests developed by authorities beyond the classroom (for example, see page **169**). It is important for policy makers and educators to understand the uses and limitations of such tests.

Simple comparisons between students, schools, districts, states, and nations are based on standardized test scores. Standardized tests are easy to give, do not require a significant loss of instructional time, and have a long history of use which gives them scientific credibility (Archibald and Newmann, 1988).

The most widely used standardized tests measure verbal, numerical, and analytical abilities. Many educators would argue, however, that over-reliance on these tests to determine school quality reduces the possibility that students will be asked to demonstrate authentic understanding and competence.

Three main concerns about standardized testing are:

1. The construction and scoring of standardized tests makes it difficult to gain useful information from them.

2. General achievement and ability tests are insensitive to curriculum in specific areas; it isn't possible to predict from such tests how students will perform when faced with more authentic forms of achievement testing.

3. Test items on standardized tests (even in specific subject areas) do not assess depth of understanding, integration of knowledge, and production of discourse. As a consequence, standardized tests of general achievement often are used and interpreted inappropriately. (Gould, in Archibald and Newmann, 1988)

But they should not be criticized for failing to measure what they were never designed to measure.

from pages 153, 202

T ests ought to measure what schools teach. There has been widespread public interest in and demand for the use of standardized tests to measure what schools teach. But critics of standardized testing are concerned that:

1. these tests only measure a narrow spectrum of abilities;

2. the nature of these tests discourages creative and imaginative thinking;

3. the results of such tests sometimes have too significant an effect on the life chances of young people;

4. the emphasis in a multiple-choice test is wrongly on the "right answer" and on simplicity instead of thoughtful judgments;

5. the tests favor the economically and culturally advantaged over the disadvantaged while claiming to be neutral; and

6. the tests are biased against those who are unfamiliar with the language and concepts of a majority culture (Ravitch, 1984).

Which of the following describes the situation in your country?

➜ **Assessment of student learning is not integrated with the curriculum taught in schools.** Go to page **203**.

➜ **Assessment of student learning is inadequate or not done at all.** Go to pages **206** and **227**.

➜ **Teachers teach to a standardized test: in effect, the test becomes the curriculum.** Go to pages **205** and **228** for alternatives to the use of standardized tests. See also page **156**.

← For more information and discussion, see page 154

The Functions of Assessment

INDIVIDUAL STUDENT

FORMATIVE ASSESSMENT	*SUMMATIVE ASSESSMENT*
Student Motivation	Selection and Social Control
Monitoring, Feedback and Guidance	Certification and Qualification
Diagnosis and Remediation	Prediction
Clear Recording and Reporting of Student Attainment	

GROUP

FORMATIVE ASSESSMENT	*SUMMATIVE ASSESSMENT*
Curriculum Evaluation	Curriculum Control
Feedback on Teaching	Accountability
Teacher Motivation	Standards

Formative assessment of student performance and learning takes place during the course of instruction. The results of formative assessment are used by both students and teachers.

Summative assessment of student performance and learning takes place at the end of the course, school year, etc. The results of summative assessment of groups of students have greater implications for the education system than do the summative assessments for one individual.

Based on Broadfoot, Murphy, and Torrance (1990).

from page 25

Which of the following best explains why teachers do not carry out the curriculum properly?

➜ **They believe the curriculum is of poor quality.** If this is true, go to page **35**.

➜ **Administrators and/or supervisors provide little or no guidance to teachers about what they should do.** If this is true, go to page **103**.

➜ **There is no way, such as an external examination, for teachers to find out how they are doing with respect to implementation of the curriculum.** If this is true, go to pages **225**, **227** and **228** for comments about the use of external examinations.

← For more information and discussion, see page 156

157

Table of Contents for Policy Options Section

from page i

A Brief List of Readings on Policy Options to Improve Basic Education

1. Periodic Sources

Bulletin of Educational Planning Documentation, International Institute for Educational Planning, Paris

International Yearbook of Education, International Bureau of Education, Geneva

Resources for Education and their Cost-Effective Use, Commonwealth Secretariat, London

Various series of papers published by the World Bank, Washington.

2. Recent Books

Chapman, David W., and Carol A. Carrier (eds.) 1990. *Improving Educational Quality: A Global Perspective*. New York: Greenwood Press.

Hallak, Jacques 1990. *Investing in the Future: Setting Educational Priorities for the Developing World*. Paris: UNESCO, International Institute for Educational Planning.

Hopkins, David (ed.) 1989. *Improving the Quality of Schooling: Lessons from the OECD International School Improvement Project*. London: The Falmer Press.

Lockheed, Marlaine E., and Adriaan M. Verspoor 1991. *Improving Primary Education in Developing Countries: A Review of Policy Options*. New York: Oxford University Press.

United States Agency for International Development 1990. *Lessons Learned in Basic Education in the Developing World*. Washington, D.C.: Bureau for Science and Technology, Office of Education.

3. Professional Journals

Comparative Education Review, US
Comparative Education, UK
Compare, UK
Educación, Organization of American States
Education Comparée, France
Educational Studies, UK
International Journal of Education Research,
International Review of Education, UNESCO
Prospects, UNESCO
Revista Latinoamericana de Estudios Educativos, Mexico

4. You may also wish to subscribe to FORUM, a quarterly popular digest of policy studies in education, published by the Harvard Institute for International Development, Cambridge, MA 02138, USA, for the USAID-funded ABEL Project.

161

from page 7

Educational Problems of Nomadic Children

Nomads are groups of people who travel and migrate in large or small clans in search of a means of livelihood. They travel within a community or a nation or across international boundaries (Ezeomah, 1990).

Nomads can be classified in three categories: hunters and food gatherers, itinerant workers, and pastoralists.

Traditionally, children of nomads are taught by their parents, older relations, and peer groups. Their teaching emphasizes survival and earning a living. Nomadic children typically assume adult responsibilities at an early age. As a consequence they may have more awareness of cultural values and their environment than do non-nomadic children. On the other hand, they may fail to gain the skills of literacy and numeracy that are more easily learned in schools.

Several countries have moved to insure the educational rights of nomads. In 1978 the Government of Kenya developed a policy favoring Arid Zone Boarding Primary Schools, for the Masai, Turkana, and Somalian nomads. In 1981 Nigeria issued a statement promising educational opportunities for all citizens, both inside and outside the formal system.

An Example of Education for Nomads

Following the Sahelian drought of 1968–1974, the American Friends Service Committee and the Government of Mali cooperated in a rehabilitation project for nomadic families in the village of Tin Aicha. A school was created in 1975, with one grade and 73 students. In 1980 permanent buildings were completed.

Most nomadic families resist formal education for their children. Typically education is provided in boarding schools, distant from the family, and often staffed with teachers not familiar with the customs of the nomads. The parents of Tin Aicha, however, were enthusiastic about their school. This enthusiasm is attributed to the location of the school in the village, and to the staffing of the school with teachers from the village.

Teachers adapted the national curriculum to the requirements of the village. They placed greater emphasis on health and on the history of the nomadic people. Students were involved in agriculture and animal husbandry.

This school is one of the few in Mali in which the majority of the students are from nomadic families. Participation rates are high, and absenteeism is low.

See Ezeomah (1990).

from page 7

Educational Problems of Refugee Children

A great deal has been said and written about the need to provide educational services to refugee children. But **there have been few studies of the educational problems of refugee children, or studies of how best to resolve these problems.** Most studies have focused on problems of adult refugees and the best methods of repatriation or resettlement.

The education solutions offered for children are generally in the form of short term emergency relief, rather than long term education. What research has been done focuses on the psychological consequences of refugee status, rather than on specific educational requirements. "Educational problems" are generally defined in terms of the actions of the organizations or countries that provide the educational services. The education of refugees in poor countries is given a lower priority than the provision of shelter and food.

The most frequently cited problems that providers of services face are the following:

1. lack of space in the school system;

2. insufficient teachers to handle the additional burden on the system;

3. inadequate supply of textbooks; and

4. inadequate supply of other instructional materials and supplies.

These may also be problems that affect children who are citizens of the country providing the education.

Problems more specific to refugee children are as follows:

5. Textbook and curriculum content are inappropriate for refugee children who come from different cultural, economic, political, or geographical contexts.

6. Language of instruction — should refugee children be taught in their mother tongue, the language of the host country, or the language of their country of destination (if that is known)? Sudan, for example, in the 1980s received a great many refugees from neighboring countries who did not speak Arabic, the language of instruction in Sudanese schools. If the decision is to offer instruction in the language of the refugee children, problem 2 looms large. A country may decide to hire as temporary teachers adult refugees with teaching experience.

7. Some refugee (parents and leaders) resist education in another language and with another curriculum, fearing that their children will lose their cultural identity.

The solutions to these problems will vary according to how long the refugees will remain in the host country.

a. If they will be permanently resettled in the host country then it may be important to begin assimilation immediately. See page **114** for a discussion of alternative approaches to language of instruction. See page **198** for a description of the factors that condition which language of instruction to choose.

b. If they will be repatriated to their country of origin in a few years, it may be acceptable to provide minimal education using instructors taken from the adult refugee problem.

c. If they will be repatriated to another country, decisions about curriculum content and language of instruction should take into account characteristics of the receiving country.

163

A Program to Train Teachers for Refugees

Refugees began arriving in Somalia from Ethiopia in 1977. By 1981 there were estimated to be 700,000 refugees in Somalia. Many of these were children of school age. Somalia, meanwhile, was having a hard time providing schooling to its own children. About one-third of the age group was enrolled in primary schools. There were not enough trained teachers.

To respond to the refugee crisis, the Somali Government, together with the UNHCR, established an Institute of In-Service Teacher Training (IITT). The Institute was modelled on the UNRWA/UNESCO Institute of Education in the Middle East, established for Palestinian refugees. Teenage or older refugees who have completed primary schooling are recruited. They are given a crash course in teaching, and placed in classrooms. Weekly seminars held locally are used to upgrade their teaching abilities. Correspondence courses are used to increase knowledge of subject matter.

Within its first year, the IITT was able to establish schools in nearly all the camps. By 1988 the IITT was providing schooling to about 40,000 students per year. More than 1,000 teachers were trained. Since that time an administrative structure has been built which is continuing and expanding the operation.

See Dodds (1986).

For more information see *Journal of Refugee Studies*.

Reducing the Cost of Schooling

The enrollment of children of poor families in schools can be increased by:

1. reducing the direct costs of schooling controlled by the education system;

2. reducing the indirect costs to the family that result from sending a child to school.

1. *Direct Costs.* This includes family expenditures on uniforms, admission fees, activity fees, examination fees, "voluntary" contributions, basic supplies such as pencils and notebooks, textbooks, transportation, lunches eaten at school. These costs can amount to as much as 20 percent of family income (Lockheed and Verspoor, 1991).

All of these costs can be met by the education system. In many countries, *none* of the above items is charged directly to families. School finance is provided through other means which place a less heavy burden on families of the poor. Textbooks are provided free in many countries. Supplies are sold at subsidized prices. The school provides a breakfast or lunch. Uniforms are not required, or are subsidized. The community or school provides free transportation. Thailand provides students in isolated rural communities with bicycles. Other countries have constructed boarding schools. Countries that have abolished fees have experienced sharp increases in enrollments, indicating the suppressive effect of fees.

Some countries, e.g., Bangladesh, have increased enrollment and graduation of girls by offering scholarships. These scholarships are awarded at the *end* of the school cycle. Parents keep their girls in school, to be relieved later of some of the costs.

Countries that want to increase access reduce costs to families for sending their children. See page **172** for suggestions of other sources of income than poor families.

2. *Indirect Costs.* These refer to benefits lost by the family as a result of sending a child to school. They include the child's contribution to the internal economy of the home, for example as a child-tender or aid in gardening. They also include the lost income that the child could have generated had she or he worked instead of going to school.

Adjustments in the annual school calendar can help with regard to reducing the conflict between the school and demand for child labor in agriculture. Changing the daily schedule can make it easier for girls, who generally have responsibility for younger siblings, to attend. Schools can also provide day care facilities for infants normally looked after by girls. Pakistan, for example, permits children to bring their younger siblings to school. This has negative effects on the classroom environment. More effective would be the construction of nursery school facilities next to the school building.

The likelihood of working outside the home increases with the child's age. Lowering the entrance age to primary and reducing repetition would raise the number of children who complete the cycle before reaching age of employment.

➜ To read more about access to school, see page **168**.

➜ For more about finance, see page **172**.

from pages 19, 90, 168, 172

Increasing Efficiency Within School Facilities

Some policy makers attribute a lack of educational supply to the low enrollment of students. If this is true, an obvious solution would be to increase the number of school facilities. Three options are most prevalent:

1. Build more schools;

2. Rent buildings constructed for other purposes;

3. Make more efficient use of current structures.

Construction of more schools requires capital outlays, by either the government or the local community or some combination of the two. Renting buildings solves an immediate need, but does not develop the capital stock of the education system. At the end of 20 years the government is still paying rent, with nothing to show for it.

In situations in which government capital funds are limited, where it is difficult to mobilize community resources for school construction, or where rents are seen as a waste of resource, it may be possible to solve space problems by making more intensive use of existing facilities.

Students can learn as much in a double shift school as in a single shift school. The critical factors are the quality of the curriculum (see page **25**) and the quality of teaching (see page **53**). Table 13 reports on six different experiments with double shifts as a way to make fuller use of facilities. The results are varied. In some cases, students in double shift schools actually learned more than students in single shifts.

from pages 166, 180, 213

Table 13
Options for Increasing the Use of Existing Facilities

Choice #1: Multiple-Shift Schooling:

One means of containing costs while raising enrollment rates is to introduce multiple-shift schools, where one school caters to two or more entirely different bodies.

Multiple shift schooling is an especially helpful option for governments with increased populations and restrained budgets.

Country:	Results:
1. Singapore (1986):	a. Difficult to arrange remedial/enrichment classes due to lack of available space. b. Double sessions effectively operated as separate institutions making it difficult to plan and run both schools efficiently. c. Lowered sense of student "belonging" to school; greater difficulty building relationship between students and teachers.
2. Malaysia (1972):	Schools used for double sessions were designed for single shifts. As a result, facilities offered students more space and could be used at other times of day.
3. Chile (1974) and Venezuela:	No noted distinction between achievement level and the number of shifts offered by schools.
4. Nigeria:	Double-shift schools found to have lower passage rate than in single-shift schools. Reason cited: lower socio-economic status of double-shift students.
5. Guyana:	Achievement within double-shift schools not adversely affected.
6. Senegal (1972):	Found double-shift school students scored higher than single-shift. Reason cited: lower student /teacher ratio increased quality of education.

Based on Bray (1987).

➜ The issue of school size is discussed on page **212**.

➜ On page **213** we make several suggestions of how to reduce demands on school building.

➜ Finally, the cost of construction can be reduced by better maintenance. See page **230**.

Choice #2: Increase Small Schools in Rural Areas:

As most governments want to get the best education for the least expense, another possible solution could be to build small schools in low population areas.

Although it may not appear cost-effective initially, in some areas it may actually decrease governmental expenditures.

Observed Results:

1. In some areas it may be cheaper to run several small schools than one large school. Establishing large schools in rural areas increases the cost of transportation.
2. Large schools become too impersonal and inefficient thereby decreasing quality and increasing administrative costs.
3. The children's fatigue from traveling long distances to large schools decreases the effectiveness of education.
4. If schools become too large, they may have to employ specialists thereby increasing costs.
5. Large schools can typically operate at a lower unit cost per pupil.
6. If large schools have poor access may need to board students thereby increasing recurrent and capital costs.

Based on Bray (1987).

➜ For additional ideas, see pages **30, 212, 213** and **230**.

from pages 23, 135, 165, 173, 215

Table 14

Policy Options to Improve Access to Primary School

BARRIERS	POLICY OPTIONS	EXAMPLES
1. **Space**	Provide more space	Build schools; some for certain groups
	Use existing space more efficiently or equitably	Double shifts; some for certain groups
	Use alternative buildings as schools	Community buildings, mosques
	Provide education at home	Distance education
2. **Distance**	Reduce distance to school	More schools; better use of space; education at home; boarding schools
	Provide safety on route to school	Transportation; chaperones; community protection
3. **Cost to household**	Financial or in-kind aid	Free schooling; free textbooks, uniforms; scholarships; incentives to keep child in school
	Reduce opportunity costs	Change schedule to permit work; provide substitute for child's labor while in school
	Increase expected returns	Increase access to higher levels; improve outcomes to training
4. **Insufficient and overworked teachers**	Recruit and put into place more teachers	Lower certification requirements; improved incentives; provide local training; place teachers near home
	Increase workload of current teachers	Double shifts with same teachers
	Enable current teachers to hand more students	Use of programmed, self-instructional materials; peer teaching; distance education
5. **Education not relevant to some groups**	Adapt education to community expectations	Reform or complement curriculum; change materials; recruit or re-train teachers
	Change community attitudes toward schooling	Fines for non-attendance; mobilize community support
	Motivate teachers to recruit students from groups not currently enrolled	Incentives for teachers with non-traditional students

→ See also page 166, 175, 215.

168

What Can Test Results Tell Us About School Quality?

In 1991, a national magazine in Mexico published a lead story with the following headline, "**Mexico: A Country of Failures.**" The article described the application of a national achievement test to primary and secondary school students. The author concluded:

> "The results of these exams are very worrisome. The great majority—83.7 percent of the primary students and 96.2 percent of the secondary students—of those examined obtained marks lower than 6 points in a scale of 10." (Guevara, 1991, p. 33).

As a result, he concluded that there is a serious decline in the quality of Mexican education.

> "The anxiety that initiated this evaluation has been converted into real alarm, taking into consideration the urgencies that the country faces with its integration into the external market and technological and scientific competition between nations." (p. 33).

Was Guevara right? Has Mexican education failed? At the same time he was publishing his critique, another study showed that productivity of Mexican automobile workers was higher than that of automobile workers in the U.S. (who have higher levels of schooling). Do the tests applied show that schools have failed to educate?

There is no doubt that students got low scores on the tests. The question is the meaning to be given to those scores. These are the critical issues:

1. Do the test items measure what children should know?

2. How much should children know about what the test items cover?

3. Do schools teach what these test items measure?

Issue 1. This is a question of *validity*, a technical term that asks whether the item measures what we want it to. The best way to estimate the validity of tests is to compare their results with those of another measure about which we are sure. A second way is to examine the items to see if they look and read like what we are attempting to measure.

The Mexican tests had the standard components, 20 multiple choice questions about mathematics, 15 about Spanish (national language), 17 about natural sciences, and 12 about social sciences. The mathematics test included questions about the basic operations (addition, etc.), use of fractions, positive and negative values, decimals, and word problems. The social sciences test included items on Mexican history, the Constitution, geography and government.

All this sounds reasonable, and is consistent with the general objectives for primary education of the official curriculum. But is that all that primary education is about? Were these the most important topics to be covered? Each country that wants to use a standardized national examination to evaluate its school system has to make sure the test covers important elements in the curriculum.

A second aspect of validity asks whether the tests measure the kind of adult behaviors we hope schools will produce. Does knowledge of high school mathematics predict the productivity of a worker? In fact, there is little research that relates test scores used to evaluate schools with adult performance.

The second part of the first issue deals with technical questions of *reliability*. Do the students answering the questions read them the same way the test makers do? Would the same test applied again produce essentially the same results? These are important questions to be asked of every test.

169

Issue 2. *Do low scores on the test reflect how much students know?* For example, on the Mexican social sciences examination there were 12 items. Only 37 percent of the students could identify the article of the Constitution (Number 123) that refers to the national education system. Is 37 percent a high or low number? Guevara assumed that students should get at least 60 percent of the items correct. The 60 percent level was arbitrarily chosen.

It is easy to change the difficulty level of multiple choice tests. One can make all the wrong alternatives obviously wrong, and scores will increase. Similarly, one can make the test harder, by making the "wrong" alternatives sound very much like the right alternative. We can only know how difficult a test is by taking it ourselves.

Issue 3. Does the test measure what the school is trying to teach? *Is the test a measure of the quality of the school?* We can be sure that a school that tries to teach its students something but fails is of low quality. If a school does not teach what the test measures, however, that school may still be of high quality.

Research shows that *opportunity to learn* is a major factor predicting to test scores. Teach-ers are asked, for each item of the test, whether the material has been covered during the school year. Students score low on items that the teachers say they have not taught. This is consistent with research on time on task (see page **92**); the more time students spend trying to learn, the more they learn.

The disastrous results reported by Guevara could be interpreted to mean not that schools are of low quality, but that they are not teaching what the test makers thought was important. Our response to a discrepancy between the *actual curriculum* and the *official curriculum* should be much different than to a demonstration that even when they try, schools do not teach enough.

What test results can tell us, therefore, is that there is a difference between what some-one expected, and what actually takes place. Test results are, therefore, *symptoms* of prob-lems, but not in themselves diagnoses. They do not by themselves tell us what we should do.

→ For a severe critique of the use of standardized achievement tests, see page **228**.

→ For a discussion of the concept of quality, see page **241**.

from page 29

School Construction: Is Revenue the Problem?

The problem in funding of school construction is principally the total cost of new buildings, rather than the expenditure per year on buildings. In most countries the annual cost of buildings is less than ten percent of the total annual expenditure on education. This proportion is low because school buildings generally last 25 or more years.

In many countries school construction is financed from currently available funds, rather than by long-term debt instruments, such as bonds. The Ministry of Education, or the school construction agency, must therefore have on hand a large amount of capital. Many countries rely on foreign sources of capital for school construction, either through loans from banks or international assistance agencies, or donations (sometimes called "soft" loans because pay back terms are very lenient).

Some governments are now resistant to increasing foreign indebtedness. The burden of "servicing" the debt by paying interest on loans often taken out by previous governments is seen as excessive. Some countries are unable to find loans at reasonable rates of interest.

There are several approaches that national governments have used to increase funding for education from national sources. First, some governments have reduced expenditures in other sectors and have transferred those funds to education. This policy requires a strong government able to withstand attacks from those benefitted by government spending in other sectors.

A second policy option is to increase government revenue for education. This can be done by increased central government direct or indirect taxes—this too poses a political problem for the central government. With the urging of international assistance agencies some central governments are looking at ways to shift some of the cost burden of education to local governments, or to private citizens.

Nigeria, for example, shifted the cost of basic education to state governments by a presidential decree. Colombia permits state governments to use taxes on some consumption goods and revenue from lotteries to finance basic education. Kenya has offered to provide salaries of teachers where local communities construct the school building at their expense. Korea relies on "voluntary funds" from parents to finance purchase of materials.

→ See pages 172 and 175 for a variety of sources of funding.

171

from pages 29, 33, 77, 85, 109, 148, 149, 151, 165, 171, 176

Financing Education in Developing Countries: Sources of Funding

There is a common belief that education is underfinanced and that government financing is limited. One limitation is due to the government's lack of will to increase educational spending out of skepticism for economic benefits and concern about unemployment for the educated (Psacharopoulos, 1986). As a result, more energy is being put in researching alternative methods for educational finance. Below are some suggested alternatives. The following page describes the positive and negative outcomes which have resulted from program implementation in specific countries.

Options for Financing Education: (According to principal sources of financing)

Government:

1. Increase general taxes (federal, state, local): Colombia, Brazil.

2. Increase school fees: Malawi, Mauritius, Peru, Brazil.

3. Increase distribution of student loans (secondary and higher ed.): Kenya, Nigeria, India.

4. Increase efficacy of current school buildings to reduce capital expenses: Colombia, El Salvador, Indonesia, United Arab Republic.

5. Reduce repetition rate at primary level: Brazil.

6. Decentralize educational financing: Arab countries, Nepal, China.

7. Relax governmental control; give part of the responsibility to the local people: Nigeria.

8. Have a national lottery, earmarking the earnings for education: Brazil.

Community:

1. Provide direct labor to build schools, cutting capital expenses: Nepal, Kenya, Tanzania, E. Nigeria.

2. Raise supplemental contribution through profits from fairs, donations, craft sales, local lotteries: Guyana.

3. Provide financial contribution through local PTA donations: Burma, E. Nigeria.

4. Create a local Board of Governors who contributes financially to the teachers' accommodations; government hires and trains the teachers: Botswana.

5. Finance all capital expenses at the local level; local contributions include building materials, labor and land: Zambia, E. Nigeria.

6. Create "community" schools, developed and financed at the local level: Kenya.

Private:

1. Accept donations or endowments from local citizens or businesses: Latin America.

2. Sponsor employer financed education (for vocational and technical education and training); businesses provide in-service training and pre-service training institutes: Arab nations, Brazil, Colombia, Peru.

3. Rent building space from private individuals or companies for educational facilities.

4. Impose levels on alumni association members: E. Nigeria.

International:

Accept outside, international aid for government capital expenses: many countries.

What has Worked, What hasn't Worked, and Why?

Increase general taxes: Increasing taxes theoretically redistributes income from rich to poor. The Colombian government taxes top income earners to help finance public secondary and higher education; the hope was that lower income groups would benefit as for they receive more benefits than they pay. But higher income groups are more likely to complete primary, and secondary school, and therefore to enroll in subsidized public universities. Conclusion: tax systems alone are not sufficient to insure equality of educational opportunity (Psacharopoulos, 1986).

Increase school fees: The more income families have, the more willing they are to pay for education of their children. On this basis it was argued that by levying school fees on upper income groups it would be possible to generate enough income to provide subsidies to the poorest children. The problem is estimating how much disposable income in fact families have to spend on education. When the government of Malawi levied fees on secondary school children, enrollments declined. When fees for primary school were removed, attendance nearly doubled.

Increase distribution of student loans: Increasing student loans can increase the demand for education by increasing access to the poor. It has worked effectively at the higher education level in Latin America, Africa and Asian countries (Kenya, Nigeria, India). However, it has been difficult to implement in some countries (Sierra Leone, Cameroon) where under-utilization of the available space resulted.

Increase efficiency of school buildings: Establishing double-shift schools for single buildings has been tried in Colombia, El Salvador and Indonesia. However, it has been difficult to implement in some countries (Sierra Leone, Cameroon) where underutilization of the available space resulted. See comments on pages **166**, **168**, and **175**.

Reduce repetition rate: In Brazil approximately 20 percent of each class in primary public schools repeat. Policy options include:

i. Automatic promotion reduces repetition rate to zero and reduces cost by 20.6 percent (Coombs and Hallak, 1987). For a criticism of this option see page **132**.

ii. Improve the quality of instruction and hence increase learning and decrease repetition; improve the quality through improved teacher in-service training. See page **52**.

Decentralize educational financing: Centralized governments spend more money and take more time allocating funds due to the bureaucratic system, leaving less money for education. Arab countries are trying to decentralize resource allocation and improve efficiency (Ghannam, 1970). Also, with empowered local governments, regional taxes can be levied as needed (earmarked specifically for education). See page **148**.

Relax governmental control: Relaxing of governmental control over finances can encourage local participation and responsibility. In Nigeria, the schools are entirely responsible for financing school facilities. The government hires and trains teachers. (Bray and Lillis, 1988).

National lottery: Between 1970-74 Brazil raised additional funds for education from a national lottery. The lottery financed 17 million people on MOBRAL (mass literary program).

Community direct labor and donation of materials: Voluntary contributions of community labor to build schools, donate materials and design structures have worked in Nepal, Kenya and E. Nigeria. These countries have strong support for education. In Eastern Nigeria respect is received through one's ability to finance projects. It may not work in every country. It is more difficult in countries such as Tanzania where equality is emphasized (Bray and Lillis, 1988).

Raise contributions through fairs: Voluntary community donations are encouraged by the Guyana government. Local communities have raised supplemental financing through activities such as fairs and craft sales. The funds are limited (Bray and Lillis, 1988).

Financial contribution through PTAs: In Burma and E. Nigeria local PTAs are expected to contribute to educational financing. In Burma the contributions are high: community construction – 21.2 percent; furniture and equipment – 63.8 percent, repairs – 63.4 percent. In E. Nigeria, the financing is used for buses and repairs. (Bray and Lillis, 1988). See also pages **54** and **74**.

Accept private donations: In Latin American countries, private donations by businesses or individuals constitute approximately 11 percent of educational income (Psacharopoulos, 1986). However, usually the contribution in developing countries is low. Could this be a source of untapped financing?

Employer financed education: Employer-sponsored education ensures education is relevant to the labor market. In Latin American countries, the government takes fees from specific institutions to help finance vocational training (Brazil, Peru, Colombia) (Psacharopoulos, 1986). In many Arab countries, businesses help finance employees' university training as needed; some firms are required by law to allocate a percentage of profits to education (Ghannam, 1970).

Impose levies on alumni association members: In E. Nigeria additional educational financing is levied from a school's alumni (Bray and Lillis, 1988). This is a limited but relatively untapped source of private income.

International aid: This is a good investment for capital expenses but can have adverse effects at the local level. As loans come due, the debt adds burden on local taxpayers. Accepting excessive aid actually postpones and increases rather than reduces educational expenditures (Psacharopoulos, 1986).

These suggested "remedies" are *supplemental*. Used in combination with current government resources, they may alleviate excessive financial burdens and contribute towards improving the overall quality of and access to education in developing countries.

➜ See also page **175.**

from pages 29, 33, 148, 149, 151, 168, 171, 172

Table 15
Suggested Financial Solutions to Educational Problems

Issue:	Action:	Fund Allocation:	Source of Funding:
1. Increase access to education.	a. Build more schools	Build schools close to students; increase the number of small schools in rural areas.	1. Increase student fees. 2. Hold national lottery. 3. Community labor and material donations. 4. Fair contributions. 5. PTA contributions. 6. Private contributions. 7. International organizations. 8. Levy alumni.
	b. Increase loans and scholarships for poor students.	1. Provide low interest loans provided for poor students. 2. Borrow initial capital; invest in secure option; use interest to fund loans and scholarships. 3. Over time, loan repayments will establish revolving fund.	a. International organizations b. Increase school fees (high-income students subsidize low-income). c. Income, property taxes. d. Private donations.
	c. Lower private costs for education at local level.	1. Allocate to children and schools based on financial need. 2. Offer tax rebate on educational expenses for low income families.	a. Replace local funding with national funds: 1) issue national texts and supplies from revenue of high-income tax bracket. 2) abolish need for uniforms. b. Fairs. c. National lottery d. Parent Teachers Association.
	d. Abolish school fees	Abolish according to financial need of students.	1. Increase income taxes. 2. Private donations. 3. Levy alumni.
	e. Introduce double-shift schools.	As needed in overcrowded areas.	1. Initial funding through international organizations. 2. Recurrent expenses funded through increased enrollment and student fees.
	f. Increase purchasing power of low-income students·	1. Parent-supplement vouchers. 2. Tax-expenditure vouchers with no supplemental income.	a. Government pays value of voucher or no strings grant. b. Money for government collected through income and property taxes.

(Table 15 continued on next page)

175

Issue:	Action:	Fund Allocation:	Source of Funding:
2. Improve quality of education	a. Lower class size	Increase number of teachers	1. Increase the number of students (in doing so increase revenue for hiring more teachers). 2. Increase taxes. 3. Increase school fees. 4. Initial increase in teachers funded by international organizations.
	b. Improve quality in teacher training	Increase frequency and quantity of teacher training (both in-service and pre-service).	1. Use international aid to construct higher quality in-service training and teacher colleges. 2. Increase school fees to fund recurrent in-service training. 3. Increase taxes (i.e. export taxes).
	c. Increase efficiency of educational system.	Establishing a more efficient system, fewer funds will be required to meet national goals.	1. Reduce costs of financing educational system by cutting excess inputs. 2. Decentralize system to redistribute spending on bureaucracy in favor of educational programs.
	d. Increase retention level.	More efficient use of system and an increase in the quality of education offered.	1. Award scholarships upon graduation. 2. Automatic promotion. 3. Subsidize based on attendance.

The above are based on Anderson (1988); Schiefelbein (1983).

➜ See also page 172.

from page 17

Educational Problems of Handicapped Children

The principal causes of childhood disability in developing countries are related to malnutrition, poor hygiene, and preventable diseases (Marfo, 1986). The four major categories of disabilities are: visual, auditory, physical impairment, and mental impairment.

Less than two percent of the children requiring special services are enrolled in educational programs in developing countries. Response to handicapped children has taken second place to efforts to provide education to children without disabilities, itself a daunting task. Tanzania, for example, has made great efforts to provide services to children with disabilities. In 1986 Tanzania had five special primary schools for the deaf, three special and 19 regular primary units for the blind, two schools for the physically handicapped, and four schools for the mentally handicapped. Unfortunately, these schools met the needs of only a portion of its handicapped children.

The Zambia National Campaign to Reach Disabled Children

Prior to 1980, special education in Zambia was in the hands of various missionary groups. In 1970 the education of the handicapped became the direct responsibility of the Ministry of Education and Culture. The Second National Development Plan (1972–1976) gave official attention for the first time to the handicapped.

In 1980 the government with assistance from the Government of Sweden launched a national campaign. Extensive use was made of training packages designed by the World Health Organization and field tested in Botswana and other countries. The WHO manual focused on mental handicaps, acceptance by the family, self-help skills for teachers, and the social integration of the handicapped into the community. The instructional packages vary according to type of disability and age group.

Immediate activities of the campaign were:

1. raise the level of public awareness of the special needs of disabled children;

2. establish provincial registers of disabled children;

3. lay the foundation for a nation-wide health and education service for disabled children; and

4. supply technical aids and prosthetic devices to as many disabled children as possible, and train them and their families to use them properly.

A District Ascertainment Team was created in each district. These teams included a primary school teacher, a medical assistant or nurse, and a community development worker.

Training courses for the teams provided:

1. exposure to educated blind, deaf and mentally retarded children, and a demonstration of how they were being educated by well-trained teachers;

2. an introduction to the nature, causes and consequences of auditory, visual, physical, and mental handicaps;

3. demonstrations of and supervised practice with procedures for assessing the various handicaps;

4. familiarization with registration and reporting procedures;

5. an introduction to community-based rehabilitation and to the development of individualized health care plans; and

6. discussion of anticipated problems and possible solutions.

During the first phase of the project 162 children were identified. Home-based interventions were designed for each. These inter-

177

ventions included teaching at home, integration into local schools, construction of low cost aids, referral for examination, treatment, and assignment to special schools. The major difficulty experienced was transportation to outlying areas.

The nation-wide campaign to register disabled children began with 3000 reporting centers in 57 districts. There were 1.7 million children between five and 15 years of age in Zambia at the time of the campaign. Some 18,000 were brought into reporting centers. About one-third of the centers did not receive any children; lack of transportation was considered to be the main reason.

Some 11,000 children were examined, of whom 7,247 were considered severely disabled, 3,209 had auditory deficiencies, 1,549 were visually impaired, 1,390 physically impaired, 626 mentally retarded and 473 multi-handicapped. These figures indicate that about 80 of every 1000 urban children and 31 of every 1000 rural children have handicaps severe enough to merit attention.

In 1987 it was estimated that less than five percent of all severely handicapped were attending school, but that the proportion of handicapped children contacted in the registration campaign was much higher. This may be because those handicapped children who were registered are those who have fewer problems of transportation. The number of handicapped children served in schools, however, was higher than that of children served in the 35 primary institutions for handicapped children.

For more information about Zambia see Csapo (1987).

For more information about education of handicapped see Baine (1988), Marfo et al. (1986), Ross (1988).

from page 105

Distance Education for Children Who Can't Attend School

In many countries there are children who by reason of distance of the nearest school or disability are unable to attend school. *Distance education* is a process in which much of the instruction is given by someone removed in space and time from the learner (Perraton, 1986). Instruction through use of printed materials that go back and forth between teacher and learners—*correspondence schools*—are a traditional form of distance education. This method works best with older students with well-established reading and study skills.

More recently printed materials have been combined with audio devices to permit volunteers or untrained teachers to assist students. The teacher speaks to students through audio cassettes or radio. Students may respond individually or in groups, and fill out worksheets or quizzes. These are returned to the teacher, who can assess whether lessons have been effective, and can provide feedback to students by marking the quizzes and returning them. Sometimes lessons include immediate information about correct answers so that students can assess their own performance. Groups meet in homes, community centers, religious buildings, even schools.

Most of the available evaluations of these programs have been carried out in Latin America. In 1982 there were at least 15 radio education programs for primary school students. Students participating in RADECO in the Dominican Republic scored as high as students in regular schools on achievement tests, with only one hour of daily broadcast and some discussions and exercises. (Hanssen, Kozlow, and Olsen, 1983). The *recurrent* costs of the program, if it were widespread, are estimated to be about 60 percent of regular school (Tilson, in Nielsen, 1991). Not available is information on promotion and drop-out rates. Ministry officials in the Dominican Republic are now considering the replacement of ineffective regular primary schools with the RADECO system.

For details of radio education programs in Mexico see Spain (1977) and Jamison and McAnany (1978). For Malawi see Mkandawire and Jere (1988).

For a general review of distance education see Nielsen (1991).

➔ See also pages **220** and **222**.

from page 45

The Cycle of School Construction in Sindh, Pakistan

The Planning and Monitoring Cell (PMC) of the Secretary of Education of Sindh Province, Pakistan is responsible for the construction and maintenance of all public school buildings. As most of the 20 million inhabitants of Sindh are widely dispersed in small rural villages, there are many schools, and many yet to be built. Each year the PMC manages about 600 construction projects.

The construction cycle begins with a proposal. The first action is a request for a school building from the community or a headmaster (in a rented building). Sometimes politicians make the request. Formal requests are supposed to flow from the petitioner to the subdistrict education officer to the district education officer, to the regional directorate, to the PMC. In fact, many requests are made in person to the PMC Director, who spends a good part of his day receiving delegations.

Although some requests are approved with review, most require a procedure that includes an estimation of the number of children not currently being served. All communities of 500 or more inhabitants with no school within 1.5 km. are supposed to be granted schools. The PMC relies on Settlement Reports produced by the Bureau of Statistics (in the Secretary of Government) to determine where schools are located. Population estimates are based on the last census.

Availability of a site is the next requirement. In most cases the village headmaster provides the school site. The PMC then estimates the cost of construction, including site preparation costs. A formal proposal is prepared (using a standard form, PC-1), and submitted to a working party that reviews all the proposals.

Proposals that are approved are included in an annual development budget submission that goes first to the Education Secretary, then to the Additional Chief-Secretary for Development, and then to the Education Ministry in the Federal Government. Once a budget is approved the PMC sends projects to the Engineering Wing, and monitors completion of the schools. The PMC's responsibility ends when the school is handed over to the community.

→ For alternatives to new school construction, see pages **167** and **213**.

from pages 39, 51, 61, 151

Primary Education Curriculum Development in India

The population of India is perhaps one of the most heterogeneous in the world. A wide variety of economic, cultural, political, and linguistic traditions are represented among its 800 million people.

Early efforts to provide uniform learning materials and common training of teachers in instructional strategies were ill-advised, given the diversity of both students and teachers. But how could the government provide relevant curriculum and appropriate instructional strategies for such a diverse population?

The proposed solution has been the diversification of the production of curriculum, while applying uniform standards for quality. In collaboration with State Institutes of Education and State Councils of Educational Research and Training, the National Council of Educational Research and Training in 1975 launched a program for Primary Education Curriculum Renewal.

The objective of this program was to provide as many students as possible with a curriculum that fits their linguistic and cultural background, and which matches the abilities of teachers. The strategy pursued was to develop the capacity of state-level groups in curriculum preparation and teacher training.

The project began in 13 states, in a set of 30 schools chosen for their wide variation in terms of characteristics of students. A detailed socio-economic and education survey was carried out to identify requirements and abilities of students and teachers. Training was provided to teachers and curriculum developers, in the elaboration of content and appropriate methods. The instructional materials produced included textbooks, teacher guides, and workbooks for students.

The success of the initial pilot program led to a second stage that involved 450 primary schools and 45 elementary teacher training institutes and their staffs. Materials were produced in regional languages and various instructional strategies were tested.

By 1984 the project was operating in all states, with 180 teacher training institutes and 2,469 primary schools actively involved in the design and production of curriculum. The project at that date had trained 11,000 teachers in the new materials and methods.

States with common languages used the same textbooks, accompanied by teacher guides that suggest alternative teaching-learning activities to match local culture and economy. Instructional practices are designed to respond to regional differences.

The various curricula set objectives for minimal learning in computation (mathematics), communication (language), health, environmental studies, artistic expression, and productive work. Emphasis is laid on promotion of desirable values and attitudes. Use of local resources is encouraged; teachers are expected to devise or adapt suitable teaching-learning strategies.

Even in the smallest states of India (e.g., Nagaland and Sikkim) teachers now use materials that are appropriate to their circumstances.

Based on UNESCO (1984).

➜ See page **35** for factors that influence the quality of curriculum.

181

from pages 97, 107

Student Discipline

There is little systematic research on the relative effects of different patterns of student discipline. On the other hand, there is widespread agreement that an orderly atmosphere is necessary in schools for effective teaching and learning to take place (Jones, 1989).

Lack of student discipline has been associated with poor class management by teachers (pages **106, 208**), and with poor school administration (page **72**). A study of student discipline in the Congo cites teacher incompetence and overcrowded classrooms as causes of student misconduct (Bafoua, 1983).

Lack of discipline reduces time on task. Examples are tardiness, temporary absences from class, disruptive behavior in the classroom, vandalism, and drug use. In addition, lack of discipline in school is associated with juvenile delinquency and the development of "bad citizens." (Bafoua, 1983).

Solutions

Discipline problems can be reduced by policies that increase:

1. student involvement in school activities;

2. expectations teachers and parents hold for student performance;

3. avoidance of coercive methods, preference for methods that attract rather than require student participation; and

4. preference for rewards rather than punishments

Table 16 (page **183**) presents examples of successful actions (Lasley and Wayson, 1982).

Table 16
School Level Actions Associated with Good Discipline

Action	Why it Works	Example
Teachers and students involved in designing a solution.	Schoolwide and class problems are responsibility of all who work in and use the school. Teachers, students, and administrators contribute to development of effective rules.	Asking students to paint murals on walls of school led to reduction of graffiti and vandalism.
Create an expectation that all students will experience some kind of success.	High rates of success are important for academic and social growth. When students learn how to do better, they value the school more and are less likely to vandalize it.	One school developed a student leadership conference that taught students how to develop more realistic and how to achieve them. Program was run by students in the following years.
Training in distinction between root causes and indications of problems.	Behavior problems are generally symptoms of other problems (e.g., fighting may be caused by overcrowding).	One school developed separate lists of symptoms, and of causes of problems. Attention was then given to designing solutions.
Train administrators and teachers in use of positive rewards rather than punishments.	Research indicates that "teachers with greater ability to handle difficult students used more total rewards... higher ability teachers used punishment less."	Schools have success with: award or honor days; positive messages home to parents; assemblies to recognize students' accomplishments.
Principal is a strong leader	Strong leadership sets standards for teacher and student.	Principal effective in creating alliances with student leaders. Principal able to delegate responsibility for discipline to others closer to students.

183

from pages 47, 65

Issues in the Selection of Teachers

A policy regarding criteria for selection of the most appropriate persons to teach makes sense when:

1. there is a surplus of candidates to be teachers;

2. the requirements of effective teaching are well-defined; and

3. it is possible to identify persons capable of meeting the requirements.

1. Can we in fact choose?

In many countries, there is a shortage of teachers. Ideal requirements have to be relaxed in order to meet demand for schooling. Selection is often based on no more than whether the candidate has a certificate or diploma. Similarly, some countries employ all graduates of their teacher training institutions. In these cases, selection is in fact determined by the candidate, and not by the government.

In these cases, the indicated policy is one that deals with **recruitment** of teachers (or candidates to teacher training institutions), rather than a policy of selection. Recruitment policies have included subsidized education for teacher trainees, forgiveness of government loans for university study, to graduates who take up teaching as a career, and salary increments.

2. What are the requirements to be an effective teacher?

The definition of "effective" depends on the goals set for the education system. The requirements to be effective depend on the instructional technology used, and the working conditions of the teacher. We have listed on page **36** a limited number of characteristics of effective teachers, but note that these are not consistent.

We can also define some fundamentals for effective teaching (see page **96**), but there is no one style of teaching that is most effective for all conditions, technologies, and goals.

3. Can we identify who will be an effective teacher?

There has been a great deal of research on teaching effectiveness in the United States. Factors used to assess teacher candidates can be grouped into seven categories. They are ordered here from most to least important in terms of relationship to effectiveness.

"1. Work samples

2. The ability to engage students in learning activities

3. The ability to perform the functions required of teachers

4. Skills related to teaching

5. Knowledge related to teaching

6. Experience with children and youth

7. Intelligence and academic ability."

(Schalock, cited in Applegate, 1987, p. 3)

This list indicates that tests, and evidence of previous academic achievement, are the *least* satisfactory predictors of teaching effectiveness. The best way to find out who will be a good teacher is to put the candidate to work and observe learning outcomes in students.

This is done in teacher training institutions which require students to carry out practice teaching under supervision, before graduation. Some countries provide teacher training only *after* the teacher has begun to teach (generally as an assistant with an experienced teacher). Certification is provided through distance education programs (see page **220**).

from page 67

Should Pre-Service Education Be Extended?

How much professional training should teachers receive before they are allowed to teach? As Table 8 on page **58** demonstrates, there is considerable variation from country to country. In wealthier countries, most teachers are educated at the university level. Would poor countries raise the quality of teachers by requiring university level education?

Perhaps, but this may not be the most important question to ask. It might be more important to ask, "In what kind of institution should teachers be educated?"

Most teachers are now educated in special teacher training institutions, at either the secondary or university level. Much of the "training" that is provided is general academic education. This emphasis on general academic education occurs for at least two reasons:

1. Countries that emphasize knowledge acquisition and use a discipline-based curriculum (see page 67), believe that teachers must have extensive knowledge of the subject matter they will teach.

2. In many countries, the persons who select teaching as a career score lowest on tests of academic achievement. It is believed that teachers need remedial education to be able to teach effectively.

The education provided in teacher training institutions is more expensive than that provided in general academic institutions. **Table 17** (on page **186**) presents data from several countries comparing the unit cost of teacher training compared to that for general secondary education. On average, teacher training at the secondary level is more expensive that general secondary education.

There is no evidence, however, that teacher training institutions are more effective than general secondary institutions. On the contrary, research (Fuller, 1987) suggests that graduates of teacher training institutions often do no better than secondary school graduates, in terms of student achievement.

Teacher training institutions may be less effective than general secondary education in imparting general knowledge. The professors in teacher training institutions often are less well qualified than professors in regular academic institutions. The high cost of teacher training comes not from high quality professors, but from subsidies to students in teacher training.

For a comparison of various methods for training teachers, see page **82**.

Table 17

Unit Cost of Teacher Training as Compared to General Secondary Education

Country	Unit Cost Compared to General Secondary
Bangladesh	1.64
Cape Verde	9.07
China	8.51
Dominican Republic	8.68
Gambia	2.96
Guatemala	1.36
Guinea-Bissau	6.31
Indonesia	1.10
Liberia	10.12
Madagascar	12.82
Malawi	4.61
Nepal	2.65
Swaziland	4.28
Zambia	3.25

Source: Lockheed and Verspoor (1991) p. 97.

Policy Alternative. Train teachers in relatively short programs that focus on pedagogical methods, and knowledge specific to the curriculum to be implemented. Provide this training to persons who have completed a general education program. See page **220**.

See Lockheed and Verspoor (1991), Chapter IV.

from pages 66, 67, 82, 89, 126

Examples of In-Service Training Programs

Bangladesh. Two months of intensive training covering general topics was provided to both teachers and assistant teachers. After the training, trainees received three days of training each month on common teaching problems.

The program focused on

a. methods of teaching the major subjects,

b. how to adapt curriculum to local environment,

c. classroom management in multigrade classrooms, and

d. community relations.

In addition, the program increased the number of supervisors, and introduced "surprise" visits to classrooms to reduce absenteeism.

Results. Enrollments increased more rapidly. Repetition and dropouts were reduced. See Verspoor and Leno (1986).

Nepal. The Ministry of Education and Culture used a programmed instructional method delivered by radio called *Interactive Radio Instruction* (see page **199** for a description) to train and upgrade unqualified primary teachers.

The ten-month course was directed at 5,592 teachers in 72 of 75 districts. The program emphasized teaching techniques; candidates received a training allowance in addition to regular salaries.

Results. More than half (2,944) of the teachers passed the final examination and were certified. A second course is now aimed at improving content knowledge. See Sedlak (1988).

Nigeria. This program was initiated following the introduction of compulsory science in the primary school curriculum. Teachers in the program met for four to six weeks during the long school vacation. They reviewed existing science programs and adapted them to the needs of their students. After applying the new programs, teachers met again during holidays to discuss difficulties and learn new materials.

Results. Students of teachers who participated in the program were more likely to gain admission into secondary schools. See Alabi (1978).

Swaziland. "Sub-qualified" teachers (1,200) participated in this program. Training included three residential courses of six weeks duration; eight correspondence assignments in five subjects; tutorial supervision in their schools; and a program of radio broadcasts.

Results. Almost all trainees completed the program. Many continued their training through correspondence courses. See Nsibande and Green (1978).

187

from page 103

Examples of Attempts to Improve Supervision

Bangladesh. The major education problems included unequal access to primary education, especially for girls and rural children; a high dropout rate; teacher absenteeism, low quality of instruction and low achievement.

Training of women as teachers was combined with production of materials, construction of classrooms, and increased community participation.

Additional supervisors were hired and trained to help teachers apply new instructional materials. Regular supervision and "surprise" visits contributed to a reduction in teacher absenteeism. Training was provided to 4000 headteachers in school supervision, administration and community relations.

Results. Enrollment increased at a rate higher than the national average, especially for girls. Attendance increased, and repetition and dropouts decreased.

Paraguay. Teacher training was coordinated with training in supervision for directors (headmasters and headmistresses). Schools were grouped into clusters of ten to 15. They shared a common "learning center" stocked with materials for teachers. The director of each cluster was provided a motorbike to permit visits to each of the schools in the cluster.

Results. School directors were not freed from teaching responsibilities and could not adequately supervise other teachers. Funds were inadequate to maintain the motorbikes of cluster directors. They made infrequent visits to schools.

Haiti. Training of teachers in pedagogy was combined with training for supervisors, who were provided transportation to visit schools.

Results. Trained teachers did poorly in a test of linguistic ability. The conclusion is that training should have included attention to subject knowledge as well as to pedagogy. Visit by supervisors did have positive results. Teachers who were visited by supervisors had higher test scores.

For more information see Verspoor and Leno (1986) and page **192**.

188

Table 18

Approaches to Pre/In-service Teacher Training

Country	Type of Training	Benefits	Programmatic Description	Works Best When:	Duration/Location	Costs
Bangladesh	Recurrent School Based **In-service** Training.	• Support reform to strengthen primary/education. • Based on needs of teachers/schools	• Each teacher and assistant teacher receives two months intensive training on general topics. • Bi-monthly, teachers receive three days of training on common teaching problems. • Content concentration on subjects important to increased student achievement.	• Nation-wide commitment to strengthening primary education. • Teachers unskilled/unaware of effective instructional strategies.	• Permanent and continuous feature at school sites.	
Brazil	"Logo II" Distance **In-service.** Tutorial activities in learning centers	• Responds to need for qualified teachers in remote/isolated areas. • Students do not need to leave posts as teachers. • Teachers do not forego salaries. • No need to recruit substitutes. • Can immediately apply what is learned.	• Curriculum consists of a number of modules on specific topics presented in different pamphlets. • Students study pamphlets at home. • Students return to learning center for testing, socializing, study groups and tutoring.	• Shortage of teachers. • All participants are currently employed, unqualified, primary school teachers. • Need to increase primary education opportunities in remote and isolated regions and to staff these schools with qualified teachers.	• Self Paced. • Usually takes 30–50 weeks. • At home and at learning centers.	• Low opportunity cost. • Generally less expensive than traditional forms of training, especially when economies of scale are reached through large enrollments.
Zimbabwe	ZINTEC Zimbabwe Integrated Teacher Education Course. **Pre/In-service**	• Professionally equivalent to conventional training course. • Efficient in use of scare education personnel. • Attracts and retains teachers.	• 16-week residential course. • 10 terms of teaching (continue studies through correspondence assessed in class by visiting mentors).	• Shortage of qualified teachers (15,000 new, untrained teachers in Zimbabwe). • Need to increase the number of trained teachers to meet the needs of school expansion.	• Four-year course.	

Table 18 (continued)
Approaches to Pre/In-service Teacher Training

Country	Type of Training	Benefits	Programmatic Description	Works Best When:	Duration/Location	Costs
Lesotho (1976–1983)	LIET Lesotho **In-service** Education for Teachers (mobile teacher training).	• Potential to engage teachers in tailoring training to their own contexts.	• Correspondence study, tutorial visits and short residential courses.	• Large numbers of unqualified teachers. • Operates in tandem with pre-service training	• Estimated five years of part time study.	• Relatively low. Few trainers move from place to place rather than moving large numbers of teachers. • Roughly similar to three year campus-based pre-service course.
Lesotho (1988-	DRT (District Resource Teacher) Program Primary **In-service** Education Program.	• Major responsibility in the hands of Lesotho trainers and teachers. • Functions within existing educational system. • DRT's offer systematic follow-up of classroom teachers. • Teachers are offered a new career path. • Community involvement is encouraged.	• School-based teacher support model based on the master teacher concept. • DRT's (experienced and qualified primary school teachers) trained to visit, advise and consult with other primary teachers. • SRT's (senior resource teachers) visit and support the DRT's in the field. • DRT's help rural teachers create instructional materials from the environment	• Remote and inaccessible areas are targeted. • Large numbers of unqualified teachers. • Multi-grade class-rooms. • Support at every educational level: national, district, classroom and community.	• DRT's (master teachers) visit about ten schools each, usually four times a year and remain there for several days.	• Approximately $20 per pupil per year (1988). • Start-up costs can now be eliminated. • Training materials will only need to be reproduced.
Malaysia	'Cascade' **In-service** Training.	• Reaches large numbers of teachers quickly. • Provision for follow-up training at school level (lends teachers support in solving implementa-tion problems).	• Top personnel (inspectors, teacher trainers, senior teachers) are brought together and trained, in cooperation with the Curriculum Development Center, to train large numbers of middle-level personnel, who in turn train teachers at state and district levels.	• Necessary to improve teaching methods and curriculum implemen-tation. • There is time to prepare and test material and training is not rushed. • Training message is simple informational and a formal, didactic style is appropriate.	• School sites. • Amount of time varies depending on content and goals. • Follow up is ongoing.	• No costs associated with traditional methods of bringing teachers to training centers.

Table 18 (continued)
Approaches to Pre/In-service Teacher Training

Country	Type of Training	Benefits	Programmatic Description	Works Best When:	Duration/Location	Costs
Nepal	Radio Education Teacher Training Project (RETT) II / Interactive Radio Instruction (IRI). **In-service.**	•Quick, economic and effective. •Apply learning immediately and contextually. •Can train large numbers quickly and inexpensively. •Teachers don't need to leave classrooms to participate.	•Printed materials complemented by radio. •Instead of oral responses, the "radio teacher" asks the listeners to read appropriate passages from accompanying materials, or to fill in sections of a workbook. •Substitutes for traditional course with the same time requirements.	•Shortage of teachers. •Teachers lack specific subject matter knowledge. •Teachers have passed school leaving exam, but have not participated in any kind of training.	•Self paced. •Broadcast daily. •Totals 150 hrs. •Listen individually in homes in evenings.	•Low opportunity cost. •Room, board, transportation, facilities costs reduced. •Fewer persons required for training.
Sri Lanka	•Teachers Colleges. **In-service.**	•Updates teachers' knowledge and skills. •Motivates teachers for long years of service.	•Traditional curriculum focused on pedagogy and includes supervised teaching and follow-up. •Lectures and teacher-centered instruction.	•Training large numbers of teachers is not urgent. •Teachers need to develop pedagogical knowledge and skills. •Resources available for selected groups of teachers.	•Full time. •Two years of course work. •Optional residency •Campus based.	•Relatively high. •Teachers receive leave pay while studying.

Based on: Dove (1986); Greenland (1983); Lockheed and Verspoor (1991); Tatto, Nielsen, and Cummings (1992).

See also page **220.**

from pages 67, 103, 188

Two Systems of Supervision

Supervision, understood as provision of guidance as training (see page **102**), is critical to the success of efforts to improve schooling. In some countries, supervision from the district level has been important (Verspoor, 1989). In other cases, countries have done well by first developing local administrative and supervisory capacity.

The school cluster system (see page **223**) has been used in a number of countries, including Sri Lanka and Papua New Guinea. Clusters help make more efficient use of both physical and human resources. When properly implemented, they permit schools to share equipment, but also talented teachers and effective principals. The cluster system moves authority closer to the scene of the action, increases teacher participation in decision making, which improves morale and leads to greater effort.

In Sri Lanka each cluster is organized as a partial federation or an amalgamation of neighboring schools. The cluster head can move staff and resources. In this system each school loses some autonomy in exchange for access to resources in other schools. In Papua New Guinea, the cluster system was used to group schools for in-service training, and for common use of Education Resource Centers.

Schools kept their authority, and the team leader has little control over their actions (Bray, 1987).

In Pakistan supervision was improved by inserting a layer of supervisory staff. The Learning Coordinator was defined as a person whose sole responsibility was to help teachers to improve instruction. Coordinators were responsible for ten to 20 schools (most with one or two teachers), which they visited at least once a month. Initially the Coordinators got around on motorbikes but these broke down and funds had not been allotted for maintenance. The Coordinators reviewed lesson plans, observed classes, did some demonstration teaching, and provided samples of instructional materials that teachers could make.

This program was highly successful in one region of Pakistan. Enrollment, attendance, and achievement scores improved. Communication from schools to district management was noticeably better. In another region, however, the District Education Officers resented the Coordinators. They were seen as receiving preferential treatment and not responding to authority (Warwick, Reimers, and McGinn, 1990).

→ See page **193** for alternatives to supervisors.

Alternatives to Supervisors

Page **102** lists three functions for supervisors:

1. to ensure compliance to ministry regulations;

2. to serve as an information link between schools and the ministry; and

3. to provide teachers with feedback about their teaching and help with improvement.

1. The first function for supervisors can be made unnecessary by the introduction of a system of performance-based management. In this system, the central ministry monitors the performance of teachers by use of standardized tests of achievement. Attention is paid to schools, directors, and teachers whose students perform at a level below that expected. See pages **225** and **227** for examples. In one sense, the ministry no longer cares whether its regulations are followed. What is important is that its goals are achieved.

2. The second function for supervisors can be supplanted by the improvement of current systems for collection, analysis, and utilization of information. Information becomes the responsibility and concern of all participants in system. In some cases there is a special officer who is responsible for making the system work, but she or he has no supervisory functions.

3. The most important function of supervisors is the third — reinforcement of the work of teachers. In effect, this function makes the supervisor part of the in-service training program. If the program provides other ways for teachers to get information about their performance, and to learn about, and learn new methods of teaching, then supervisors are not necessary.

This replacement of the supervisor can be done in at least two ways.

1. Training of the school director to be an instructional leader, and trainer for teachers. Examples of this approach are seen in pages **223** and **226**. The school director becomes a *master* teacher, who provides models of good teaching for the teachers in the school. The director is trained in methods of observation of teacher performance in the classroom, and in techniques of instruction that motivate teachers to welcome suggestions for change. This policy is most feasible in large schools in which directors have few or no instructional duties, and a staff that can handle routine administrative matters.

In principle, directors are preferable to visiting supervisors. Because they are always present, they can observe teachers under a wide range of conditions. They are more likely to establish a relationship with teachers that permits them to suggest changes. They are more knowledgeable of the conditions in which teachers work. Costs of transportation are eliminated.

2. Development of peer coaching relationships among teachers. A common observation is that teachers have only limited repertories of teaching techniques. Exposure to other models and methods of teaching allows teachers to expand the range of activities they can carry out with their children. Research has shown that range of activities is directly linked to levels of learning (see page **96**). *Peer coaching* refers to teachers learning from each other.

This can be accomplished in teacher meetings that focus on issues of pedagogy and curriculum.

These meetings may not be formal. Pakistan introduced a program to convert all one-teacher schools to two-teacher schools when research showed reduced teacher absence and greater variety of teaching methods in schools with more than one teacher.

from pages 44, 50, 218

Sustainability, or What Happens After the Funder Leaves?

Many countries now depend on loans or grants from international assistance agencies to fund new programs in education. But experience shows that many externally-funded projects fail to reach their objectives. Many projects that are actually implemented fail when external funding ends. There are several reasons why this happens.

1. Most projects are not designed with sustainability in mind. Both funders and borrowing countries devote their efforts to planning the installation of the project. Cost and personnel requirements of keeping the project going into the future are generally overlooked.

2. In their concern for installation, lending agencies insist on the establishment of special units to oversee implementation. These implementation units often are given special authority and resources. When the project funding ends, the unit can not be integrated into the regular structure of the ministry and the project dies.

3. Few ministries carry out the kind of monitoring and evaluation that is necessary for long-term project development. Most statistics are collected to permit observation of the annual cycle of the ministry. It may take five or more years for a new project to begin producing results.

4. As a consequence, new projects often are not designed to support earlier projects. There is too little "follow-up" activity.

The projects most likely to continue and prosper after the funder leaves are those:

a. designed to continue without external support,

b. integrated into the structure of the ministry, and,

c. that enhance the capacity of the ministry and the government to solve their own problems.

Based on World Bank (1990).

Keeping Failing Students in School

Children who fail are more likely to be absent during the school year. The relation of cause and effect works both ways: absences lead to failure; failure lowers motivation to keep attending. A common pattern for weak students is to attend faithfully until they have their first failure. This might come on a quiz in the middle of the semester. Then their attendance becomes spotty. There are more failed quizzes. Eventually the child stops coming altogether, but enrolls again the next year, as a repeater.

Success, or the avoidance of failure, is the means to break this chain. Success with students prone to failure will require more effort than will success with bright students. But the result can be a student who completes the year, does not repeat, and does not form the negative self-attitudes associated with failure.

Remedial work designed to help failing students to succeed can be carried out by teachers, or by student peers. In most cases the parents of failing students themselves lack academic abilities. They are not in a position to help their child succeed. Teacher remediation can be carried out during class time, using self-instructional activities for other students. Teachers and peers can also work with the failing student after hours.

Remediation requires an adequate understanding of the failing student's learning problems. These may be a result of failure to learn requisite concepts or skills in an earlier level, or it may be difficult with a new concept or skill. The teacher must identify the learning problems. Once those are identified the teacher can then design exercises and materials that can be used by a teacher, or by peers, to help the student.

Teachers with large classes, who live far from the school, or who must work a second job in order to support their family, are unlikely to be able to spend time with failing students. A policy to maintain failing students will, therefore, require additional resources. Mexico, for example, required its teachers to identify at mid-year all students likely to fail the year. The education system then provided additional funds for remedial teaching. This could be carried out by the classroom teacher, or by another teacher. The Mexican experiment demonstrated that it was possible to reduce significantly the failure rate, and that the cost of the remedial program was less than the cost to the system of the student repeating.

→ See also page 125.

195

from pages 109, 197

School Libraries

The importance of libraries in instruction is well understood. We lack, however, research on how best to organize libraries to be effective. There have been few evaluations of initiatives to improve library services.

Libraries provide an opportunity for students to learn on their own, without the intervention of the teacher. Because they contain many books, they supplement the narrow range of information and values found in the textbook. In Papua New Guinea, school libraries are important to be provide information about the wide variety of cultures in the nation. Libraries contribute to programs to teach students how to do research, how to generate information. For example, the library was a central element when Nigeria decided to move away from emphasis on memorization toward "inquiry and discovery" methods of learning.

Libraries can also provide the books required for classes that families cannot afford to buy. When children are not allowed to take textbooks home, they may spend more time in school. Books last longer when they are not taken home. In the Escuela Nueva (see page **199**), students copy the text from their workbooks into notebooks, which then become their property.

The most common problems faced by libraries are lack of trained staff and physical resources. Library personnel often lack specialized training. Learning materials are limited, inappropriate and culturally irrelevant. The building or room of the library is often inadequate. Facilities and collections of books are planned centrally without taking into account local circumstances.

The Department of School Libraries in Oman in 1987 established a university level program in Library and Documentation Studies (Karim, 1991). In Ghana, the Ministry of Education enabled the Ghana Library Board to make books available to students through a mobile library system (Alemna, 1983). In Nigeria, a "Book Depot" was established to help libraries build their collections (see page **197**).

For more information see Trask (1984).

from page 196

The "Book Depot" in Bendel State, Nigeria

Most of the primary schools in Bendel State have a library. However, the quality of their collections, staff, and accommodations vary widely. The improvement of these libraries is a large task, given the many schools. The State has relatively few booksellers that stock relevant books and materials. Teacher-librarians have not been trained in book selection, organization and leadership of libraries.

The State Library Board is responsible for improvement of school libraries. The Board has been successful in setting up a working "book depot" designed to meet the collection requirements of school libraries. The State Library centrally acquires and processes materials, using funds deposited by the schools. Schools are by law required to deposit 75 percent of their library fees with the State Library. The State Library then distributes materials to the school libraries.

The "book depot" program involves:

1. periodic visits to assess school library facilities;

2. use of professional advice for the reorganization of existing school library collections;

3. bulk deposit of books in schools;

4. provision to schools of mobile library services;

5. provision of training to teacher-librarians and library assistants; and

6. availability of reference and information services from the State Library.

The "book depot" program has been evaluated to have these advantages:

1. cost effectiveness. Costs of book purchasing and cataloguing to schools are reduced. Deliveries of books take less time.

2. collections of good and uniform quality. This insures that students and teachers have access to a library that is well-balanced in terms of subject, type of material and variety of content. High standards are maintained for selection of materials.

Source: Apeji (1990)

→ See also page 196.

197

from pages 41, 61, 114, 115, 123, 163

Figure 14

A Process for Assigning Children to Language of Instruction

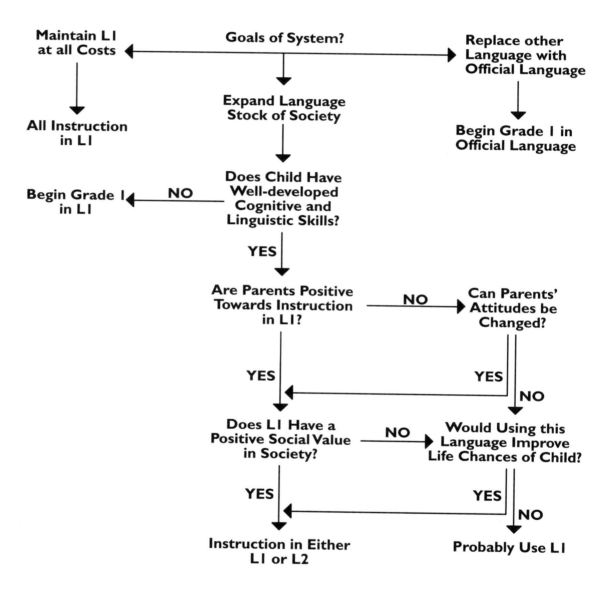

Based on Dutcher (1982).

from pages 24, 32, 66, 87, 90, 98, 106, 108, 119, 126, 187, 196, 208, 216, 222, 231

The Use of Self-Instructional Materials

Dependence on the teacher as the sole source of instruction can be reduced by the introduction of instructional materials designed to:

1. match the learning psychology of the children;

2. require children to work in small groups and to "teach" each other; and

3. provide teachers with ample information about the pace of learning of the student.

This approach to curriculum uses "instructional design" in which emphasis is on sequencing and pacing according to the psychology of the child. Material is presented in small modules. These permit a child, even a slow learner, to master content in a reasonable amount of time. Each module includes methods for self-assessment. The child can decide whether he or she is ready to go on to the next module.

The role of the teacher is changed from sole source of information about what is to be learned, to facilitator of the learning process of the child. Much less time is spent on *teaching* by the teacher, much more time is spent on studying by the student. Emphasis is on *mastery* by the student of the material in the module.

In the conventional curriculum design approach, evaluation tells the teacher what proportion of the total material has been learned, but does not indicate what level of understanding has been reached. This contributes to heterogeneity in upper grades. The instructional design or mastery learning approach indicates exactly what level of understanding has been attained. The conventional approach attempts to reduce heterogeneity by *streaming*, assigning all fast students to one teacher, all slow students to another. This is an expensive and inefficient solution. It also widens the gap between slow and fast students.

The instructional design/cooperative learning approach takes advantage of student heterogeneity, and reduces differences.

Examples

1. The Learning Technology Project of USAID uses instructional design materials from transmission through radio. Approximately 30 minutes per day of instruction (mathematics, English have been evaluated, others are now being used). The instruction presents material in small modules and asks students to respond out loud in class, or to respond in notebooks. Teachers monitor student responses. The program has been used in Nicaragua, Thailand, Dominican Republic, Kenya, Bolivia, and Honduras.

The major source of costs for this program is production and transmission of programs. Estimates of these costs are not available. Estimate of costs for operation (once materials have been developed) range between US$.30 and $.50 where large numbers of students (one million or more) are involved. In Nicaragua where 120,000 students were involved, the operating cost for an additional student was $1.64.

Research is clear that instruction by radio of the type described above is as effective as conventional instruction. When directed to schools with crowded classrooms and teachers with low levels of qualifications, radio instruction of the type described above is more effective than conventional instruction; students learn more in less time. Teachers are willing to cooperate with radio instruction of this kind, in part because it takes only a half hour of their class day.

For more information see Anzalone (1988).

2. The term "low-cost learning systems" has been used to describe a program based on instructional design concepts that has been

199

applied (under different names) in Philippines, Indonesia, Liberia, Thailand, Bangladesh, Malaysia, and Jamaica.

This program replaces traditional textbooks and other instructional materials with programmed instructional materials. The set of materials includes a teacher's guide with detailed, programmed instructions for the entire school year, and texts and workbooks for students. The instructional material is modularized, that is divided into relatively small units, with attention to sequencing and pacing. The material includes assessment devices. The curriculum is re-written with attention to the learning psychology of the child.

Problems have been experienced in the implementation of this program in some countries. Low-skilled teachers welcomed the material, but teachers with more skills resisted learning the new approach which reduces their autonomy and freedom to innovate. In Thailand the program was adopted but then slowly abandoned.

The method is clearly effective in comparison with conventional teaching methods. Students do as well or better than students in conventional schools on conventional achievement tests.

Cost for the entire package ranges between US$2 to $23. A more useful comparison: low cost learning system materials cost less than half the cost of conventional materials. In the Philippines, for example, the conventional package of materials cost $47, the low cost package $23. The cost savings of the low cost system are most clear with respect to teacher/ pupil ratios. The *optimal* class size for the low cost system in Liberia was estimated at 60 students. This then leads to substantial savings when compared to the conventional approach.

For more information see Thiagarajan and Pasigna (1988).

3. The *Escuela Nueva* or "New School" combines the instructional design and programmed instruction concepts of the Radio Learning Project and low cost learning systems, with a re-organization of the structure of the primary school. This system, now implemented in 20,000 rural primary schools in Colombia, seeks to increase time spent studying in and out of school, and to link the school more closely to the community.

All teachers in the New School were already in service when they began their new assignments. Teachers who volunteered to transfer were screened during their participation in a two-week training program in a demonstration school. The most difficult requirement for the new teachers is to learn to not attempt to control all aspects of the classroom.

A key element in the program is the creation of a student government which makes students (under the authority of the teacher) responsible for all aspects of the functioning of the school. This includes discipline, maintenance of the school garden, sweeping and cleaning, organizing and maintenance of the library, organization of the sports program. A significant amount of time is given over to election of student officers and participation in committees for decision making about the school.

In contrast with the Radio Learning and low cost learning projects, almost no direct instruction occurs in the New School. All student work, especially after the first year, is programmed through modularized workbooks. These books are kept in the school; students copy out of the books both the lesson content and their assignments. Each lesson is divided into activities. Students choose which grade they wish by electing the number of activities they wish to complete. When a lesson has been completed the student moves on to the next lesson. When the lessons for a given year have been completed the student can move to the next year's book. No students fail grades, as grades no longer need to exist. Some students can and do finish the five-year program in less than five years, others take more than five years.

Each unit requires students to pose questions based on the material they have read, and to then collect evidence to answer these questions. This work is done in small groups; students work around small movable tables (there are no desks). A classroom can have any number of "grades" within it, and one teacher works with students at several different levels. Many of the New Schools have two teachers for all five grades.

At the beginning of the year the teacher visits the home of every student and interviews the parents using a standard questionnaire. The teacher identifies skills and interests of the parents, and later involves the parents in demonstrations of their skills in the school. The students collectively develop a map of the community which locates all houses and other landmarks. Each month parents are invited to the school where children put on a demonstration of what they have learned. The school's link to the community is further reinforced by the lesson units which require students to collect information from and about their parents and others.

Students from the New School do better than students from conventional schools on the standard achievement tests. Evidence that the program teaches children to think creatively and independently is suggested by their experiences in secondary school. Reports are that New School students find the conventional secondary program dull and slow; teachers complain that New School students ask too many questions, want to work on their own.

The New School program is slightly more expensive because of the instructional materials. Teachers are required to spend more time working in the New School, designing new materials and new activities for students. This has been accomplished in Colombia without salary increments, but with much higher levels of job satisfaction because teachers feel more like professionals.

For more information about the New School see Schiefelbein (1991).

General Comments

All three of the options described are *centralizing*, in that they attempt to improve the quality of education by *reducing* unwanted variation in teacher coverage of the curriculum, and in teacher quality. The radio approach does this through a single master teacher; the low cost learning approach programs the classroom teacher's behavior using a programmed teacher's guide; the New School substitutes a programmed text for the teacher. See pages **150-151** for issues related to decentralization.

The radio approach is *homogenizing*, in that all students are exposed at the same time to the same material at the same pace. The low cost learning and New School approaches take into account the heterogeneity of students in the classroom and allow each to learn at their own speed; this is more true in the New School approach.

The radio and low cost learning approaches maintain the *teacher as the source of all knowledge*, while the New School approach encourages students to see others, including themselves, as sources of knowledge. The New School approach is therefore intrinsically much more connected to the local community, and makes much more use of parents and other adults as instructional resources.

The radio approach requires almost *no preservice teacher training* and could be implemented as soon as materials were made available. The low cost learning approach requires little or no training but has provoked resistance from teachers who do not wish to be "programmed." The New School approach requires in-service training of teachers, but this can be done without interrupting the school year.

The New School and low cost learning approaches have the *lowest infrastructure (fixed capital) costs and higher expendable material costs*. The radio approach has high fixed capital costs unless it uses existing transmitters. Costs can also be reduced by using a generic approach to script-writing. All programs require an up-front investment in a radical transformation of the curriculum, with attention to instructional design concepts. See pages **216** and **217**.

from pages 44, 236

Management Information Systems

A management information system includes procedures for the collection, organization, retrieval, and presentation of information to decision makers. Not all collections of statistics serve as management information systems.

1. The indicators (measures of performance) may not be linked to goals.

2. Data may not be available in time to inform current decisions.

3. Decision makers may not be able to extract useful information from complex tables.

Most collections of statistics were designed originally to keep track of inputs to the education system. For example, data are collected on numbers of students, numbers of teachers, numbers of classrooms, each classified in a number of different ways. This information may be useful for accounting purposes, but it does not help in assessing how well schools are doing. In an effort to keep track of every input to the schools, some countries collect so much information they can not process it within the annual school cycle.

Some education management information systems include information about what can be called process indicators. Generally these tell about actions. For example, some countries collect information about student attendance. Not collected in any systematic way, however, is information about coverage of the curriculum (see page 92).

There is increasing effort to collect information about the outputs of the education process, about student learning in the form of achievement scores (see pages 4, 154, 155, 227, 228).

A management information system (MIS) shifts attention away from accounting for inputs, to identification of those combinations of inputs and processes that maximize outputs. Less effort is paid on counting everything, more on explaining why things happen. For example, with a properly designed MIS it is possible for a manager to:

a. identify those units (regions, schools, classrooms) with highest and lowest rates of student attendance;

b. list the characteristics of those units (for example size, location, qualifications of teachers, grade level); and

c. estimate what it would take (for example, how much training for teachers) to raise units with low student attendance up to the average level.

This kind of analysis is not possible using the traditional statistical yearbook kind of information system. The yearbook is a collection of two-dimensional, or flat file, tables. The categories in the tables can not be changed or recombined. Because the data are aggregated it is not possible to know the value of a particular unit.

An MIS is like a set of files in a cabinet. Each file is a case, with information on all the indicators for that case. This makes it possible to relate any one indicator with all other indicators. For example, the manager can go through the files picking out all the cases that meet certain criteria, for example, classrooms with more than 60 students and under-qualified teachers. This characteristic makes it possible to design and carry out a wide variety of analyses.

All the data in the education management information system of a large country can be stored in a microcomputer. This low cost technology makes MIS available to all countries. Also, it is now possible to design simple programs that allow decision makers to interact easily with data about inputs and performance. The MIS makes it possible for the decision maker to have more rapid access to information, and to explore a much wider variety of possibilities than is possible with traditional approaches.

For more information about management information systems in education see Chapman and Mahlck (1993).

from page 155

Classroom Assessment of Student Learning

Every school day classroom teachers make a wide variety of decisions. They concern themselves with the academic, personal, and social characteristics of their students. They make decisions about planning, teaching, and evaluation of learning outcomes and student performance. Assessment, the process of gathering and organizing information, helps teachers make these and many other decisions (Airasian, 1991).

Paper-and-pencil tests are frequently used for classroom assessment. Such tests may be teacher-constructed, developed by the text-book publishers, or standardized to be taken by all students in the education system.

Successful classroom assessment requires integration of assessment with the curriculum. Teachers can control this integration by developing their own tests and by using alternative forms of assessment (see pages **152, 205** and **207**).

There are two basic types of test questions: **selection items** and **supply items**. Selection items require students to make a choice among options while supply items require students to provide a response (Airasian, 1991).

Table 19
Comparison of Selection and Supply Test Items

	Selection	Supply
Type of item	Multiple choice, matching, true-false, interpretive exercise.	Short answer, essay, completion.
Behaviors Assessed	Memory, recall, and comprehension; thinking and reasoning behaviors such as application and analysis using interpretive exercises.	Memory, recall, and comprehension; thinking and reasoning behaviors such as organizing ideas, defending positions, and integrating points.
Major Advantages	Items can be answered quickly so broad sample can be surveyed; items are easy and objective to score; test constructor has complete control over the test items.	Preparation of items relatively easy; only a few questions needed; students have a chance to construct own answers; students less likely to guess.
Major Disadvantages	Time-consuming to construct; most teacher time is spent before testing; many items must be constructed for testing; guessing is a problem.	Time-consuming to score; most teacher time is spent after the test; sample of of instructional topics is small.

continued on page 204

The type of assessment a teacher chooses should depend on the purpose of that assessment. Teachers should be encouraged to use a variety of methods when assessing student learning and performance. The following chart compares various types of assessment.

Table 20
Comparison of Various Types of Assessment

	Objective Test	Essay Test	Oral Question	Performance Assessment
Purpose	Sample knowledge with maximum efficiency and reliability	Assess thinking skills and/or mastery of a structure of knowledge	Assess knowledge during instruction	Assess ability to translate knowledge and understanding into action
Typical Exercise	Test items: Multiple-choice True/False Fill-in Matching	Writing task	Open-ended question	Written prompt or natural event framing the kind of performance required
Student's Response	Read, evaluate, select	Organize, compose	Oral answer	Plan, construct, and deliver original response
Scoring	Count correct answers	Judge understanding	Determine correctness of answers	Check attributes present, rate proficiency demonstrated, describe performance via anecdote
Major Advantage	Efficiency—can administer many items per unit of testing time	Can measure complex cognitive outcomes	Joins assessment and instruction	Provides rich evidence of performance
Potential Sources of Inaccurate Assessment	Poorly written items, overemphasis on recall of facts, poor test-taking skills, failure to sample content representatively	Poorly written exercises, writing skill confounded with knowledge of content, poor scoring procedures	Poor questions, students' lack of willingness to respond, too few questions	Poor exercises, too few samples of performance, vague criteria, poor rating procedures, poor test conditions
Influence on Learning	Overemphasis on recall encourages memorization; can encourage thinking skills if properly constructed	Encourages thinking and development of writing skills	Stimulates participation in instruction, provides teacher immediate feedback on effectiveness of teaching	Emphasizes use or available skill and knowledge in relevant problem contexts
Keys to Success	Clear test, blueprint or specifications that match instruction, skill in item writing, time to write items	Carefully prepared writing exercises, preparation of model answers, time to read and score	Clear questions, representative sample of questions to each student, adequate time provided for student response	Carefully prepared performance exercises; clear expectations; careful rating and time to do rating

➜ For more on assessment, see pages **205** and **206**.

Based on R.J. Stiggins in Airasian (1991).

from pages 137, 152, 155, 203, 206

Alternative Forms of Assessment: Portfolios

What is a portfolio?

- A purposeful collection of student work which exhibits a student's efforts, progress and achievements in one or more areas;

- a collection which includes student participation in selecting the contents; the criteria for selection and judging merit of the contents; and

- evidence of student self-reflection and thinking about learning.

What do portfolios do?

- Portfolios reveal information about the learner;

- permit an understanding of the process of education at the individual level;

- serve as means for students to take control over their own learning;

- require students to collect and reflect on their work; and

- act as an intersection of instruction and assessment.

What are some of the guidelines for implementing the use of portfolios?

1. A completed portfolio should contain evidence that the student has thought about his or her own learning.

2. For students to learn to value their work, they must be involved in choosing the contents of the portfolio.

3. Portfolios will not usually contain test scores or other cumulative information.

4. A portfolio will convey the student's activities.

5. Portfolios may serve different purposes throughout the school year. They may contain works in progress or materials ready to be made public (to other students, to teachers and/or parents).

6. Portfolios should illustrate a student's progress towards attaining instructional goals.

7. The portfolio should demonstrate student growth. For example, evidence of changes in a student's attitudes, interests, opinions, and the like may be kept in a portfolio.

8. Students should see examples of portfolios and receive help in developing their own portfolios.

Based on Paulson, Paulson, and Meyer (1991).

➜ Read page 228 for risks of standardized achievement tests.

from pages 137, 155, 203, 204

Principles of Assessment

There are two important things to remember about assessment: the entire process of assessing student achievement should be positive; and testing must never become more important than instruction.

The following questions will help you evaluate the assessment process in your education system:

1. Is assessment explicitly purposeful and related to one of the following educational needs: screening, referrals, and/or instruction?

2. Is assessment related to the requirements of the curriculum?

3. Do teachers choose the priorities for assessing subject areas most related to school success, the skills needed for the next level, and the skills needed for participation in activities in and out of school?

4. Are assessment instruments and techniques related to the purpose of the assessment?

5. Does assessment proceed from evaluating broad, general areas to specific skills?

6. Are student errors analyzed and used in approaches to prevent failure?

7. Are assessment findings substantiated through several assessment trials on the same skill, on reassessment of skills, and on student application of skills in every day situations?

8. Are results of assessment recorded and reported? Are the written reports brief and understandable? Do they contain lists of the skills assessed? Are achievement records maintained?

9. Are efforts made to continually improve assessment practices?

Based on Poteet (1985).

➜ Read also about portfolio assessment (page **205**), curriculum based assessment (page **207**) and risks in the use of standardized tests (page **228**).

from pages 25, 97, 125, 203, 206

Curriculum Based Assessment: Why Use It?

The *curriculum* defines for teachers the skills that students should learn. This curriculum may be established by the state, or developed by a committee. It may be determined by the official textbook, or in a list of learning objectives. No matter its origin or form, the curriculum is meant to guide the teacher's behavior.

Given a curriculum, the teacher chooses: developmental strategies to introduce skills; corrective strategies to re-teach material the student has forgotten; and/or maintenance strategies to make sure that the student practices using the material in order to insure retention. At each point the teacher must assess students' knowledge and skills. This comparison of current student level of knowledge and skill, with curriculum specifications is often called *curriculum based assessment,* sometimes "continuous assessment." It is this assessment, and not the results of standardized tests, that governs what teachers teach each day.

Curriculum based assessment contributes to the continuous improvement of quality of teaching in five ways:

1. Immediate assessment of students to determine if they have reached an instructional objective. Good teachers build this assessment into their instructional practice. As part of the instructional process, the assessment is an efficient way to insure student mastery of a given skill or unit of knowledge.

2. Regular charting of student progress. This makes it possible for teachers to identify students who are failing, or units or themes in the curriculum that are more difficult than others. Teachers can then adjust their instructional strategies, changing the pace, or introducing new material. In effect, this assessment practice makes it possible for teachers to study systematically their own teaching.

3. Generation of reliable and valid information about achievement. Curriculum based assessment is valid because it uses material from the student's curriculum. Standardized test items may not measure what the student has been taught. Curriculum based assessment is reliable because it provides repeated samplings of student performance. Traditional standardized norm referenced achievement tests cannot measure every skill on every curriculum. Such tests tend to be not very reliable because they are usually given only once during a school year or only to targeted grade levels (see page **228**).

4. Focus on mastery of curriculum skills. Research has shown that when curriculum based assessment is used to develop controlled instruction matched to the curriculum, it is effective in promoting the achievement of low performing students by increasing time-on-task, task completion, and task comprehension (Gickling and Thompson, 1985).

5. Identification of students who can benefit from external assistance. Curriculum based assessment can help the teacher make referral decisions about low performing students. Regular classroom teachers can use curriculum based assessment to identify students who may need some form of extra help and the area(s) for improvement.

Based on Poteet (1985).

from pages 126, 127, 182, 231

What Factors Make Multigrade Classrooms Effective?

1. *Classroom management* (page **106**). Teachers can vary use of time, space, and materials. They can organize students in different combinations. The correct instructional practices can produce academic learning outcomes that match those of single grade classrooms. These practices can generate superior social and affective learning.

Effective teachers group students by ability, according to the particular subject matter. In resource-poor classrooms, the teacher spends more time with slower students. Advanced students work alone or in small groups. Groups may shift during the day, for example to be able to see the blackboard. In richer settings, students work in activity centers, reading corners or libraries.

Effective multigrade teachers give less class time to direct instruction (e.g., lecturing). They give more time to student-led group discussions, or individual or group exercises. Where possible, students work on workbooks or exercise sheets, or read in their textbooks. Sometimes teachers have written exercises on the blackboard in advance. More advanced students are used to help slower students while the teacher attends to another group.

This method works well when lessons are carefully sequenced. Teachers break up the day into units with well-defined objectives, and frequently test for student understanding. Student motivation is maintained by linking exercises to the local situation, and by frequent rewards for progress.

2. *Curriculum.* Some subjects can be taught effectively to a whole class. These subjects include art, health, literature, oral language, and science. Other subjects are best taught to small groups of students. These subjects include mathematics and reading (Pratt and Treacy, 1986).

Heavy dependence on the textbook as the source of curriculum reduces the effectiveness of multigrade teaching. Teachers in multigrade settings have to adapt objectives, content, and methods to match the current knowledge, abilities, and interests of different groups of students.

The more the official curriculum prescribes specific objectives, methods, and time for each subject, the more difficult is the task of a teacher in a heterogeneous classroom. Students learn when the sequence and pace of information presentation matches their abilities to attend and absorb. Multigrade teaching requires flexible presentation of information, varied across groups, and according to subject.

Instructional design (page **34**) approaches take into account differences in the interests and rate of learning of students of different ages. See page **199** for examples of their application in multigrade settings.

Based on Rowley (1992).

from page 115

Nutrition and Learning

There is a strong link between the nutritional status of children and their attendance and performance in school (Levinger, 1989). Nutritional deficiencies in childhood reduce enrollment in school, increase absenteeism, and lower performance leading to early dropout (Pollitt, 1990).

Malnutrition takes three different forms that affect student achievement. Most common is protein-energy malnutrition. Second is temporary hunger, followed by micronutrient (iodine, iron, Vitamin A) deficiency.

Table 21 outlines the causes of these three forms of malnutrition, and their effects on students.

Table 21

Causes and Effects of Different Forms of Malnutrition

Nutritional Status	Cause	Effect
Protein energy deficiency	Deficient diet, exacerbated by parasites; poverty	School absence; reduced enrollment
Temporary hunger	No breakfast	Distractability; poor classroom performance
Micronutrient deprivation	Deficient diet	Decreased mental performance; reduced attention span; nutrition-linked blindness; stunted growth; school absence

For more information see Dobbing (1987).

Programs to Offset Malnutrition

The most common solution to protein-energy malnutrition and temporary hunger has been the supplementary feeding program. School feeding programs have been used to offset the immediate negative effects of hunger and malnutrition. They also act as an incentive that increases attendance, and they serve as an income transfer to the poor. The most common programs have provided some form of lunch. Others provide breakfast, or a snack.

For the most part, these programs have not been designed to meet nutritional goals. As a consequence, evaluations often report no effect on feeding and student achievement. Successful programs lead to improved attendance and, as a consequence, greater learning. A school breakfast experiment in Jamaica resulted in higher rates of attendance and improved scores on arithmetic tests. School feedings programs are expensive to maintain. They also take students away from their classrooms, that is, reduce instructional time (Pollitt, 1990).

Deficiencies in iron, iodine and Vitamin A can be reduced through supplementation, fortification, and elimination of parasites.

Nutritional programs are most effective when combined with health care and intellectual stimulation. The social and economic factors that bring about malnutrition also are associated with the general health and intellectual environment of the child. The broad effects of poverty are best overcome through an integrated approach.

→ For more on student attendance, see page **104**.

from pages 40, 115

Should Pre-Primary Education be Expanded?

Almost all countries have some kind of pre-primary education. Some countries offer a Grade Zero, or pre-primary program through public primary schools. The most common form is privately organized. Child-tending services are provided along with some minimal amount of formal instruction. A small number of pre-primary schools serve as feeders to selective primary schools, and provide formal instruction in letters and numbers.

Research on the impacts of pre-primary education in developing countries is relatively limited. **There is, however, clear evidence that pre-primary education can improve the performance of children in the early primary grades.**

Some pre-primary programs are successful in reducing the rate of failure, and repetition of children. In Thailand, for example, grade 3 children who had attended pre-primary schools scored higher on standardized tests of language and mathematics than did children of similar background, sex, and age who had not attended (Raudenbush, Kidchanapanish, and Kang, 1991). Pre-primary programs have been effective in reducing school failure in Argentina, Bolivia and Chile. The impact of these programs is attributed to improved nutrition, intellectual stimulation, and socialization into the behavior patterns expected in formal schools (Halpern and Myers, 1985; International Development Research Center, 1983).

Not all pre-primary programs make a difference. The Sandinista government in Nicaragua made great efforts to extend pre-primary education to rural youth. Enrollments grew from three percent of the eligible population in the late 1970s to 20 percent by the mid 1980s. But there was no noticeable change in overall rates of promotion and repetition. It is likely that the quality of the programs suffered as a consequence of the war (Chesterfield,

1991). Under the right circumstances, however, pre-primary education can improve the internal efficiency of the primary school, by reducing student failure.

Should a country invest in expansion of public pre-primary education? **The question is better stated as: Should investments be made in expansion of pre-primary education, or in expansion and/or improvement of primary education?** Expansion of pre-primary education is an additional cost, even when it improves the efficiency of primary schools. If resources are constrained, money for pre-primary schools has to be taken from primary schools.

1. When not all children are in school, expansion of pre-primary education means less funds are available to expand primary school. Pre-primary education benefits some children at the expense of others.

2. When all children are enrolled, but failure and repetition rates are high, expansion of pre-primary education can reduce repetition rates. But the funds spent to expand pre-primary education could also be spent to improve the quality of primary education, which would also reduce repetition rates. **No research has been done to compare the cost-effectiveness of pre-primary education to that of improved primary education.**

3. A program of pre-primary education could be a way to extend the length of time that all children are in school. This would be appropriate when all children are enrolled, and failure and repetition rates are low (which could be taken to mean that quality is high).

4. An untested alternative would be to move the school entry age downward, without making the cycle longer. Here the question is: can children learn more and faster if we start their schooling younger?

The most effective pre-primary programs are radically different from conventional primary school programs. The effective programs emphasize individualized and active learning. In these programs the teacher is a *manager of the learning process* rather than the sole source of knowledge for the student. Pre-primary programs often have smaller class sizes, more highly trained teachers, and make more use of instructional materials.

All of the methods that are effective in pre-primary programs can be implemented in primary schools as well.

Figure 15
Impacts of Pre-School Programs

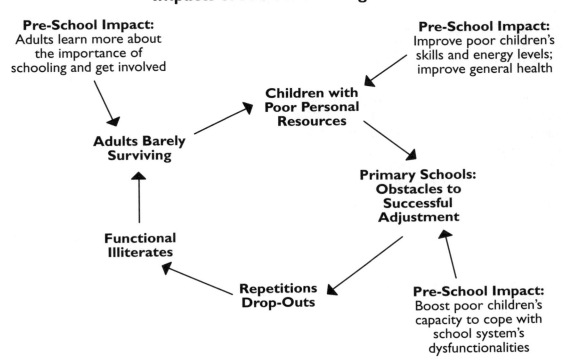

Pre-School Impact:
Adults learn more about the importance of schooling and get involved

Pre-School Impact:
Improve poor children's skills and energy levels; improve general health

Children with Poor Personal Resources

Adults Barely Surviving

Primary Schools: Obstacles to Successful Adjustment

Functional Illiterates

Repetitions Drop-Outs

Pre-School Impact:
Boost poor children's capacity to cope with school system's dysfunctionalities

from pages 45, 167

Issues of School Size

Larger schools make more efficient use of certain school resources than do smaller schools. This is because of *economies of scale.* (Kenny, 1982). In a small school, the cost per student of special facilities such as laboratories, libraries, audio-visual rooms, and gymnasiums can be very high. With more students, the unit cost goes down. Especially at the secondary level, large schools provide a more varied curriculum (Monk, 1987).

The same is true with respect to provision of special teachers, for example for art, music, guidance and counseling, physical education. There are economies of scale with respect to school administration. Provision of health care and supplementary nutrition programs is also less expensive, per student, in larger schools.

Land preparation and per square meter construction costs are also less for larger schools as compared to smaller schools.

For all these reasons, it has been argued that countries should favor larger over smaller schools.

Arguments for construction of smaller schools are:

1. Where population is dispersed, as in rural areas, construction of large schools means each building is farther apart. The greater distance between schools requires students to travel farther. This reduces enrollment, and increases dropout, especially among the poor, and girls.

2. In the United States, larger secondary (grades 9–12) schools have a broader range of physical inputs and more diversity in course offerings and teachers, but also show lower levels of student attendance and morale (Lindsay, 1982). It should be kept in mind that the average size of American secondary schools may be large (e.g., 1,600 students) compared to those of other countries.

For an example of a policy study on school size, see Ahlawat (1991).

For more discussion of advantages of small schools in rural areas see Bray (1987).

Alternative Sites for Schools

Eventually, of course, schools should be located in buildings designed according to the requirements of the curriculum. Where this is not possible there are several options. These have been used as a temporary solution to the problem of shortage of school sites.

Option 1: Rent private buildings.

Some countries have found it useful to rent buildings as locations for schools. This may be appropriate in urban areas, where construction costs are high, and sites often not available. In Egypt, a progressive government eager to provide universal primary education to a rapidly growing urban population, took possession of private buildings and compensated owners for their use. Some of these buildings were former private residences, others were office buildings.

Over time, land prices and therefore building rents in growing cities will increase far beyond their original level. If rents for schools do not increase, their owners will not maintain them, and the quality of the school building will decline. If rents are allowed to increase they may become too expensive for the government to pay. This is likely to happen as the area in which the school is located changes from residential to commercial use.

Option 2: Expand the capacity of existing school sites with low-cost temporary facilities.

Where a school site already exists, existing capacity can be generated for the short term by use of temporary buildings. These are structures that use low-cost materials such as those ordinarily used in construction of warehouses, and are not as well-equipped (for example with water and electricity) as are regular buildings. This solution is *tolerable for a limited length of time. Cheap buildings do not last long, even with maintenance.*

Option 3: Use other public buildings.

Some countries have used as schools other public or community buildings not in active use during the time when schools are in session. For example, Pakistan has used **mosques** as the site of **public** schools. Mosques are found in almost every village in Pakistan. Most are constructed with a large patio, sometimes covered. Mosques have access to water for purification before prayers. The **imam** or **mullah** responsible for the mosque is often a respected man in the community. In rural areas where there are no school buildings, the Ministry of Education rents the mosque. The imam receives a small stipend for teaching religious studies. Teachers are regular Ministry employees. This program has permitted enrollment of at least 300,000 children in more than 17,000 communities. It has been particularly helpful in increasing enrollment of girls (Anderson, 1989).

→ See page **166** for a discussion of increasing efficiency within school facilities.

→ See page **167** for more ways to increase space.

213

from pages 21, 47

Options to Increase Training for Rural Teachers

Teachers can be trained before entering the profession—this is called *pre-service* training. It is also possible to admit untrained persons into teaching and to provide training *in-service.*

Pre-Service Training. Supply of trained rural teachers is limited by two factors:

a. many urban-born teachers are unwilling to serve in rural areas.

b. too few candidates come from rural areas. This occurs because too few persons attain enough education to be admitted to pre-service training programs (see pages **66** and **87**), and because training institutions are often located in distant urban areas.

To solve this problem in Rajasthan, India, the National Council for Educational Research and Training (NCERT) recruited local villagers and provided economic support for them to attend regional teacher training colleges. Training emphasized teaching in skills and content most relevant to village life; textbooks were developed as aids for teachers. Student attendance rose from 41 percent to 80 percent of age group (Aruna, 1980).

214

from pages 14, 23, 168

Interventions to Raise Female Enrollment

1. Increase Supply of Schools for Girls

A. *Provide more places where girls can be taught.* See page **168**.
- Add classrooms to existing schools in rural areas.
- Renovate existing buildings.
- Use public buildings (e.g., mosques) for classes.

B. *Provide more female teachers.*
- Train rural women with secondary education as teachers.
- Recruit teachers from rural areas.
- Provide residences for rural teachers.
- Establish incentive systems to attract more women.
- Build teacher training institutes in rural areas.

C. *Provide alternative settings.*
- Build lower primary schools in rural areas (feeders).
- Set up evening schools for dropouts.

2. Reduce Direct Costs of Schooling

A. *Provide free uniforms or abolish use of uniform.*

B. *Provide scholarships.*
- Offer scholarships at secondary level only.
- Offer scholarships at primary level.

C. *Provide school breakfasts, lunches.*

3. Reduce Indirect Costs of Schooling for Girls

A. *Relieve girls of child-tending responsibilities.*
- Build work-site day care centers, preschool centers.
- Provide sibling care at primary schools.

B. *Adapt labor-saving home technologies.*
- Distribute labor saving machines.
- Distribute or disseminate fuel-efficient stoves.

C. *Change schedule to permit work at home.*
- Introduce programmed instruction in schools.
- Introduce multigrade teaching.
- Use self-teaching materials.

D. *Provide training in non-traditional occupations.*
- Centers to train middle level technicians.
- Training located near primary schools.
- Open programs for women in industrial occupations.

4. Overcome Gender Bias

A. *Revise textbooks, curriculum, make gender-neutral.*

B. *Launch media campaigns to promote education of girls.*

C. *Offer incentives to delay onset of pregnancy (e.g., scholarships)*

Adapted from Bellew and King (1991).
See also Herz, Subbarao, Habab and Raney (1992).

215

Figure 16
Conceptual Model of Mother's Education and Daughter's Educational Intentions

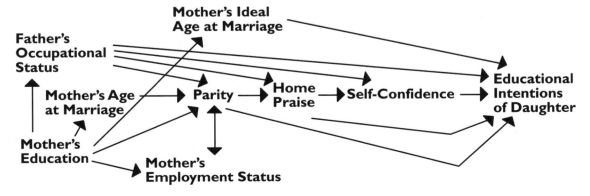

from pages 34, 201, 219

Instructional Materials Based on Principles of Instructional Design

Instructional design encourages the use of multiple media in instruction. Among the less expensive media are those based on print, the most common medium used in instruction in developing countries, and the medium most likely to have been produced nationally. However, these textbooks often:

1. do not match the scope and sequence of the official curriculum and

2. are beyond the reading level of students for whom they are intended.

Here are examples of instructional design materials.

A. *Modularized Materials.* This approach replaces the traditional textbook with a number of separate units or modules. These permit greater flexibility in teaching and use of self-instruction. Modular materials are more expensive, but increase learning outcomes.

B. *Programmed Learning Materials.* These are self-instructional materials that require students to make frequent responses, and which provide feedback on response correctness.

Programmed materials have been shown to be highly effective with older learners. The *Escuela Nueva Program* (see page **199**) has used programmed materials with students in grades 2 though 5; students learn more than those taught with traditional methods.

C. *Workbooks.* These are collections of exercises and drills that permit students to practice what they have learned, without direct supervision by the teacher. They are most effectively used in combination with textbooks. Costs can be reduced by having students copy exercises from workbooks into their own, less expensive copybooks.

D. *Posters.* These are large visual displays of graphic and text material. Posters can reduce dependency on textbooks for carrying curriculum content.

E. *Instructional Games.* The best teachers develop a number of instructional games on their own. Games can be highly motivating and effective for mastering basic skills and for drill and practice.

Based on Thiagarajan and Pasigna (1988).

from pages 34, 126, 201, 219, 220

An Example of Use of Instructional Design Materials

The Improved Efficiency of Learning (IEL) Project began in Liberia in 1979. The IEL Project was a *response to two major problems:*

1. lack of instructional materials in classrooms; and

2. shortage of trained and qualified teachers.

The Project was highly cost-effective compared to conventional methods, and was adopted for all primary schools.

The Project used the following approaches:

1. programmed teaching and learning;

2. self-instructional materials;

3. peer group learning; and

4. peer and cross-age tutoring.

All subjects in primary school were included. In the lower grades, use of programmed materials overcame the lack of knowledge of under-trained teachers. In the upper grades, students used self-instructional materials.

Materials were produced by Liberians trained in instructional design principles, and were printed using high quality equipment. The final products included modules; an implementation handbook; training manuals for students, teachers, supervisors and module writers; and arts and crafts manuals. By 1986 the Project was in operation in 109 schools with 23,000 students.

On average, IEL Project students scored 17 percentile points higher on standard assessment instruments than did students taught traditionally. Enrollments in IEL schools were expanded 71 percent with no additional teachers. Class sizes in the lower grades were increased to 60 students per teacher; in the upper grades the ratio was 70 to one. Student failure and dropout rates declined.

The annual *additional* cost per student of the Project was US$3.05 in 20-student classes, and US$2.13 in 60-student classes, about the same as the cost of textbooks in conventional classes. Teacher training costs were significantly less.

For additional information and other examples see Cummings (1986) and page **222**.

217

from page 50

Factors that Affect the Implementation of Policies and Programs

1. *Organizational intelligence.* Implementation requires two kinds of information, or intelligence. At the beginning of the process, analysts and planners must have some knowledge or understanding of whether a new policy is feasible, and whether it is desirable. Managers require information during the implementation of the policy, in order to work out faults in the design that could lead to failure.

2. *Sense of ownership.* Policies and programs are more likely to be implemented when those involved believe in what they are doing. This belief is generated by participation in the process of defining the policy issue and designing a solution.

3. *Tasks and technology.* It must be possible to carry out the policy, which is to say that the means to do so must be known. Clarity about what is expected is essential, as is ability.

4. *Management and organization.* Implementation takes place within an organizational context, and requires sustained management capability.

5. *Culture.* Implementation also takes place in a cultural context. New proposals must not deviate too much from existing norms and beliefs about what can and should be done.

6. *Politics.* Implementation takes place in a political context. Most changes of any consequence affect the balance of power among groups, and therefore have important political considerations. Reforms that are contrary to the prevailing powers are likely to fail.

7. *Implementors.* The major reason why plans fail and policies are not implemented faithfully is because those responsible for their implementation are not aware of what is expected of them, are not convinced that they should do what is asked, or are not able to do what is asked.

8. *Clients.* Plans and policies are more likely to be implemented when there is a clearly defined set of stakeholders, beneficiaries, or clients. These may be parents, the community-at-large, or employers. Clients help provide resources, as well as motivation to implementors.

9. *Resources.* Plans fail when they are not adequately financed, or if required resources are not mobilized from client groups.

10. *Benefits of the Policy.* Policies and plans are implemented over time, generally in stages. If obtained results are less than expected, or if costs are much higher than promised, or if much more effort is required than was thought, then clients and funders and implementors may reduce their support. The program may die, or be killed, before it becomes fully institutionalized.

"Implementation means transaction. To carry out a program, implementers must continually deal with tasks, environments, clients, and each other...the key to success is continual coping with contexts, personalities, alliances, and events...crucial to such adaptation is the willingness to acknowledge and correct mistakes, to shift directions, and to learn from doing."

Warwick, Reimers, and McGinn (1991).

See also Verspoor (1989).

➜ Implementation over time brings up issues of sustainability. See page **194**.

from page 106

The Reduced Instructional Time Project: Thailand

The Reduced Instructional Time (RIT) Project was begun to compensate for a shortage of teachers. The Project combined programmed instructional materials (see pages **34**, **216**, and **217**) with procedures for management and evaluation. The objective was to increase student involvement in direction of the learning process, and to reduce the amount of teachers' time required for instruction and supervision of students. The Project was successful in maintaining or improving levels of student achievement, while also increasing class sizes.

About the same time, however, Thailand began an Open University (distance education) program for teacher training (Nielsen, 1991). This program also was successful, to the point that by the mid-1980s class sizes had dropped sharply, and in mostly urban areas it was considered that there were too many teachers.

Attention focused on the problem of isolated rural villages. These have populations too small to permit assignment of teachers for each grade; teachers have to work in a multigrade context. RIT was used to permit these teachers to work with more heterogeneous classes. By 1988 RIT was being used in 6,800 schools in 72 provinces.

An evaluation carried out in 1984 reported:

1. Students using the RIT materials scored higher on achievement tests than did students using traditional textbooks and taught by traditional, teacher-directed methods.

2. Students in small RIT schools gained more from the use of materials than did students in large RIT schools. That is, the Project was successful in reducing inequities in quality of teaching and learning.

3. The RIT Project reduced the overall need for teachers. The savings were greater than the cost of materials and training for the RIT Project.

Based on Wheeler, Raudenbush, and Pasigna (1989).

For more information see Thiagarajan and Pasigna (1988).

219

from pages 33, 85, 88, 179, 184, 186, 191, 222

Use of Distance Education for Teacher Training

Distance education methods employ print, audio, or visual media to communicate with students without the direct presence of the teacher. These methods are most appropriate when one or more of the following conditions hold:

a. there is an acute shortage of qualified teachers

b. regions vary widely in the quality of teachers

c. some groups, e.g., girls, lack access to schools because there are not enough female teachers

d. the costs of conventional teacher training make expansion unfeasible

e. infrastructure for transportation and communication are in place.

More than 40 countries have used some form of distance education for teacher training, 18 in Africa, 11 in Latin America, eight in Asia. One model is the "Open University" or university extension model (Kenya: Coldevin and Naidu, 1989; Pakistan: Abbas, 1987; Thailand: Nielsen, 1991). Some countries, such as Swaziland, have established special centers.

The various models differ in terms of emphasis on subject matter knowledge vs. pedagogy, and the number of media used. About half the projects combined academic training with pedagogy, and used some combination of correspondence, face-to-face training, and mass media.

Distance education is an effective way of training teachers. A recent evaluation of 14 programs rated nine as effective, four as ambiguous, and one negative (Nielsen, 1991). Cost information was available for 12 programs; the distance programs were less expensive for ten of the cases, and the same for the other two. Of the 11 rated for *cost-effectiveness,* seven were cost-effective compared to alternatives, two were not cost-effective.

Distance education is a less expensive method for training teachers than are teacher colleges. The critical factor affecting cost-effectiveness is *size.* Programs with few participants are not cost-effective. Programs that are extended to reach many trainees have economies of scale. Costs per student trained, for equal level of ability, are lower than alternatives. An evaluation of programs in Sri Lanka and Indonesia reports costs that are one-sixth to three-fifths those of campus-based programs.

Distance education training for teachers reaches those who would not otherwise become teachers. Distance education methods make training and teacher certification available to those who are not able to attend residential training colleges. Because it reaches people in rural areas, it helps to increase the supply of rural teachers. Most rural teachers trained in this fashion remain in rural areas.

Distance education programs transfer some costs from the government to the participant. Most residential programs provide free materials and may even include subsidization of living expenses. Distance education programs typically expect the participant to bear those costs. Some programs even charge fees. Despite these transfers, however, *distance education programs impose less of an absolute cost on participants than do conventional programs.*

Distance education programs can be stopped or altered once they meet their original goal. Faced with a serious shortage of teachers, Tanzania instituted a distance education program for teacher training in the 1970s. Within eight years it had trained more than 45,000 teachers, and reduced the teacher shortage significantly. The program was then stopped. Once the Open University in Indonesia had trained enough

220

teachers to meet the expected shortage in junior secondary, it switched to upgrading primary school teachers in service. (See Nielsen, 1991, for more examples.)

Conditions for Success

a. There must be adequate demand to permit expansion to scale.

b. Instructional methods and materials must be of high quality. See page **217** on *instructional design*.

c. Formative evaluation is the preferred method.

d. Participation of local groups helps insure program success.

For more information see Nielsen (1991) and Nielsen, Tatto, Djalil, and Kularatne (1991).

from pages 105, 179, 217

Distance Education for Improved Learning

The impact of interactive radio instruction is greater than that of improved teacher training, or textbooks (Lockheed and Hanushek, 1988).

When good teachers are in short supply, distance education can provide instructional processes that contribute to high levels of learning. The most effective programs *supplement* the work of teachers but do not replace them.

The most common method of distance education uses radio to deliver instructional units. Radio lessons are provided daily for 20 to 30 minutes for each subject. During the radio lesson students are encouraged to respond out loud. For this reason the programs are sometimes called *interactive radio instruction.* The radio lesson generally is followed by a teacher-led activity that reinforces the radio lesson. In the best programs, teachers are guided in this activity by use of a workbook keyed to the radio lesson. Some programs also provide materials to be used at home.

Radio instruction programs have been used in a number of countries. *Interactive* radio instruction programs are more effective than conventional classrooms. Studies in Bolivia (mathematics), Honduras (mathematics), Kenya (English), Nicaragua (mathematics) and Thailand (mathematics) report higher levels of student achievement on standardized exami-

nations. Both students and teachers respond favorably to the program.

Adding radio increases costs of instruction slightly. Recurrent costs are estimated at between US\$.50 and US\$1 per year per student.

The advantages of using distance education methods in the classroom include:

1. Can be used to reduce differences in the quality of instruction provided in different regions. Distance education can help improve quality and expand access simultaneously.

2. Can contribute to teacher improvement by providing examples of alternative instructional strategies.

3. Upgrading of teachers can take place in the classroom, that is, without removing the teacher for long periods of training.

4. Are relatively low cost. Radio requires a relatively small capital investment.

For more information see *Development Communication Report,* volume 48, 1985, published by the Institute for International Research, Rosslyn, Virginia. Other published evaluations include: Anzalone (1988); Friend (1989); Friend, Searle and Suppes (1980); Friend and Kemmerer (1985).

→ See also pages **199** and **220**.

222

from pages 30, 102, 192, 193, 231

The School Cluster Reform in Sri Lanka

Prior to the Reform, control over schools was exercised through 26 Districts, each with three to five Circuits. Each Circuit Officer or Supervisor was responsible for between 50 to 100 schools. Visits to schools were infrequent, many schools were visited only once in two or three years. Central bureaucrats were unsure about the validity of the statistics they received, and were aware that central dictates were not always carried out faithfully.

After a period of experimentation, the Ministry settled on the following structure. Each District was divided into four to six Divisions. Each Division had seven to 15 Clusters. Clusters were collections of seven to 12 schools located close together. One school in each cluster was designated as a core school, and its principal as the executive head of the cluster.

An evaluation of the reform after four years found the following:

1. Frequency of communication *downward* to the school increased by about 60 percent. Frequency of communication *upward* from the school increased by about 90 percent. Communication among schools also increased by about 90 percent. Increases in communication were greatest in urban areas.

2. Sharing of resources among schools doubled for rural schools, but declined for urban schools.

3. The number of in-service training seminars increased by about 100 percent in rural schools, only slightly in urban schools.

4. Schools that implemented the cluster system fully experienced:

   a. increases in support from the local community;

   b. increases in levels of teacher morale;

   c. some improvements in student achievement.

Overall school autonomy declined; schools in clusters have less autonomy than those existing before the Reform.

For more information see Bray (1987); Cummings, Gunawardena, and Williams (1991).

For another example, see Wheeler, Raudenbush, and Pasigna (1989) and page **226**.

223

from pages 75, 81, 98, 125

Common Features of Effective Schools

1. *A guiding philosophy* that provides a framework for all the activities of the school. This philosophy can be understood as a vision, as a set of guiding principles, as a "mission statement." It should talk about fundamental changes in the school, not just marginal adjustments or refinements.

2. *An overall strategy,* a global plan for fulfilling the vision stated in the philosophy. This strategy, to be comprehensive, has to include curriculum teachers, administration, students, community, facilities. As a global statement, the strategy makes it possible for both the central administration of the school and individual teachers to make adjustments and improvements over time.

3. *Responsibilities are assigned to all the stakeholders,* that is, all the persons who will be affected by the changes proposed. This includes administrators, teachers, support staff, parents, students, and other members of the community. These responsibilities include financial support (from the community and parents), volunteer labor and donation of materials, parental support in helping teachers to carry out the program, school participation in and support of other community activities.

4. *Stakeholders participate in decision making.* Small schools may use some form of consensual decision making. In larger schools, groups of stakeholders may elect representatives, or they may be chosen by the school administrator, with approval by the stakeholders. In all forms, it is understood that some decisions are made centrally or collectively, and others can be made locally or individually. The school is most effective when there is clarity about which decisions are left to teachers, parents and students, and which are reserved to all the stakeholders.

5. *Active Learning.* Effective schools assign responsibility to students for their own learning, and therefore adopt methods in which the student is highly engaged in the teaching-learning process. This may include learning contracts, in which students set their own objectives, peer teaching, in which some students are responsible for others, and instructional units built around projects which are carried out by teachers and students together.

6. *Focus.* Clarity of objectives and emphasis on involvement requires that schools narrow the range of objectives they hope to achieve. The philosophy that effective schools work out delimits what can and should be achieved. It is not clear, however, that this means that the total learning in effective schools is less. On the contrary, it appears that curriculum clarity and active learning methods tend to expand the range of learning that occurs.

7. *Standards.* Effective schools set clear, and high standards for the behavior and performance of all their members. This may include dress codes for teachers and students, discipline codes for students. It includes high standards for student achievement. Combined with teacher commitment to the program, this translates into expectations by teachers that all children will achieve at higher levels than is normally expected. It is important to note that as standards are consensually defined, they do not act as bureaucratic regulations that are evaded or applied punitively.

8. *Resources.* Effective schools require more resources. This statement does not mean that spending more will necessarily produce an effective school. Instead, it refers to the fact that change requires an additional expenditure of energy, and hence resources, at least until the reform is successfully established. Most effective schools have accomplished this by mobilization of resources from the community.

Based on Levin (1992). For additional information on effective schools see Bickel (1990), MacKenzie (1983), and Teddlie and Stringfield (1993).

from pages 144, 157, 193

Use of Indicators to Monitor Quality of Education: Zimbabwe

The Ministry of Education decided to assess the quality of students in grade 6 of primary school. They posed the following as critical questions:

1. Which (of essential) inputs do schools currently receive?

2. What percentage of schools are below the norm?

3. How are inputs distributed across regions?

4. How does academic achievement vary by region?

5. What inputs contribute to achievement? Which should be increased?

Inputs were defined in three categories: 1) school buildings, 2) teachers and their living conditions, 3) facilities in schools and classrooms.

Reading achievement in English was defined as the critical *output* variable.

Questionnaires and tests were applied in a national sample of 145 schools to 2,600 students and their teachers. Field work required two weeks time. Some of the findings were:

Inputs were low.

1. Ministry norms for provision of notebooks, pencils and ballpoint pens were met in 11 percent, 25 percent and one percent of the schools respectively.

2. Only 18 percent of classrooms had sufficient sitting spaces for students, and only 12 percent had sufficient writing spaces.

3. Only 24 percent of classrooms had sufficient supplies to meet Ministry norms.

As a consequence, outputs were also low.

4. Levels of mastery on reading test items were below criteria set by teachers. About 38 percent of the students were able master half of the 33 items on the test. Only 13 percent mastered more than 70 percent of the items.

The most important inputs are those that directly improve quality of instruction.

5. Teachers believe that increased quantity and quality of classroom supplies is most important for improving their satisfaction with their work, even more important than improvements in their salaries.

6. Teacher listed furniture as least important as an input.

Based on Ross and Postlethwaite (1992).

➜ For more information about the importance of instructional materials see page **60**.

➜ For a discussion of teacher motivation see page **96**.

➜ For definitions of "quality" see page **241**.

225

In–Service Training for School Principals: An Example from Thailand

Thailand provided in–service training to all of its primary school principals between 1985 and 1988. In addition, it changed procedures for the selection of principals. Now all candidates must have approval at the district and provincial level, and complete a training program in educational administration. Candidates are ranked according to scores on a test applied at the end of training, and on the quality of a brief research paper on some issue in administration.

The in–service training program was designed by 15 experienced principals and supervisors. Development of the program required one year, and included pilot testing of video tapes, slide presentations, and 20 booklets describing various aspects of the principal's job. The materials also provided suggestions of activities for principals.

Training was carried out using a *cascade* method. The core group trained provincial supervisors, who then met with principals in district offices. Emphasis was put on the seriousness of the training, and linked to the development of accountability indicators that would be used to judge the principal's performance (see page **227**).

The program began with a one–day session in which trainees took a test of their knowledge of six areas of responsibility: academics, personnel, clerical and finance, student affairs, physical facilities, and school–community relationships. These six areas are described in the basic manual provided by the Ministry.

Trainees then did exercises in three of the booklets, and returned to their homes to complete another five booklets.

The second phase of the training lasted five days. The remaining booklets were completed, and trainees participated in simulations on common problems in school administration. The initial test was readministered. Trainees who scored less than 60 percent correct were asked to review all the booklets and other training materials, and to take the test again in one month.

As other principals, and teachers, found out about the high standards of the program, levels of motivation increased and the quality of later training sessions improved.

During the year following training, principals were monitored in their schools to see if they had carried out the activities recommended by the booklets. Those principals who had passed the final test, and who had implemented the program, received a certificate. An evaluation in 1987 indicated that more than 60 percent of the principals trained were ranked "high" in their performance. During this period of time student achievement scores began to increase.

As a consequence of the program, about 2,000 principals either resigned, or were assigned to teaching positions.

For more information see Wheeler, Raudenbush, and Pasigna (1989).

from pages 4, 155, 157, 193, 202, 226, 228, 235

Use of Standardized Achievement Tests to Improve Quality: The Case of Thailand

In 1984 the Office of the National Primary Education Commission (ONPEC), the top educational policy organization in Thailand, began development of a national test of achievement for grade 6 students.

The action was motivated by a judgment that the quality of education in primary schools was lower than it should be. Low quality was thought to be a consequence of inadequate implementation of the official curriculum. Public comparison of the performance of provinces on the achievement test would motivate provincial education directors to work harder to get district officials to pressure principals to improve the quality of education. In effect, the test would increase the control of ONPEC over the performance of teachers in schools. The test would be a form of indirect supervision to insure compliance with objectives. (See page **102**).

Each year ONPEC hosted a meeting of all provincial education directors. The directors were presented with information comparing the performance of schools by province. ONPEC presented them with mean scores, standard deviations, current ranking for the year, and ranking in terms of amount of improvement from the previous year.

The directors from the provinces with highest average scores, and those with greatest gains, were asked to make presentations explaining their strategies. Directors from the provinces ranked in the bottom third had private meetings with ONPEC officials. These directors were asked to explain reasons for the low performance, and plans for improvement.

The meetings were reported to make the provincial directors "very nervous." The directors were embarrassed by having been singled out, and left the meeting motivated to work on raising the average level of achievement in their province.

One strategy used by the provincial directors was to rank each of their districts on the test, and to meet with the heads of the district offices to review results, much as ONPEC had done at the national level. Districts then began their own testing systems, and ranked schools and individual teachers according to average student performance.

By 1988 a common practice was for district officers to grant double promotions to school clusters with high rankings, and for principals to recommend promotions for teachers with high average scores.

The policy had immediate effects on test results. Average test scores rose from 49.08 in 1984 to 56.84 in 1985 in Thai (national language), and from 33.11 to 36.52 in mathematics. Gains were less in Thai, but much larger in mathematics in 1986. Gains were also recorded in the subjects titled "Life Experience" and "Work–Oriented." Small gains were reported in "Character Development".

It is important to note that this program was accompanied by an in–service training program for teachers, and another for principals. Both were evaluated as successful (see page **226**).

Source: Wheeler, Raudenbush and Pasigna (1989).

→ For a critique of the use of achievement tests see page **228**.

→ For definitions of "quality" see page **241**.

from pages 4, 151, 155, 157, 169, 202, 205, 206, 207, 227

Dangers in the Use of Standardized Achievement Tests

The main arguments for the use of standardized achievement tests are that tests provide an objective standard by which parents, teachers, and managers of the education system, can measure progress.

1. Parents can tell whether their children are learning.

2. Teachers can assess the effectiveness of their teaching practices.

3. Managers and planners can, over time, evaluate the impact of different policies.

Although there is relatively little research on the impact of achievement tests on education in developing countries (for one example, see page 227), **there is an abundance of research on the impact of testing in the United States and other early–industrialized countries.**

Some research says the impact is negative. The argument is not that all testing is bad, but that **the use of achievement tests alone to make critical decisions about students, teachers and schools** *reduces* **the quality of education.**

Testing has been on the increase in the United States at least during the past 20 years. A number of states have required local districts to apply standardized achievement tests and to report their results. Test results have been used to evaluate students, and schools and school districts. This policy has had effects on instructional practices, curriculum, and students.

1. *Impact on instructional practices.* There is no doubt that the use of a standardized test to evaluate student (and teacher) performance has an impact on what takes place in schools. Parents, eager that their children succeed, pressure teachers to cover the material covered in the test. Teachers, concerned about their own evaluation, give students practice using the same kinds of questions used in the test.

Most standardized tests rely on multiple choice questions, as these are more easily scored. When teachers teach students how to answer multiple choice questions, they spend less time on activities that develop higher order thinking skills. These activities such as carrying out experiments, cooperative learning, free compositions, critical discussions, and interviews in the community permit students to go beyond the simple facts presented in books and lectures, as well as on multiple choice tests.

Research has shown that with proper coaching individual scores on achievement tests can be raised significantly. The most effective coaching teaches students how to identify the correct answer by attention to format, rather than by learning the content, or by learning how to think about the question posed.

The performance of American students on multiple choice tests of basic skills has on average improved since 1970. At the same time, however, scores in higher order thinking, in almost every subject area, have been declining. Research also has shown that these higher order thinking skills begin to develop in the primary school years. Emphasis on drill and practice, as opposed to thinking and problem solving, limit students' acquisition of these skills. It is important to note that the most successful (often private) primary schools, emphasize thinking and learning skills over drill and practice.

2. *Impact on Curriculum.* A number of studies have shown that the use of tests with important consequences (for students, teachers) leads to *reduced* content in the curriculum. In the primary grades, use of achievement tests has meant not only less time spent on "luxury" subjects such as art or citizenship, but also less time on science and social studies. More attention is given instead to the "basics," reading and mathematics.

3. *Impact on Students.* Mistakes are made when a test with less than perfect reliability is used to make decisions about the future of individual students. Some students are promoted who should not be. More seriously, some students are failed who deserve to be promoted.

In the United States, tests are often used in early grades to assign students to "tracks" or "streams" according to their supposed ability to learn. The argument is made that teachers do better in more homogeneous classes (for example see page **126**). What in fact happens is that teachers set lower standards, which leads to lower student achievement (see pages **36** and **104**). Studies of tracking show that students in the "slow" tracks are limited to rote–oriented teaching, and receive less of the school's physical and human resources than students in the "faster" tracks. The net effect is to insure that students identified by the test as having low learning ability learn less.

Tests are sometimes used to assess *minimum competencies*, "gates" through which students must pass. Student failure and repetition (for any reason) is likely to *further depress* learning, by its effect on students' motivation (see page **128**). Even the best achievement tests are selective in their content, presenting situations, concepts, and words more familiar to some social groups than others. Research shows that tests often are biased against members of ethnic and linguistic minorities, and girls.

Based on Shann (1991).

For additional information see *Phi Delta Kappan*, 73(3), November 1991.

from pages 19, 45, 71, 167

The Importance of School Maintenance

Maintenance refers to actions to repair and restore to original functioning condition buildings, equipment, materials. **Proper maintenance of buildings and equipment prolongs their useful life, avoids premature replacement and thus reduces the costs of construction.** Some research suggests that the physical condition of the school affects levels of student learning. Whether or not this is true in all circumstances (see page **18**), there is evidence that the condition of buildings and equipment affects the morale of teachers (see page **78**).

The preventive care and repair of facilities is one of those issues in which the proper response is not always the most obvious. Managers faced with limited resources may defer maintenance until funds are available. New buildings may be constructed instead of repairing those that are old. But cost analysis shows that **it is more expensive to respond to emergencies than to do preventive maintenance**, and that routine maintenance can reduce the requirements of new construction.

Problems and Solutions

Most managers in education have no training in how to tell when maintenance is required or in how to set up a maintenance plan. Some countries have developed special departments dedicated solely to issues of maintenance. This is most appropriate in large systems. Small systems with relatively few facilities might rely on private contractors to provide maintenance services. For an example from Maldives see Luthfi and Zubair (1986).

Another approach has been to make local districts or communities responsible for the maintenance of facilities. Community involvement in facilities maintenance is recommended because it promotes more careful and responsible use (Almeida, 1988).

In Paraguay the Ministry of Education built schools in communities that promised to maintain them in good condition. A follow up evaluation after six years found that buildings were still in good condition, with maintenance provided by the communities.

"Through direct contributions, fees, school canteens and parties, teachers, parents and others have not only maintained but have improved the schools left in their stewardship." (Nicholson, 1983, p. 14)

The Maldives Community Schools Project made communities responsible for construction of their own schools. These schools were designed to make use of traditional types of spaces and indigenous building materials. The communities' commitment to their buildings insured their maintenance of them (Luthfi and Zubair, 1986).

In some areas of the Sudan, parents' council take on the responsibility of school maintenance. Fees or donations are levied on parents of students. Fund raising also includes sale of agricultural products grown on donated lands (Lyons, 1981).

Community–based maintenance of schools can be part of reforms to transfer some aspects of governance to local districts or communities.

→ See page **54**.

230

from page 133

What to Do When There are not Enough Students

In some countries or regions the ratio of students to teacher, or students per classroom is below the national standard because:

1. population density is low;

2. population has declined because of migration; or

3. enrollments have declined because of declining birth rates and aging of the population.

In these circumstances, what can be done to provide full educational services, and to maintain quality?

Policy Option 1. Admit Students Every Other or Third Year

The opportunity to complete all six grades (in a six–year primary cycle) is generated by admitting new classes every other or every third year. If students are admitted every other year, teachers work with grade 1, 3, or 5 in the first year, and grade 2, 4, or 6 in the second year. In the third year the process is repeated. In a *triennial* system, the first year offers grades 1 and 4, the second year grades 2 and 5, and the third year grades 3 and 6. Other combinations are possible.

This policy requires teachers to stay with the same group of students for one or more years, and to be able to shift from teaching grade 1, for example, to grade 2 the following year.

Policy Option 2. Set up a Network of Schools

This policy generates access to all six grades by locating lower grades in some schools, and higher grades in others. The schools with the lower primary grades are located in the least accessible areas, so that small children do not have far to travel to school. These schools "feed" children who have completed the lower grades to schools with the higher grades. These schools may be located in the center of several small schools.

The policy is similar to the **cluster school** approach (see page **223**). The success of this policy depends on the quality of school administration (see page **140**) and on sufficient resources to permit communication between teachers in the various schools in the network. Parents often do not want to send children away from their communities.

Policy Option 3. Use Multigrade Teaching

Schools with small student populations can achieve efficiency in the use of resources, and offer all grades of instruction, by combining students at different levels in a single classroom. Because several grades of students are taught by a single teacher, this is called a *multigrade* classroom.

The major requirements for an effective multigrade classroom are found on page **208**. Examples of application are found on page **199**.

Details of how to organize and operate a multigrade school are found in Thomas and Shaw (1992).

from page 146, 151

Latin American Experiences with Decentralization

Decentralization of education from national control was begun in Argentina in 1976; Mexico in 1978; Chile in 1981; and Colombia in 1986. In none of the countries is the process complete. And in none of the countries is there a thorough evaluation of the experience. We can, however, learn something from these attempts to shift control over education.

Each country kept some responsibilities at the central level, and shifted others downward in the system. The government units to which responsibilities were transferred varied. In Argentina, Colombia, and Mexico, responsibility passed to state (province) governments. In Chile, responsibilities were given to 325 municipalities. Table 22 shows some of the responsibilities and how they were affected.

Table 22

Distribution of Some Responsibilities for Education Following Implementation of Decentralization

Responsibility	Argentina	Chile	Colombia	Mexico
Resource allocation	D	C	C	C
School calendar	C	C	C	C
Curriculum design	C	C	C	C
Teacher accreditation	C	C	C	C
Hiring of teachers	D	D	D	D
In–service training	D	D	D	D
Teacher salary schedule	D	D	C	C
Data collection	D	D	C	D
School construction	D	D	D	D

C= Centralized   D= Decentralized

Source: Prawda (1992).

Implementation of decentralization has been completed in most but not all of the governmental units involved. In each country some of the local governmental units were either unwilling to take on the responsibilities assigned to them, or were not competent to take them on. Resistance to decentralization in Colombia, for example, came from wealthy and well–organized departments that felt they had little to gain by taking on the responsibility of the central government. In Chile some municipal governments lacked the skills necessary to assume responsibility for running schools.

Results

Argentina was successful in getting provincial governments to assume the financial burden for primary education. Total spending on education as a percentage of GNP increased from 3.89 to 4.91 percent. This was not true in the other countries. Central government's share of spending on primary education actually increased in Mexico. Chile was successful in reducing government spending on higher education (shifting the burden to the private sector) and increasing spending on primary education. The decentralization reform had little impact on patterns of finance in Colombia.

Evidence that decentralization contributed to improved efficiency is ambiguous. Internal efficiency (repetition, drop out, and completion rates) did improve after decentralization. But these rates also improved in other countries in the region that did not decentralize. Student–teacher ratios remained essentially the same in both decentralizing and non–decentralizing countries.

The impact of decentralization on student learning has been assessed only in Chile. Scores on grade 8 achievement tests administered between 1982 and 1984 were compared with scores on a updated version of the test administered in 1988 and 1989. Scores in 1989 were lower than scores in 1982, for Spanish and mathematics. In addition, the gap between high–scoring and low–scoring schools widened.

If the social class of students is taken into account, the most effective schools (in terms of student achievement) are the subsidized private schools. Taking social class into account, there is no difference in test scores between the fee–charging private and public schools.

The subsidized private schools have been particularly effective in low income neighborhoods. These private schools organize drum and bugle bands, require students to wear uniforms, assign more homework, involve parents in fund–raising. It is likely that families with high educational aspirations for their children prefer these private schools to less–disciplined public schools. There is no evidence that the quality of teaching is better in the subsidized private schools.

Summary

Decentralization of basic education can be achieved, but full implementation may take a number of years. Obstacles to implementation include: resistance from government units that feel they may lose from the shift of authority and/or resources; lack of competence by local governments to manage responsibilities; lack of consensus with regard to objectives to be achieved through decentralization.

Decentralization does not necessarily lead to increased local spending on education. In addition to transferring responsibility for finance to local units, the central government has to give these units the capacity to mobilize resources.

Decentralization does appear to improve internal efficiency, in terms of repetition, promotion and completion rates. On the other hand, there is as yet no evidence that local control of schools improves quality of teachers or levels of learning overall. Improved quality depends on increased participation by teachers in the design and implementation of innovative programs.

Decentralization requires that the central ministry carry out continuous monitoring of local units, in order to correct problems of incompetence and inequity. In effect, the central ministry has to become more informed about local schools than it is at present.

Based on Prawda (1992).

➔ For more on centralization and finance see page **148**.

from pages 143, 145

Improving Administration at the Local Level

There is a strong relationship between effective schools and the role of the school administrator or manager. Research says that effective school administrators are instructional or curriculum *leaders*; student–centered, persistent, aggressive; and, that they initiate action for change (Leithwood, 1989).

The following is a partial list of policies to develop and maintain effective school administrators or managers.

1. Identify how schools should be improved, internally and in terms of school–community relationships. Assess the relative importance of each problem in terms of the capabilities of the education system and its personnel.

2. Involve district officials and school administrators in efforts to prepare, design, plan, and execute programs to accomplish school improvement.

3. Create policies for identification, recruitment, and career movement of school administrators.

4. Establish programs for careers in school administration. These programs should include general competence in fields not covered by academic courses; contact between administrative trainees and active school administrators; and, opportunities for supervised practice as school administrators or managers.

5. Create programs to support and guide newly appointed school administrators or managers. One suggestion would be to pair new administrators with more experienced colleagues (mentors).

6. Specify the general direction and standards for categorizing school administration or management positions. Develop guidelines for duties and responsibilities.

7. Develop methods to assess administrators' or managers' performance of professional duties.

8. Provide opportunities for school administrators to familiarize themselves with and analyze far–reaching social questions.

9. Develop external support for such activities as the recruitment and selection of school administrators or managers; the development and/or improvement of pre–service and in–service training; the selection of models for self–assessment, etc. Such support may come from universities, consultants, international organizations, professional organizations, etc.

Based on Stego (1987).

➜ See page **226** for an example.

234

from page 137

Evaluating and Reporting about School Programs

Education authorities, policy makers, district and school administrators, and managers often have to evaluate school programs and prepare reports on their findings. Sometimes specific data are misused to make incorrect statements about the state of education systems. Sometimes the reports do not communicate effectively the accomplishments of the system. This may weaken public support for education. It may decrease parents' confidence in the importance of education for their children.

What can educators and policy makers do to prepare effective reports about the education system? The following profile offers a format that might be useful when evaluating and reporting about school programs.

Program Description. Include here a description of the program. The evaluation may have already taken place or you may be preparing for an upcoming evaluation process.

If you are writing about a particular school or school district, include information about the students, their families, and the community. Include information about any other important variables in your education system.

Program Objectives. Include in this section objectives for knowledge, skills, attitudes, understandings, and appreciations. State the objectives in terms of expected student performance.

Describe the criteria against which the program will be evaluated. Explain how students, teachers, parents, administrators, and policy makers will know that the objectives have been attained.

Program Content. In this section describe information such as the concepts, knowledge, curricula, etc. that the students have already learned or that they will be learning. A description of the program content should be limited to this particular program and its objectives.

Program Processes. What are the processes that students will learn? Some examples are classifying, deciding, solving, performing, and creating. What are the attitudes and values that students will acquire? These might be respect, fairness, honesty, sense of humor, cooperation.

Program Evaluation. You may decide not to evaluate all the objectives of the program. However, once you have chosen the objectives to be evaluated, you should decide how they will be evaluated and when the evaluation will occur.

After you establish what is to be evaluated, you must decide who will be evaluated. In most cases you will be considering student performance, but the objectives might require evaluations of parents or even teachers as part of the evaluation design.

Evaluation Package. Prepare an outline that includes the objectives, which factors will be evaluated for each objective, and the instrument(s) (achievement tests, checklists, etc.) that will be used in evaluating the factors.

Data Analysis. Before you prepare this portion of the report, you should have examined the data with various constituencies. These can include teachers, administrators, supervisors, etc. Your discussions will center around the meaning of the data, the conclusions you can draw, the likely recommendations, any alternatives, factors to be discussed, and so on.

When it is completed, this section of your report will present the data in summary form.

Program Report. What can be included in a public report? In addition to a brief description, the objectives, and evaluation procedures, include a summary of the results and what they

235

mean. Include any concerns or cautions that should be considered when interpreting the data.

The report should be concise. Present data using diagrams and charts. You will probably want to hold meetings to discuss the report with groups most directly affected by it, such as parents, teachers, community groups, etc.

Agenda for the meetings should include discussion of the report, alternative programs that might be considered and the impact on personnel, finances, and resources.

Based on DeRoche, 1987.

→ To read about management information systems, go to page **202**.

→ To read about curriculum evaluation, go to page **237**.

→ To read about standardized achievement tests, go to page **227**.

from pages 25, 35, 121, 153, 235

A Matrix for Curriculum Evaluation

To use this matrix, fill in the blanks with a curriculum focus or component. You might choose, for example, *problem solving in primary math*. You would then write "problem solving in primary math" in the blanks and answer the questions.

The answers to the matrix questions will aid you in evaluating the existing curriculum as well as provide an agenda for curriculum revision/reform.

Table 23
A Matrix for Curriculum Evaluation

	Planning	**Implementation**	**Outcomes**
Design	What are the needs for _____ in today's society?	What are today's priorities for _____ in society, business, communication, and in schools?	What expression of _____ can be found in the education system's goals, philosophy, and written curriculum?
Instructional Means	What lessons, activities, and methods enhance the teaching of _____ ?	What classroom communication, environment, and sequence of events are required to facilitate _____ ?	How do we know that the teaching for _____ has been successful?
Resources	What curricular material, media, facilities, teachers and resources are needed to facilitate the teaching of _____ ?	By what criteria have we acquired the best resources to facilitate _____ ?	Are these resources used and do they facilitate the teaching and learning of _____ ?
Staff Development	What type of preparation will the teachers and staff need to teach or facilitate _____ ?	Is the in–service consistent with the actual strategies and process that the teacher will use in the classroom?	What _____ teaching strategies were actually developed in the teachers through the in–service staff development?
Learner	How does the learner recognize and respond to situation which demands a _____ response?	What are the optimum conditions and personal style of the learner engaged in _____ ?	In what situations can our learners apply _____ ?

Based on Hill (1989).

from page 121

Textbook Evaluation: Characteristics and Properties of Good Textbooks

The check list that follows may be helpful in evaluating textbooks.

1. The textbook contributes to helping teachers and students attain curriculum goals.

2. The text has a recent copyright date (within five years).

3. The content of the text:
   - covers all or most of the course to be taught;
   - is up–to–date;
   - accurately portrays minority groups;
   - accurately reflects ethnic cultures and life styles;
   - is free of racist and sexist connotations;
   - presents controversial issues objectively, and accurately reflects representative points of view; and
   - provides material or examples of how the concepts or contents are correlated with other subjects.

4. Concepts, generalizations, and relationships are clearly and accurately presented. They are developed from concrete to abstract when and where it is appropriate.

5. Students find the textbook interesting to read.

6. Most students find the textbook easy to read.

7. The textbook highlights new and difficult words.

8. Graphs and tables are clearly illustrated and easy to read.

9. Diagrams and scale drawings are clearly illustrated and easy to read.

10. The text has:
    - a table of contents;
    - an index;
    - main ideas at the beginning of each chapter or subsection;
    - directions that are clear and complete;
    - summaries appropriately placed throughout the chapter; and
    - chapter summaries and reviews of the concepts, generalizations, and relationships.

11. New ideas are introduced through motivating social or personal situations or issues.

12. Quotations or other authoritative sources are used to highlight concepts or content.

13. The textbook contains recommended readings for students.

14. End-of-the-chapter activities:
    - are interesting and stimulating;
    - require students to apply concepts or contents;
    - emphasize creative problem solving;
    - provide for immediate practice of a skill;
    - and include several forms of questions.

15. The textbook is attractive, colorful, well–designed with a type–size that is easy for students to read.

16. The textbook binding and page–paper is strong enough to withstand student use over a number of years.

Based on DeRoche (1987).

from page 44

Towards Democratic Planning

Although the planning of education can be done by isolated individuals, the intended results are always social or collective: planners use their knowledge to devise strategies to affect the actions of others. This separation of knowledge and action is problematic. How can the planner gain an objective knowledge of the subjectivity that conditions the actor? In other words, if I as planner want to affect your behavior, how can I know why you do what you do?

One way to minimize this problem is to reduce the size of the unit for which planning is carried out, and to increase participation in the planning process. The form of decentralization called school–based management/shared decision making (Hanson, 1990) is one example; teachers participate in planning the activities of the school in which they work, they are both planners and actors.

This type of planning has been called transactive (Friedmann, 1987; Warwick, 1980) or interactive (Adams, 1988), to suggest that planning is based on the dialectics between plan and reality (or action and consequence) and between the persons attempting to shape their collective future.

There is another kind of educational planning, which until recently dominated the field. This kind locates the planner (as individual or group) outside the reality which is the object of planning, and applies the methods of objective science in an effort to overcome problems of subjectivity. The term "rational" has been preempted to apply to this kind of planning, an unfortunate choice that has caused much confusion because all planning requires the use of reason and information to choose among alternative methods to achieve goals.

The major difference between the two types of planning (and their many variants) is not their degree of rationality (or systematic use of information in the choice among alternatives for future action), but their assumption about the extent to which the necessary information exists **prior** to the planning process.

The rationalist approach focuses on *plan–making*. If objectives are fixed, alternative policies already identified, and the environment stable, then planning can be effective as a technical exercise in which manipulation of data is sufficient for discovery of the alternative with the most likelihood of achieving that objective.

An alternative to plan–making is to understand the process of planning as the construction of possibilities for the future. Not all possibilities can be seen in advance because some will depend on the actions of others who also engage in planning. From this perspective successful planning requires the generation of consensus about both goals or objectives and means.

This approach to planning is overtly political. It includes the distribution of power as a central variable to be modified by the process of planning. In one variant, called *policy dialogue* by the international assistance agencies, conventional definitions of sovereignty or domain of authority are set aside and foreign lenders and donors insist that certain conditions be met by the government seeking funding.

There has been no systematic treatment of the practice of policy dialogue, or its effects on the content and effectiveness of educational plans. It will be important to distinguish between instances of genuine dialogue, in which outcomes cannot be predicted from either set of planners' objectives, to instances of political manipulation in which the powerful impose their plans based on "rational" planning.

Policy dialogue as a form of planning is similar to the *strategic planning* carried out by private sector organizations in a competitive environment. An effective planning approach in this situation is fundamentally inductive rather than "rational deductive." The model is one of political decision–making. Strategy is required to guide actions beyond the foreseeable future (Bryson, 1988).

The concept of strategic planning has also been adopted for public education in the United States, but with an important change (McCune, 1986). Now emphasis is on the development of community–wide consensus about what the goals of the education system should be. The task is not to plan to beat out competitors in the market but rather to satisfy multiple client populations often with competing goals. Once again politics is explicit; goals and ideologies have to be made clear for groups to be able to communicate effectively with each other.

Strategic planning begins with definition of the mission (long–term objective) of the organization. The planner acts to collate and synthesize the expressions of the various groups within the organization. At each stage, from definition of performance standards to specification of budgets, the planner both suggests alternatives and attempts to synthesize suggestions made by the participants. In the process, mission and short–run objectives may be rewritten, as constituent groups become dissatisfied with what they are likely to achieve. The dominant method in these processes is communication rather than analysis.

The "rational" approach to planning has been described as a "search through a solution space of alternatives," while the interactive approach is one that treats "designing as making sense together" (Forester, 1989, p. 121).

In strategic planning, the important alternatives do not yet exist when planning starts, therefore, they cannot be discovered; instead they are brought into existence, they are constructed. Who participates in the construction process is critical to the success of the planning exercise; political criteria are primary and overt.

Tending toward the moribund at the beginning of the 1980s, educational planning is regaining attention as a means for working through political differences and designing the future. Although educational planning as a centrally controlled activity carried out by a handful of highly trained experts may never regain the importance it was given in the 1950s and 1960s, planning is likely to proliferate in the future.

The major impetus to the "rebirth" of planning has been, ironically, democracy — once considered threatened by the power of centralized and "rational" planning because it excluded the voice of the people. The democratic revolution that will matter is not just the movement to replace self-appointed princes with elected representatives, but especially that which results in more control over representatives in the hands of citizenry. Decentralization, understood as moving the locus of control of education from larger toward smaller civic units, requires more rather than less planning. Decentralization requires planning in and by local units, and a new role for central planning in the promotion of equity and system–wide efficiency.

➜ See page **146** for more about decentralization.

from pages 10, 11, 170, 225, 227

Definitions of the Concept of Quality

The quality of something is an attribute assigned by humans. The judgment is most reliably made when there are pre-established criteria about what constitute high or low quality, and what exactly will be judged.

The assessment of the quality of education systems, schools, and teachers has often been controversial because of a failure to specify not only the criteria for quality, but also what would be judged. For example, one person might focus on the methods a particular teacher uses for instruction, while another judges the teacher's quality in terms of what is taught, a third focuses on the instructional materials used, and a fourth looks only at how much students learn.

Until the early 1960s, almost all research on education used the term "quality" to refer only to the content, materials and methods used in teaching. When researchers evaluated teachers, they seldom, if ever, measured amount of student learning as an indicator of quality.

In recent years, attention has shifted from an assessment of the inputs and process of teaching, to measurement of how much learning has taken place. There are several reasons for this shift. First, we now have much better methods for assessing student learning than before. Second, education systems have been recognized as important elements in the development of a society, and their management has been taken over by persons not necessarily trained as teachers. Third, there has been a shift in perspective from management by pre-determined rules, to management in order to reach objectives.

Here are five definitions of education quality currently in use:

1. *The quality of inputs.* Refers to whether resources (materials, personnel, physical facilities, etc.) meet pre-established standards.

2. *The quality of process.* Includes not only what teachers do in classrooms, but also management practices, school traditions, school climate.

3. *Quality as outputs.* As a result of inputs and process, students are transformed in certain ways. We call this learning. We can assess the quality of this learning by comparing it with standards we have established.

4. *Quality as outcomes.* The evaluation and valuation of graduates of an education system, by themselves, parents, employers, society in general, can produce outcomes such as improved social standing, employment, higher incomes. These outcomes are not direct products of the education system, but many people argue that education is not relevant unless it affects their economic, political, social, and spiritual lives.

5. *The amount of value added.* A simple assessment of how much a student knows, or how much a graduate earns, does not tell us whether the education system actually transformed the student. What seems like a "good" school could merely be one that managed to enroll bright students (who learn outside of school), but didn't teach them anything. At the end of the process, the students may have increased knowledge, but not because of the school. The highly paid graduates of a prestigious institution may not know anymore than graduates of a lesser institution, but receive higher wages because of the reputation of their school, not its ability to transform them.

When we assess value added, we are asking whether the current state of the individual (in terms of knowledge, values, behavior) can in any way be attributed to the school attended. If so, then we can say that the school "added some value." The state-of-the-art in assessment of education systems, schools, and teachers is not yet far enough advanced to assess how much value has been added. We are still in the stage of assessing outputs and outcomes.

continued on page 242

241

Standards for Quality

Until now, quality has been defined situationally and subjectively. This has made it difficult for planners and policy makers to compare the effectiveness of alternative programs. If "quality" is what anyone wants it to be, it is not a very useful concept.

There have been at least two kinds of efforts to rescue the concept of "quality." One approach has focussed on identifying education systems or schools that people are willing to agree are of high "quality," whatever is meant by the term. Then the characteristics of that system or school have been carefully described. For example, if you choose this alternative, you can read what some people have said are the characteristics of an "effective" school (meaning a school with high value added).

A second approach has attempted to develop a consensus about the minimal requirements that every system or school should meet. One version of this approach has produced a Fundamental Quality Level list, which includes indicators of inputs, process, and outputs against which schools can be compared (Horn, 1992).

The major difficulty with both approaches is that they require agreement about a complex process that varies considerably according to characteristics of students and teachers, that changes over time based on its own internal dynamic and external events, and that pursues multiple, sometimes conflicting, goals. As a consequence, these attempts to generate consensus may have generated even more contention and confusion.

At present, the term quality continues to be used widely, and with wildly different meanings.

For more information, see Adams (1993), Organization for Economic Cooperation and Development (1989), and Richardson and Skinner (1991).

from pages 11, 110

Stages of Improvement in Quality

Read the following stages and determine which one most closely describes the situation in your country. At the end of each stage, there are suggestions for change(s) which can help your education system advance towards the next stage(s) of development.

It should be noted that an attempt to introduce elements of more developed stages into less developed ones results in mismatches that prevent successful implementation of innovation or change. For example, providing untrained teachers from stage one with instructional materials that were designed to be used by well–educated teachers from stage four will probably result, at best, in inadequate use of those materials.

Table 24
Stages of Improvement in Quality

Stage One: *Unskilled*

Teachers:	Untrained, little mastery of subject content or teaching techniques, poorly motivated
Curriculum:	Emphasis on basics, low standards, subject content is limited, high dropout rates
Textbooks and Other Materials:	One textbook/class used by teacher, few or no other materials
Teaching Techniques:	Recitation, rote learning, memorization, students copy from chalkboard
Supervision:	Limited to control and compliance with regulations
Teacher Reaction to Innovation:	Ignorance, confusion, doesn't apply innovations/changes
Possible change(s):	Provide structured teachers' guides, textbooks and minimal instructional materials Provide teacher training in subject matter and basic teaching techniques Provide teachers with opportunities to understand need for improvement

Stage Two: *Mechanical*

Teachers:	Lower secondary education, little professional training, some in–service training
Curriculum:	Highly structured, standards are set by examinations, high rate of repetition
Textbooks:	One or two textbooks for each student in main subjects
Teaching Techniques:	Memorization, curriculum strictly followed, short–term activities/objectives
Supervision:	Emphasizes compliance and standardized use of curriculum and teaching materials
Teacher Reaction to Innovation:	Uncertain, innovations are adapted to personal/professional capacity/motivation
Possible change(s):	Broaden the curriculum Increase training in subject area mastery and introduce simple teaching techniques Teachers' guides and textbooks set standards that are enforced by exams Increase teacher confidence through training and school–level support

243

Table 24 continued on page 244

Stage Three: *Routine*

Teachers:	Secondary education with training, subject area mastery, some contact with colleagues
Curriculum:	Broader goals, opportunities for adaptation/experimentation exist, concern with prevention of failure
Textbooks and Materials:	Several textbooks available, small school library, selective use of textbooks
Teaching Techniques:	Increasing attempts to introduce "learning by doing," more goal–oriented planning, tracking
Supervision:	More frequent supervision and in–service emphasizing teaching
Teacher Reaction to Innovation:	Will try to adapt innovation to make classroom management easier
Possible change(s):	Focus on teaching for understanding Promote flexibility and diversity in curriculum Develop broader objectives to include emotional/creative development of students Encourage professional exchange between teachers

Stage Four: *Professional*

Teachers:	Well–educated/trained, read professional publications, interested in improving student performance
Curriculum:	Emphasizes meaning/understanding, variety in content and methods, considerable attention to emotional and creative development of students
Textbooks and Materials:	Broad availability of textbooks, supplementary materials, reference books, other instructional materials, well–supplied school library
Teaching Techniques:	Ability to investigate new ideas, longer–term planning to adapt curriculum/materials to student needs, individualized and group instruction
Supervision:	Training emphasizes professional skills development, principal is source of pedagogical support
Teacher Reaction to Innovation:	Focus on student needs, willing to try/test alternative approaches, able to master and adapt innovations to particular group of students
Possible change(s):	Innovation is a permanent feature Teachers behave and perceive themselves as professionals

Verspoor (1989) adapted from Beeby (1966, 1986).

Even Numbered Pages Index

246

Index of Tables

Index of Figures

Index of Key Topics

Index of Authors

References

Abbas, R. (1987) "Training of primary school teachers at Allama Iqbal Open University." *Pakistan Journal of Distance Education* 4(1), 41–50.

Adams, Don (1988) "Extending the educational planning discourse: Conceptual and paradigmatic explorations." *Comparative Education Review* 32(4), 400–415.

Adams, Don (1993) *Defining Educational Quality*. Arlington, VA: Institute for International Research, IEQ Publication No. 1.

Ahlawat, Kapur (1991) *Analysis of School Size and Grade Structure in the Public Schools of Jordan: Policy implications*. Amman: National Center for Educational Research and Development, Publication Series No. 7.

Airasian, Peter (1991) *Classroom Assessment*. New York: McGraw Hill.

Alabi, Rufus O. (1978) "Training teachers for school science in Nigeria." *Prospects*, 8(1).

Alemna, A. A. (1983) "The development of school libraries in Ghana." *International Library Review* 15, 217–223.

Almeida, Rodolfo (1988) *Handbook for Educational Buildings Planning*. Paris: UNESCO, Educational Building and Equipment # 9.

Anderson, L. and Postlethwaite, N. (1989) "What IEA studies say about teachers and teaching." In A.C. Purves (ed.) *International Comparisons and Educational Reform*, Washington, D.C.: Association for Supervision and Curriculum Development.

Anderson, Mary B. (1988) *Improving Access to Schooling in the Third World: An Overview*. Cambridge, MA: Harvard Institute for International Development, BRIDGES Research Report Series No. 1.

Anderson, Mary B., et al. (1989) *A Study on School–Community Relations in Sri Lanka*. Cambridge, MA: Harvard Institute for International Development, BRIDGES Casual Paper.

Andrews, John, and David Thomas (1986) *Effective Programs of Inservice Training for Teachers in Developing Countries: A study of expert opinion*. Vancouver: University of British Columbia.

Anzalone, Steven (1988) *Using Instructional Hardware for Primary Education in Developing Countries; A review of the literature*. Cambridge: Harvard Institute for International Development, BRIDGES Casual Paper.

Apeji, E. Adeche (1990) "The development of school library services." *International Library Review* 22, 41–51.

Applegate, Jane H. (1987) "Teacher candidate selection: An overview." *Journal of Teacher Education* 38, 2–7.

Arancibia, Violeta (1987) *Manejo instruccional del profesor en la sala de clases*. Cambridge: Harvard Institute for International Development, BRIDGES Casual Paper.

Archibald, Doug A., and Fred M. Newmann (1988) *Beyond Standardized Testing: Assessing authentic academic achievement in the secondary school*. Reston, VA: National Association of Secondary School Principals.

Armitage, J. and others (1986) *School Quality and Achievement in Brazil*. Washington, D. C.: World Bank, Education and Training Department Discussion Paper EDT No. 25.

Aruna, Roy (1980) "Schools and communities: An experience in rural India." *International Review of Education* 36(3), 369–378.

Avalos, Beatrice (1986) "Teacher effectiveness: An old theme with new questions." Paper presented at seminar on Quality of Teaching in Lesser Developed Countries, International Movement Toward Educational Change, Bali, Indonesia.

Bach, Rebecca, Saad Godalla, Hind Abu Seoud Kattab, and John Gulick (1985) "Mothers' Influence on Daughters' Orientations toward Education: An Egyptian Case Study." *Comparative Education Review* 29(3), 375–384.

Bafoua, Justin (1983) *An Examination of Indiscipline in Secondary Schools in the Congo*. Nairobi: Kenya Institute of Education.

Baine, David (1988) *Handicapped Children in Developing Countries: Assessment, Curriculum and Instruction*. Edmonton, Canada: Alberta University.

Baker, Victoria J. (1988) "Schooling and disadvantage in Sri Lankan and other rural situations." *Comparative Education* 24(3), 377–388.

Beeby, Charles E.(1966) *The Quality of Education in Developing Countries*. Cambridge, MA: Harvard University Press.

Beeby, Charles E.(1986) "The Stages of Growth in Educational Systems." In Stephen P. Heynemann and Daphne Sienv White (eds.) *The Quality of Education and Economic Development*, pp. 37–44. A World Bank Symposium. Washington, D.C.: World Bank.

Bellew, Rosemary, and Elizabeth M. King (1991) *Promoting Girls' and Women's Education: Lessons from the Past*. Washington, D.C.: World Bank, Policy, Research and External Affairs PRE Working Paper, WPS 715.

Benavot, A., and D. Kamens (1989) *The curricular content of primary education in developing countries*. Washington, D.C.: World Bank, Staff Working Paper No. 237.

Bequele, Assefa, and Jo Boyden (eds.) (1988) *Combating Child Labour*. Genevia: International Labour Office.

Bickel, W. E. (1990) "The effective schools literature: Implications for research and practice." In *Handbook of School Psychology*. New York: Wiley & Sons.

Bray, Mark (1987) *Are Small Schools the Answer? Cost Effective Strategies for Rural School Provision*. London: The Commonwealth Secretariat.

Bray, Mark (1987) *School Clusters in the Third World: Making Them Work*. Paris: UNESCO-UNICEF Cooperative Programme.

Bray, Mark, (1989) *Multiple-Shift Schooling: Design and operation for cost-effectiveness*. London: The Commonwealth Secretariat.

Bray, Mark, and Kevin Lillis (1988) *Community Financing of Education: Issues and policy implications in less developed countries*. London: Commonwealth Secretariat, Pergamon Press.

British Council (1987) *International Guide to Qualifications in Education*, Second Edition London: Mansell Publishing, Ltd.

Broadfoot, Patricia, Roger Murphy, and Harry Torrance (eds.) (1990) *Changing Education Assessment: International perspectives and trends*. London: Routledge.

Bryson, John M. (1988) *Strategic Planning for Public and Nonprofit Organizations*. San Francisco: Jossey-Bass.

Chakravarty, B. (1989) *Education and Child Labour*. Allahabad, India: Chugh Publications.

Chapman, D. W. (1983) "Career satisfaction of teachers." *Educational Research Quarterly* 7, pp. 40–50.

Chapman, David W., and C. A. Carrier (eds.) (1990) *Improving Educational Quality: A Global Perspective*. Greenwich, CN: Westview Press.

Chapman, David W., and Lars O. Mahlck (eds.) (1993) *From Data to Action: Information systems in Educational Planning*. Paris: UNESCO: International Institute for Educational Planning, Pergamon Press.

Chapman, David W., and Conrad W. Snyder (1989) "Is teacher training associated with teachers' classroom behavior in the Third World?" Albany, NY: State University of New York at Albany, IEES Project, unpublished paper.

Chapman, David W., Conrad W. Snyder, Jr., and Shirley A. Burchfield (1991) *Teacher Incentives in the Third World*. Tallahassee, FL: Florida State University, Learning Systems Institute, IEES Project.

Chesterfield, Ray (1991) *Nicaragua Primary Education Subsector Assessment*. Washington, D.C.: Academy for Educational Development.

Chivore, B. (1988) "Factors determining the attractiveness of the teaching profession." *International Review of Education* 34(1), 59–77.

Coldevin, G., and S. Naidu (1989) "In-service teacher education at a distance: Trends in Third World development." *Open Learning* 9–15.

Coombs, Philip H., and Jacques Hallak (1987) *Cost Analysis in Education: a tool for policy and planning*. Washington, D.C.: Johns Hopkins University Press.

Cope J., C. Denning, and L. Ribeiro (1989) *Content Analysis of Reading and Mathematics Textbooks in Fifteen Developing Countries*. London: Book Development Council.

Corvalan, Graziella (1985) *Estado del Arte del Bilinguismo en America Latina*. Santiago, Chile: REDUC.

Crouch, Luis A., Jennifer E. Spratt, and Luis M. Cubeddu (1992) *Examining Social and Economic Impacts of Educational Investment and Participation in Developing Countries: The Educational Impacts Model (EIM) Approach*. Cambridge, MA: Harvard Institute for International Development, BRIDGES Research Report No. 12.

Csapo, Marg (1987) "Special education developments in Zambia." *International Journal of Educational Development* 7(2), 107–112.

Cuadra, Ernesto, Mary Anderson, and Frank Dall (1990) *Female Access to Basic Education: Trends, Policies and Strategies*. Cambridge, MA: Harvard Institute for International Development, BRIDGES Casual Paper.

Cummings, William K. (1986) *Low–cost Primary Education: Implementing an Innovation in Six Nations*. Ottawa: International Development Research Centre.

Cummings, William, and Abby Riddell (1992) *Alternative Policies for the Finance, Control and Delivery of Basic Education*. Cambridge: Harvard Institute for International Development, ABEL Project.

Cummings, William K., G. B. Gunardwardena, and James H. Williams (1992) *The Implementation of Management Reforms: The Case of Sri Lanka*. Cambridge, MA: Harvard Institute for International Development, BRIDGES Research Report Series No. 11.

David, Jane (1989) "Synthesis of research on school-based management." *Educational Leadership* May 255–292.

DeBevoise, Wynn (1984) "Synthesis of research on the principal as instructional leader." *Educational Leadership* February 14–20.

DeRoche, Edward F. (1987) *An Administrator's Guide for Evaluating Programs and Personnel: An Effective Schools Approach*. Boston: Allyn and Bacon, Inc.

Dobbing, John (1987) *Early Nutrition and Later Achievement*. London: Academic Press.

Dodds, Tony (1986) *Refugee Education: The Case for International Action*. Cambridge, UK: World University Services.

Dove, Linda (1986) *Teachers and teacher education in developing countries*. London: Croom Helm.

Dutcher, Nadine (1982) *The Use of First and Second Languages in Primary Education: Selected Case Studies*. Washington, D.C.: World Bank, Staff Working Paper No. 504.

Eisemon, Thomas, John Schwille and Robert Prouty (1989) "Empirical results and conventional wisdom: Strategies for improving primary school effectiveness in Burundi." Cambridge, MA: Harvard Institute for International Development, BRIDGES Casual Paper.

Eisemon, Thomas, Robert Prouty and John Schwille (1990) "Can Schooling Make a Better Farmer?" Cambridge: Harvard Institute for International Development, BRIDGES Casual Paper.

Ellwein, M. C., and G. V. Glass (1989) "Ending social promotion in Waterford: Appearances and reality." In Lorrie A. Shepard and Mary Lee Smith (eds.) *Flunking Grades: Research and policies on retention*. London: The Falmer Press. pp. 151–173.

Ezeomah, Chimah (1990) *Educating Nomads for Self Actualization and Development*. Geneva: International Bureau of Education.

Farrugia, C. (1986) "Career choice and source of occupational satisfaction and frustration among teachers in Malta." *Comparative Education*, 23(2) pp. 225–236.

Fielding, Glen D. (1989) "Improving curriculum and assessment through a school–university partnership." *NASSP Bulletin* 73(513).

Fisher, C., et al. (1980) "Teacher behavior, academic learning time and student achievement." in C. Denham and A. Lieberman (eds.) *Time to Learn*, Washington, D. C.: National Institute of Education.

Floro, Maria and Joyce M. Wolf (1990) *The Economic and Social Impacts of Girls' Primary Education in Developing Countries*. Washington, D.C.: Creative Associates.

Forester, John (1989) *Planning in the Face of Power*. Berkeley, CA: University of California Press.

Fraser, B., H. Walberg, W. Welch and J. Hattie (1987) "Syntheses of educational productivity research" *International Journal of Educational Research*, 11(2), pp. 147–252.

Friedman, Isaac (1991) "High and Low-Burnout Schools: School Culture Aspects of Teacher Burnout." *Journal of Education Research* 84(6) pp. 325–333.

Friedmann, John (1987) *Planning in the Public Domain: From Knowledge to Action*. Princeton, NJ: Princeton University Press.

Friend, Jamesine (1989) "Interactive radio instruction: Developing instructional methods." *British Journal of Educational Technology*, 20(2).

Friend, Jamesine, Barbara Searle and Patrick Suppes (1980) *Radio Mathematics in Nicaragua*. Palo Alto, CA: Stanford University.

Friend, Jamesine, and Frances Kemmerer (1985) "Strategies and costs for disseminating the Radio Language Arts Project throughout Kenya." in *Interactive Radio in Education.* Washington, D.C.: United States Agency for International Development and Institute for International Research, Communications Support Project.

Fuller, Bruce W. (1987) "What factors raise achievement in the Third World?" *Review of Educational Research* 57(3), 255–292.

Fuller, Bruce (1989) "Is primary school quality eroding in the Third World?" *Comparative Education Review* 30, pp. 491–507.

Gagne, R. M., and L. J. Briggs (1979) *Principles of Instructional Design.* New York: Holt, Rinehart & Winston.

Gardner, R. (1982) *Textbooks in Developing Countries* London: University of London, Institute of Education.

Georgiades, W., and H. Jones (1989) *A Review of Research on Headmaster and School Principalship in Developing Countries.* Washington, D. C.: World Bank, Background Paper PHREE/89/11.

Ghannam, Muhammad A. (1970) *Financing Education in the Arab States: a survey of recent trends and future prospects.* Paris: International Institute for Educational Planning.

Gickling, and Thompson (1985) "A Personal View of Curriculum-Based Assessment" in Joyce S. Choate, et al. *Assessing and Programming Basic Curricular Skills.* Boston: Allyn and Bacon.

Glass, G., L. Cahen, M. Smith, N. Filby (1982) *School Class Size: Research and Policy.* London: Sage Publications.

Gould, William T. S. (1978) *Guidelines for School Location Planning.* Washington, D.C.: World Bank, Staff Working Paper No. 308.

Gould, William T.S. (1978) *Guidelines for School Location Planning.* Washington, D.C.: World Bank, Staff Working Paper No. 308.

Greenland, Jeremy. (1983) *Inservice Education and Training of Primary School Teachers in Anglophone Africa.* Baden-Baden: Nomos Verlagsgesellschaft.

Grissom, James B., and Lorrie A. Shepard (1989) "Repeating and dropping out of school." in Lorrie A. Shepard and Mary Lee Smith (eds.) *Flunking Grades: Research and Policies on Retention.* London: The Falmer Press, pp. 151–173.

Guevara Niebla, Gilberto (1991) "Mexico: Un pais de reprobados?" *Nexos,* 163, pp. 33–44.

Gumbert, Edgar B. (ed.) (1990) *Fit to Teach: Teacher Education in International Perspective.* Atlanta: Georgia State University.

Guthrie, J., et al., (1976) *Impacts of Instructional Time in Reading.* Newark, DE: International Reading Association.

Haddad, Wadi (1978) *Educational Effects of Class Size.* Washington, D. C.: World Bank, Staff Working Paper No. 280.

Hallak, Jacques (1977) *Planning the Location of Schools: An Instrument of Educational Policy.* Paris: UNESCO, IIEP.

Hallak, Jacques (1989) "The future of education planning." *Prospects* 19(2), pp. 165–167.

Halpern, Robert (1986) "Effects of early childhood intervention on primary school progress in Latin America." *Comparative Education Review,* 30, 193–215.

Halpern, Robert, and Robert Myers (1985) *Effects of Early Childhood Intervention on Primary School Progress and Performance in the Developing Countries.* Ypsilanti, MI: High Scope Educational Research Foundation.

Hamel, J. P. (1977) *Educational Facilities Design: Educational Training Material.* Bangkok: UNESCO.

Hanson, E. Mark (1986) *Education Reform and Administrative Development: The Cases of Colombia and Venezuela.* Stanford, CA: Hoover Institution Press.

Hanson, E. Mark. (1990) "School-based management and educational reform in the United States and Spain." *Comparative Education Review* 34(4), 525–537

Hanssen, A., S. Kozlow and A. Olsen (1983) "RADECO: Radio–Based Primary Education in the Dominican Republic," *Development Communication Report.*

Heise–Baigorria, Cornelia (1991) *Language of Instruction and Achievement.* Cambridge, MA: Harvard Institute for International Development, Education Discussion Paper No. 392.

Herz, Barbara, K. Subbarao, Masooma Habib, and Laura Raney (1992) *Letting Girls Learn: Promising approaches in primary and secondary education.* Washington, D.C.: World Bank Discussion Paper No. 133.

Heyneman, Stephen P., Dean Jamison, and Xavier Montenegro (1984) "Textbooks in the Philippines: Evaluation of the pedagogical impact of a nationwide investment." *Educational Evaluation and Policy Analysis* 6(2), 139–150.

Heyneman, Stephen P., and William Loxley (1983). "The distribution of primary school quality within high- and low-income countries." *Comparative Education Review* 27, pp. 108–118.

Hill, John C. (1989) "A matrix for curriculum evaluation: The author's approach." *NASSP Bulletin* 73(516).

Hopkins, David (ed.) (1989) *Improving the Quality of Schooling: Lessons from the OECD International School Improvement Project.* London: The Falmer Press.

Horn, Robin (1992) *The Fundamental Quality Level Indicator System for Primary Schools.* Washington, D.C.: United States Agency for International Development, Bureau for Africa, draft memorandum.

Husen, Torsten, L. Saha and R. Noonan (1978) *Teacher Training and Student Achievement in Less Developed Countries.* Washington, D.C.: World Bank.

International Development Research Centre (1983) *Preventing School Failure: The Relationship between Preschool and Primary Education.* Ottawa.

International Institute for Educational Planning (1989) "Conditions in the teaching profession: a current problem." *IIEP Newsletter* VII (4), p. 1.

Jamison, Dean, and McAnany, N. (1978) *Radio for Education and Development.* Beverly Hills, CA: Sage Publications.

Jamison, Dean, Barabara Searle, K. Galda, and Stephen Heyneman (1981). "Improving elementary mathematics education in Nicaragua: An experimental study of the impact of textbooks and radio on achievement." *Journal of Educational Psychology* 73(4), pp. 556–567.

Jenkinson, F., and Chapman, D. W. (1990) "Job satisfaction of Jamaican elementary school teachers." *International Review of Education* 36, pp. 299–313.

Jones, Neville (1989) *School Management and Pupil Behavior.* London: The Falmer Press.

Joyce, Bruce, and B. Showers (1980) "Improving inservice training: Messages of the research." *Educational Leadership* February, 379–385.

Karim, Badri Musa A. (1991) "The emergence of libraries in the Sultanate of Oman." *International Library Review* 23, 229–236.

Keith, Sherry, and Robert H. Girling (1990) *Education: Management and Participation*. Boston: Allyn & Bacon.

Kemmerer, Frances (1990) "An Integrated Approach to Primary Education Incentives." in David W. Chapman and Carol A. Carrier (eds.) *Improving Educational Quality*. New York: Greenwood Press. pp.135–152.

Kemmerer, Frances N, and Sivasailam Thaigarajan (1989) *Teacher Incentive Systems: Final Report*, Tallahassee, FL: Florida State University, IEES Project.

Kenny, Lawrence W. (1982) "Economies of scale in schooling." *Economics of Education Review* 2(1), pp. 1–24.

King, Elizabeth (1990) *Educating Girls and Women: Investing in Development*. Washington, D.C.: World Bank.

Lasley, Thomas, and William Wayson (1982) "Characteristics of schools with good leadership." *Educational Leadership* 28–31.

Lee, D., et al., (1981) "Successful practices in high–poverty schools." In *The Study of the Sustaining Effects of Compensatory Education on Basic Skills*. Santa Monica, CA: System Development Corporation.

Leithwood, Keith (1989) *A Review of Research on the School Principalship*. Washington, D.C.: World Bank, Population and Human Resources Department.

Lembert, Marcella (1985) *The Impact of Mothers' Expectations and Attributions on Children's Primary School Dropout*. Stanford: Stanford University, Unpublished doctoral dissertation.

Levin, Henry M. (1992) "Effective schools in comparative focus." In Robert F. Arnovew, Philip G. Altbach and Gail P. Kelly (eds.) *Emergent Issues in Education: Comparative Perspectives*. Albany: State University of New York Press. pp. 229–248.

Levin, Henry M., and Marlaine E. Lockheed (eds.) (1991) *Effective Schools in Developing Countries*. Washington, D.C.: World Bank, PHREE Background Paper Series.

Levinger, Beryl (1989) *Nutrition, Health and Learning*. Newton, MA: Action Group for School Nutrition and Health, Educational Development Corporation, Technical Monograph No. 1.

Lewin, Keith M. (1988) "Perspectives on Planning: Initiatives for the '90s." *Educational Review* 40(2), pp. 175–183.

Lindsay, P. (1982) "The effect of high school size on student participation, satisfaction and attendance." *Educational Evaluation and Policy Analysis*. 4(1), pp. 57–65.

Lockheed, Marlaine, and Eric Hanushek (1988) "Improving Educational Efficiency in Developing Countries: What Do We Know?" *Compare* 18 (1), pp. 4–38.

Lockheed, Marlaine, and A. Komenan (1989) "Teaching quality and student achievement in Africa: The case of Nigeria and Swaziland." *Teaching and Teacher Education* 5(2), 93–113.

Lockheed, Marlaine, and Adriaan Verspoor (1991) *Improving Primary Education in Developing Countries: A Review of Policy Options*. Oxford: Oxford University Press.

Luthfi, Mohamed, and Habeeba Zubair (1986) *Innovation in Primary School Construction: Maldives Community Schools*. Bangkok: UNESCO Regional Office for Education in Asia and the Pacific, Educational Building Report No. 12.

Lyons, Raymond (1981) *The Organization of Education in Remote Rural Areas*. Paris: International Institute for Educational Planning.

Mackenzie, D.E.(1983) "Research for school improvement: An appraisal of some recent trends." *Educational Research* 12(4), pp. 5–17.

Marfo, Kofi, Sylvia Walker, and Bernard Charles (eds.) (1986) *Childhood Disability in Developing Countries: Issues in Habilitation and Special Education*. New York: Praeger.

McCune, Shirley D. (1986) *Guide to Strategic Planning for Educators*. Alexandira, VA: Association for Supervision and Curriculum Development.

McGinn, Noel F. (1990) "Forms of governance" In R. Murray Thomas (ed.) *International Comparative Education: Practices, Issues and Prospects*. New York: Pergamon Press. pp. 109–138.

McGinn, Noel F. (1992) "Reforming educational governance: Centralization/decentralization" In Robert F. Arnove, Philip G. Altbach and Gail P. Kelly (eds.) *Emergent Issues in Education: Comparative Perspectives*. Albany: State University of New York Press. pp. 163–172.

McGinn, Noel F., Fernando Reimers, Armando Loera, Maria del Carmen Soto, and Sagrario Lopez (1992) *Why Do Children Repeat Grades? A Study of Rural Primary Schools in Honduras*. Cambridge, MA: Harvard Institute for International Development, BRIDGES Research Report No. 13.

Mendelievich, Elias (1979) *Children at Work*. Geneva: International Labour Office.

Miller, Bruce A. (1987) *The Multigrade Classroom: A Resource Handbook for Small, Rural Schools*. Portland, OR: Northwest Regional Educational Laboratory.

Mkandawire, D. S. J., and D. R. Jere (1988) "Democratization of education through distance learning and problems of assessment with special reference to Malawi." *Studies in Educational Evaluation* 14.

Monk, David H. (1987) "Secondary school size and curriculum comprehensiveness." *Economics of Education Review* 6(2) pp. 137–150.

Montero–Sieburth, Martha (1989) *Classroom Management: Instructional Strategies and the Allocation of Learning Resources*. Cambridge, MA: Harvard Institute for International Development, BRIDGES Research Report Series No. 4.

Morales Gomez, Daniel (1989) "Seeking new paradigms to plan education for development." *Prospects* 19(2), pp. 191–203.

Munoz Izquierdo, Carlos (1979). "Sindrome del atraso escolar y el abandono del sistema educativo." *Revista Latinoamericana de Estudios Educativos* IX(3), pp. 1–60.

Munoz Izquierdo, Carlos, and Sonia Lavin de Arrive (1987) *Strategies for Improving Access to and Retention in Primary Education in Latin America*. Cambridge, MA: Harvard Institute for International Development, Education Discussion Paper.

Murnane, Richard J., and David K. Cohen (1986) "Merit pay and the evaluation of the problem: Why some merit plans fail and few survive." *Harvard Educational Review* 56(1), 1–17.

Mwamwenda, Tuntufye, and Bernadette B. Mwamwenda (1987) "School facilities and student academic achievement." *Comparative Education* 23(2), 225–236.

Nicholson, Ronald (1983) *US Aid to Education in Paraguay: the Rural Education Development Project*. Washington, D.C.: United States Agency for International Development, Project Impact Evaluation Report No. 46.

Nielsen, H. Dean (1991) "Using Distance Education to Extend and Improve Teaching in Developing Countries." in International Development Research Center, *Perspectives on Education for All*. Ottawa: pp. 123–155.

Nielsen, H. Dean, Maria Teresa Tatto, Aria Djalil and N. Kularatne (1991) *The Cost-Effectivess of Distance Education for Teacher Training*. Cambridge: Harvard Institute for International Development, BRIDGES Research Report No. 9.

Nsibande, M. J., and Clifford Green (1978) "In-service teacher training in Swaziland." *Prospects* 8(1), 110–116.

Organizaton for Economic Cooperation and Development (1989) *Schools and Quality: An International Report*. Paris: OECD.

Paulson, F. Leon, Pearl R. Paulson, and Carol A. Meyer (1991) "What makes a portfolio a portfolio?" *Educational Leadership* 48(5).

Paxman, B., C. Denning, and A. Read (1989). *Analysis of research on textbook availability and quality in developing countries*. London: Book Development Council.

Pearce, Douglas(1982) *Textbook Production in Developing Countries—Some problems of preparation, production and distribution*. Paris: UNESCO.

Pearce, Douglas(1988) *A Guide to Planning and Administering Government School Textbook Projects*. Paris: UNESCO.

Perraton, Hilary (ed.) (1986) *Distance Education: An Economic and Educational Assessment of its potential for Africa*. Washington, D. C.: World Bank.

Planning Institute of Jamaica (1992) *Attendance Patterns in Schools Offering Primary Education September–December 1990*. Kingston.

Pollitt, Ernesto (1990) *Malnutrition and Infection in the Classroom*. Paris: UNESCO.

Postlethwaite, T. Neville (ed.) (1988) *Encyclopedia of Comparative Education and National Systems of Education*. Oxford: Pergamon Press.

Poteet, James (1985) "Educational Assessment" in Joyce S. Choate, et al. *Assessing and Programming Basic Curricular Skills*. Boston: Allyn and Bacon.

Pratt, C. and K. Treacy (1986). *A Study of Student Grouping Practices in Early Childhood Classes in Western Australia Government Primary Schools*. Melbourne: Education Department of Western Australia, Cooperative Research Series No. 9.

Pratt, D. (1986) "On the merits of multiage classrooms." *Research in Rural Education* 3(3).

Prawda, Juan (1992) *Educational Decentralization in Latin America: Lessons Learned*. Washington, D. C.: World Bank, Views from LATHR No. 27.

Prophet, B. and P. Rowell (1988) *Botswana: Curriculum-in-Action: Classroom Observations in Botswana Junior Secondary Schools*, 1987–1988. Tallahasee, Florida: Florida State University, Learning Systems Institute, IEES.

Psacharopoulos, George (1986) *Economics of Education: Research and Studies*. New York: Pergamon.

Psacharopoulos, George, and Ana Maria Arriagada (1989) "The determinants of early age human capital formation: Evidence from Brazil." *Economic Development and Cultural Change*, 37(4) 683.

Psacharopoulos, George, and Maureen Woodhall (1985) *Education for Development: An Analysis of Investment Choices*. New York: Oxford University Press.

Purkey, S., and Marshall Smith (1983) "Effective schools: A review." *The Elementary School Journal* 83(4), pp. 427–452.

Ramirez, Francisco, and John Boli (1987) "The political construction of mass schooling: European origins and worldwide institutionalization." *Sociology of Education* 60:1, 2–17.

Ramirez, Francisco, and Richard Rubinson (1979) "Creating members: the political incorporation and expansion of public education." in John W. Meyer and Michael T. Hannan (eds.) *National Development and the World System*. Chicago: University of Chicago Press, pp. 72–82.

Raudenbush, Stephen W., Somsri Kidchapanish, and Sang Jin Kang (1991) "The effects of preprimary access and quality on educational achievement in Thailand." *Comparative Education Review*, 35(2), 255–273.

Raudenbush, Stephen W., Suwanna Easmsukkawat, Ikechuku Di–Ibor, Mohamed Kamali, and Wimal Taoklam (1991) *On-the-job Improvements in Teacher Competence: Policy Options and Their Effects on Teaching and Learning in Thailand*. Cambridge, MA: Harvard Institute for International Development, BRIDGES Casual Paper.

Ravitch, Diane (1984) "Value of Standardized Tests In Indicating How Well Students Are Learning." in Charles W. Daves (ed.) *The Uses and Misuses of Tests*. San Francisco: Jossey-Bass.

Reimers, Fernando (1990) *Education, Adjustment, and Democracy in Latin America*. Cambridge, MA: Harvard Institute for International Development, Development Discussion Paper No. 363.

Richardson, R. C., and E. F. Skinner (1991) *Achieving Quality and Diversity*. New York: Macmillan.

Richey, R. (1986) *The Theoretical and Conceptual Basis of Instructional Design*. New York: Nichols Publishing Co.

Rondinelli, Dennis A., John Middleton, and Adriaan M. Verspoor (1990) *Planning Education Reform in Developing Countries: The Contingency Approach*. Duke University Press, Durham and London

Rosenshine, B., and D. Berliner (1978) "Academic time engaged." *British Journal of Teacher Education* 4, 3–26.

Ross, D. H. (1988) *Educating Handicapped Young People in Eastern and Southern Africa*. Paris: UNESCO.

Ross, Kenneth N., and T. Neville Postlethwaite (1992) *Indicators of the Quality of Education: A National Study of the Primary Schools in Zimbabwe*. Paris: International Institute for Educational Planning, Research Report No. 96.

Rowley, Samuel Dunham, Jr. (1992) *Multigrade Classrooms in Pakistan: How Teacher Conditions and Practices Affect Student Achievement*. Cambridge, MA: Harvard University, Graduate School of Education, Unpublished Ed.D. dissertation.

Rucker, Walter E., Clyde A. Dilley and David W. Lowrey (1985) *Heath Mathematics, Teacher's Edition*. Lexington, MA: D. C. Heath.

Rugh, Andrea, with Ahmed Nawaz Malik and R. A. Farooq (1991) *Teaching Practices to Increase Student Achievement: Evidence from Pakistan*. Cambridge, MA: Harvard Institute for International Development, BRIDGES Research Report Series No. 8.

Rust, Val, and Per Dalin (eds.) (1990) *Teachers and Teaching in the Developing World*. New York: Garland Publishing.

Sack, Richard (1992) "Making education ministries more effective." *IIEP Newsletter* 10(2), p. 11.

Schiefelbein, Ernesto (1991a) *In search of the school of the XXI Century: is the Colombian Escuela Nueva the right pathfinder?* UNESCO/UNICEF.

Schiefelbein, Ernesto (1991b) *Efficiency and Quality of Latin American Education.* Santiago, Chile: OREAL–UNESCO.

Schiefelbein, Ernesto, and Joseph P. Farrell (1982) *Eight Years of Their Lives.* Ottawa: International Development and Research Centre.

Schiefelbein, Ernesto, and Seppo Heikinnen (1991) *The LAC Region: Access, Repetition and Efficiency in Primary Education.* Santiago, Chile: OREALC–UNESCO.

Schwille, J., T. Eisemon, F. Ukobizoba, R. Houang, D. Kown and R. Prouty (1991) *Is Grade Repetition Always Wasteful? New Data and Unanswered Questions.* Cambridge, MA: Harvard Institute for International Development, BRIDGES Research Report Series No. 7.

Searle, Barbara. (1985) *General Operational Review of Textbooks.* Washington, D.C.: World Bank, Education and Training Department EDT No. 1.

Sedlak, Philip A. S. (1988) "Radio Education Teacher Training Project." *Development Communication Report* (USAID).

Shann, Mary (1991) "Debating national education tests." Washington, D.C.: *Washington Times* 91, pp. 97–101.

Spain, Peter L. (ed.) (1977) *Radio for Education and Development: Case Studies,* Washington, D. C.: World Bank.

Stego (1987) "Perspectives on School Leader Development." in David Hopkins, et al. *Improving the Quality of Schooling: Lessons from the OECD International School Improvement Project.* London: Falmer Press.

Stiggins, R.J. (1987) "Comparison of Various Types of Assessment." in Peter W. Airasian, *Classroom Assessment.* New York: McGraw Hill.

Stromquist, Nelly P. (1989). "Determinants of educational participation and achievement of women in the Third World: A review of the evidence and a theoretical critique." *Review of Educational Research* 59:2, 143–183.

Tatto, Maria Teresa, Dean Nielsen and William Cummings (1991) *Comparing the Effects and Costs of Different Approaches for Educating Primary School Teachers: the Case of Sri Lanka.* Cambridge: Harvard Institute for International Development, BRIDGES Research Report No. 10.

Teddlie, C. and Stringfield, S.(1993) *Schools Make a Difference: Lessons Learned From a 10-Year Study of School Effects.* New York: Teachers College Press.

Thiagarajan, Sivaisalam, and Aid Pasigna (1988) *Review of the Literature on the Soft Technologies of Learning.* Cambridge: Harvard Institute for International Development, BRIDGES Research Report No. 3.

Thomas, Christopher, and Christopher Shaw (1992) *Issues in the Development of Multigrade Schools.* Washington, D.C.: World Bank

Toronto, James A. (1990) *An Organizational Analysis of the Ministry of Education: Arab Republic of Egypt.* Cambridge, MA: Harvard Institute for International Development, Development Discussion Paper No. 346ES.

Trask, Margaret (1984) *South Pacific Region Pilot Project on School Library Development: Training Programmes for Teachers.* Paris: UNESCO.

Tsang, Mun (1989) *Private Resources and Educational Quality: The Case of Primary Education in Thailand.* Cambridge, MA: Harvard Institute for International Development, BRIDGES Project, Casual Paper.

Tsang, Mun (1990) *Resource Mobilization to Primary Education in Pakistan: An Exploration of Policy Options.* Cambridge, MA: Harvard Institute for International Development, BRIDGES Casual Paper.

UNESCO (1984) *Diagnostic Studies on Educational Management: Country Studies.* Bangkok: UNESCO Regional Office for Education in Asia and the Pacific.

UNESCO (1989) *Multigrade Teaching in Single Teacher Primary Schools Bangkok: Regional Office for Education in Asia and the Pacific.*

UNESCO (1990) *Statistical Yearbook.* Paris: UNESCO.

UNESCO/OREALC (1990) *The State of Education in Latin America and the Caribbean,* 1980–1987. Santiago, Chile.

United States Agency for International Development (1990) *Lessons Learned in Basic Education in the Developing World.* Washington, D.C.: Bureau for Science and Technology, Office of Education.

Verspoor, Adriaan (1989) *Pathways to Change: Improving the quality of education in developing countries.* Washington, D.C.: World Bank Discussion Paper No. 53.

Verspoor, Adriaan, and Janet Leno (1986) *Improving Teaching: A Key to Successful Educational Change: Lessons from World Bank Experience.* Washington, D.C.: World Bank.

Warwick, Donald P. (1980) "Planning as transaction." In Russell G. Davis (ed.) *Issues and Problems in the Planning of Education in Developing Countries.* Harvard University, Center for Studies in Education and Development, Cambridge, MA.

Warwick, Donald P. and Fernando Reimers (1992), "Teacher Training in Pakistan: Value–Added or Money Wasted?" Cambridge, MA: Harvard Institute for International Development, BRIDGES Annual Conference Paper.

Warwick, Donald, Fernando Reimers, and Noel McGinn (1989), *Teacher characteristics and student achievement in Math and Science.* Cambridge, MA: Harvard Institute for International Development, BRIDGES Papers on Primary Education in Pakistan, No. 5.

Warwick, Donald, Fernando Reimers and Noel McGinn (1990) *How Do Government Primary Schools in Pakistan Differ?* Cambridge, MA: Harvard Institute for International Development, Casual Paper.

Warwick, Donald P., Fernando Reimers and Noel McGinn (1992) "The implementation of educational innovations: Lessons from Pakistan." *International Journal of Educational Development* 12(4), 297–307.

Weiner, Myron (1991) *The Child and the State in India: Child Labor and Education.* Princeton, NJ: Princeton University Press.

Weinstein, C. S. (1979) "The physical environment of the school: A review of the research." *Review of Educational Research*, 49(4), pp. 577–610.

Wheeler, Christopher, Stephen Raudenbush and Aida Pasigna (1989) *Policy Initiatives to Improve Primary School Quality.* Cambridge, MA: Harvard Institute for International Development, BRIDGES Research Report No. 5.

Winkler, Donald (1988) *Decentralization in education: An economic perspective.* Washington, D. C.: World Bank, Education and Employment Division.

World Bank (1990) *The Sustainability of Investment Projects in Education.* Washington, D.C.

World Bank (1991) *World Development Report 1991.* Washington, D. C.